Hellenic Studies 44

PLATO'S COUNTERFEIT SOPHISTS

Recent Titles in the Hellenic Studies Series

http://chs.harvard.edu/chs/publications

PLATO'S COUNTERFEIT SOPHISTS

HÅKAN TELL

CENTER FOR HELLENIC STUDIES
Trustees for Harvard University
Washington, D.C.
Distributed by Harvard University Press
Cambridge, Massachusetts, and London, England
2011

Plato's Counterfeit Sophists
  by Håkan Tell
Copyright © 2011 Center for Hellenic Studies, Trustees for Harvard University
All Rights Reserved.
Published by Center for Hellenic Studies, Trustees for Harvard University, Washington, D.C.
Distributed by Harvard University Press, Cambridge, Massachusetts, and London, England
Production: Ivy Livingston
Cover design: Joni Godlove

LIBRARY OF CONGRESS CATALOGING-IN-PUBLICATION DATA
  Tell, Håkan.
  Plato's counterfeit Sophists / by Håkan Tell.
    p. cm. — (Hellenic studies ; 44)
  Includes bibliographical references and index.
  ISBN 978-0-674-05591-9 (alk. paper)
  1. Sophists (Greek philosophy) 2. Plato. I. Center for Hellenic Studies (Washington, D.C.)
  II. Title. III. Series.
  B288.T45 2010
  183'.01--dc22

                                                        2010045614

Contents

Acknowledgments

I AM GRATEFUL for the encouragement and support I have received while writing this book. I owe special thanks to my teachers, Leslie Kurke, Mark Griffith, and Tony Long, who all, in different ways, inspired me with their teaching, and who sparked my interest in the Greek wisdom tradition. Without their intellectual engagement and generosity of spirit this book would not have been possible.

Loïc Wacquant introduced me to the cultural sociology of Pierre Bourdieu and helped me develop a critical framework to analyze the development of the field of Greek philosophy in the fifth and fourth centuries BCE.

I would also like to thank my colleagues at Dartmouth College for their unwavering support. Jim Tatum, especially, read through several versions of the manuscript at different stages and proved to be an invaluable critic.

The Center for Hellenic Studies provided an ideal scholarly environment to bring this project to completion, with its knowledgeable and accommodating staff. I am especially grateful to Greg Nagy for his encouragement and advice.

There are many others—friends, teachers, and colleagues—who have read portions of this book and generously offered their criticism. Thanks to Pascale Brillet-Dubois, Paul Christesen, Elizabeth Irwin, Giuseppe Lentini, Gauthier Liberman, Richard Martin, Bill Scott, Roberta Stewart, Ronald Stroud, Leslie Threatte, Roger Ulrich, Bob Wallace, and Margaret Williamson.

John Zaleski provided crucial editorial assistance at the last stages of the book and saved me from many errors.

Thanks are due also to Jill Curry Robbins of the Center for Hellenic Studies for her encouragement and steady stewardship of the project.

Last, I would like to express my gratitude to Sophie Tell for her commitment and love, to which no words can do justice. I dedicate this book to her.

Portions of chapters 2, 4, and 5 have appeared in print: "Sages at the Games: Intellectual Displays and Dissemination of Wisdom in Ancient Greece," *Classical Antiquity* 26:249–275 (2007), and "Wisdom for Sale? The Sophists and

Money," *Classical Philology* 104:13–33 (2009). Permission to reprint is gratefully acknowledged.

Introduction

*The philosophical field is undoubtedly the first scholastic field to have
constituted itself by achieving autonomy with respect to the developing
political field and the religious field, in Greece in the 5th century BC.*

Bourdieu *Pascalian Meditations*

Competing Articulations of Philosophy

I T IS WIDELY ACCEPTED TODAY that philosophy as a specialized discipline was
not developed before Plato, but that he was instrumental in creating and
defining this new field of intellectual practices.[1] His articulation of philosophy
was so powerful that it remained largely uncontested into modern times.[2] But
the establishment of the discipline of philosophy in antiquity was anything
but a straightforward or uncontested process.[3] There was a fierce debate about
the meaning and successful appropriation of the term *philosophia*, and this
debate was pursued as much in terms of what *philosophia* was not as in terms
of what it was. In this context omissions and misrepresentations of competing
articulations become an essential strategy. In expressing his own view of

[1] Nightingale 1995:10: "Indeed, as a careful analysis of the terminology will attest, φιλοσοφεῖν
     does not take on a specialized and technical meaning until Plato appropriates the term for his
     own enterprise. When Plato set forth a specific and quite narrow definition of this term, I will
     suggest, he created a new and specialized discipline." But see Laks 2006, esp. 55–82, for a critique
     of this position. According to Laks, the development of philosophy as an autonomous field of
     activities had already emerged before Plato, as evidenced by the discussions in Gorgias *Helen* (13),
     Hippocrates *On Ancient Medicine* (20), and Plato *Euthydemus* 305c. If we take into consideration the
     doxographical nature of Hippias' *Synagoge* (see discussion below), it seems very likely that Laks is
     right in his critique of the view of Plato as philosophy's inventor. What matters to my argument,
     however, is not that Plato was the first to establish philosophy as an autonomous field, only that
     his articulation was among the first ones and that it deliberately portrayed philosophy as an old
     discipline without acknowledging either its newfangled or contested status.
[2] Cf. Schiappa 1991:7.
[3] For the Platonic and Isocratean contestation over the correct meaning and application of philos-
     ophy, see Nightingale 1995:1–59. Cf. Lloyd 2005:12–13, who makes the intriguing point that the
     first historical invocations of philosophy did not always have positive connotations.

philosophy, Plato simultaneously designates sophistry as philosophy's opposite, its "daemonic double," to quote Michael MacDonald.[4]

Plato systematically associated a specific group of practitioners of wisdom with the derogatory label sophist and then projected onto them a set of unflattering characteristics. Edward Schiappa has called attention to this Platonic practice, which he labels "dissociation:"[5]

> In this instance Plato was attempting to dissociate the general and traditional meaning of *sophistês* as a wise person or teacher into two concepts, one of which (the Sophist as a possessor of counterfeit knowledge) would be negatively valued, the other (the philosopher as the seeker of true wisdom) would be positively valued.[6]

The intellectual ostracism of the sophists was upheld and furthered by Aristotle.[7] Michael Frede's recent exploration of the Aristotelian history of Greek philosophy in the *Metaphysics* illustrates this development. Frede calls attention to how interrelated Aristotle's conception of philosophy is with his discussion of its origin and first practitioner:

> So there is reason to think that Aristotle in [*Metaphysics*] A.1–2 also tries to advocate a certain conception of wisdom and thereby of philosophy, that his account of the beginnings and early history of philosophy reflects this conception, and that this conception itself also is influenced by reflection on this history and supposed to be borne out by it.[8]

Of particular interest are the temporal limits that Aristotle imposes on the development of philosophy. He traces its origin back to Thales and no further. Though he acknowledges that some (τινες) claim that Thales' views that water was the origin of everything had already been expressed by others, Aristotle staunchly rejects any attempt to lend the name of philosophy to these earlier expressions.

---

[4] "The refutation of sophistry constitutes one of the founding acts of philosophy. Philosophy, it seems, creates itself by purging the sophists as its other, its daemonic double, even its 'counteressence' (*Gegenwesen*)," MacDonald 2006:39.

[5] "Dissociation is a rhetorical strategy whereby an advocate attempts to break up a previously unified idea into two concepts: one which will be positively valued by the target audience and one which will be negatively valued," Schiappa 1991:6.

[6] Schiappa 1991:6.

[7] I would like to establish from the beginning that I do not mean to imply that the philosophical systems of Plato and Aristotle are identical or even similar. Their treatment of the sophists, however, is, for the most part, very similar. Only in this respect do I assume correspondences between them.

[8] Frede 2004:17.

But who were the ones who wanted to trace the history of philosophy beyond Thales? Plato for one, argues Ross, referring to a passage in the *Cratylus* (402a–c) that matches the view expressed in Aristotle.[9] Frede, following Bruno Snell, sees a common source for both Plato and Aristotle, and identifies Hippias of Elis as its originator. Through great detective work, Snell has shown that the discussions of the poetic predecessors of Heraclitus and Thales in the *Cratylus* (402a–c) and the *Metaphysics* (983b20–984a5) are derived from the work of Hippias (contemporary of Socrates). In this work, argues Snell, Hippias contrasted Thales' opinions to those of such older poetic predecessors as Homer, Hesiod, and Orpheus. In the *Cratylus* Plato substitutes Thales with Heraclitus because it better fits his purposes and also because Plato is making a joke.[10] Despite this difference in the two accounts, however, the common source, according to Snell, is Hippias. Carl Joachim Classen has taken this investigation further and found other traces of Hippias in Plato's *Symposium* and Aristotle's *Metaphysics*.[11]

Building on Snell and Classen, Jaap Mansfeld has convincingly argued that the sophists were instrumental in developing the early forms of doxography, and that the organizing principles of these works—for example the exposition of related ideas—are reflected in the discussions of the history and origin of philosophy in both Plato and Aristotle.[12] In addition to Hippias, both Protagoras and Gorgias exhibited an interest in cataloguing the opinions of their predecessors, though the evidence regarding them suggests a more polemical stance than that found in Hippias.[13]

Much of the evidence relating to the early development of doxography has to be painstakingly reconstructed through a patchwork of references and crossreferences. When it comes to Hippias' contribution, however, we are on slightly firmer footing. Clement of Alexandria in the *Stromateis* (6.2.15 = DK 86B6) quotes what is supposedly the proem of Hippias' *Synagoge* (*Collection*):[14]

τούτων ἴσως εἴρηται τὰ μὲν Ὀρφεῖ, τὰ δὲ Μουσαίῳ κατὰ βραχὺ ἄλλῳ ἀλλαχοῦ, τὰ δὲ Ἡσιόδῳ τὰ δὲ Ὁμήρῳ, τὰ δὲ τοῖς ἄλλοις τῶν ποιητῶν, τὰ δὲ ἐν συγγραφαῖς τὰ μὲν Ἕλλησι τὰ δὲ βαρβάροις· ἐγὼ δὲ ἐκ πάντων

---

[9] Ross 1953, 1:130.

[10] But see the objections raised against this assumption in Mansfeld 1990:43–55.

[11] Classen 1965.

[12] "The assumption that the rudimentary beginnings of the historiography of Greek philosophy may be dated to the period of the Sophists is a very safe one," Mansfeld 1990:27. "Their [*sc.* Plato's and Aristotle's] famous discussions of the problems of being and becoming, of unity and plurality, and of genesis and change or motion, are ultimately rooted in the preliminary doxographies of the Sophists," Mansfeld 1990:69.

[13] Mansfeld 1990:22–83.

[14] For a discussion of the origin of this title, see Patzer 1986:97–99. All translations are mine, unless otherwise indicated.

τούτων τὰ μέγιστα καὶ ὁμόφυλα συνθεὶς τοῦτον καινὸν καὶ πολυειδῆ
τὸν λόγον ποιήσομαι.

Some of these things have probably been said by Orpheus, others by
Musaeus briefly in different places, yet others by Hesiod and Homer,
others by the other poets, others in the prose writings of Greeks and
non-Greeks alike. But I will make this account new and varied by
putting together the most important and related sayings from all of
them.

It seems that Hippias' ambition was to present in the *Synagoge* an overview of
contemporary and ancient thinking on an encyclopedic scale, and that the work
was organized according to themes that were illustrated by short quotations
from the primary sources.[15] Hippias also seems to have assumed that all contemporary thinking was derived from older predecessors;[16] or, to be more precise,
Hippias seems to have believed that all contemporary thinking that we today
might characterize as philosophical was ultimately derived from older, mythological expressions, though these older expressions might lack the sophisti-
cation and explicit articulation found in later writers.[17] The exposition in the
Synagoge most likely started with a statement from one of Hippias' contemporaries or predecessors and then traced it back to the works of one of the poets of
old, such as Musaeus, Homer, or Hesiod.[18]

---

[15] See Patzer 1986:32.

[16] Patzer 1986:110.

[17] Both Patzer 1986 and Baulaudé 2006 argue that the ideas that underpin Hippias' *Synagoge* were
revolutionary. Patzer points out that Hippias' assumption that everything new is of ancient
origin broke with the traditional view of the past: Xenophanes, Hecataeus, and Heraclitus all
invoked their predecessors with polemical intent and to underscore their difference with and
superiority over their intellectual predecessors. It was only in the late fifth century and in the
thinking of the sophists, argues Patzer (110–111), that this new conception of the past developed—a conception based upon the realization that a new era had begun, which had liberated
itself from and even overcome the previous era. Baulaudé (287–304), in turn, stresses the novelty
of how Hippias relates to knowledge. He breaks with his predecessors in not wanting to transmit
the opinions of his predecessors for the purpose of putting the reader in a position to understand nature, but rather for the purpose of understanding what has been said about nature, so
that this knowledge can be applied to the political sphere. In Baulaudé's view, Hippias' project
was fundamentally political.

[18] For an attempt at reconstructing the *Synagoge*, see Snell 1944 and Patzer 1986:33–42. One
remaining question is what purpose the *Synagoge* had. Whereas Aristotle quoted earlier thinkers
only to point out their inadequacies compared to his own philosophical system—especially as
their thinking related to the four causes—it is not clear that Hippias had similar intentions.
From the little we know about the *Synagoge*, it appears that Hippias was aiming at the opposite,
namely to show how the ancients had already anticipated—though in cruder form—what later
practitioners of wisdom would claim as their own intellectual accomplishments.

This, then, seems to be the competing articulation of the origin of philosophy that Aristotle rejects in the first book of the *Metaphysics*. As opposed to Hippias, Aristotle will not allow philosophy's origin to stretch back to the poetic past, be it Greek or non-Greek.[19] But why does Aristotle settle with Thales? This question can of course be answered in numerous ways, but what matters at present is how it relates to Aristotle's conception of philosophy, a point that Frede has explored. He sees Aristotle's decision to let philosophy begin with Thales as anything but arbitrary. He reminds us that when Aristotle wrote the *Metaphysics* there was no consensus about what philosophy was or should be.[20] Part of Aristotle's ambition was to champion his view of philosophy, to present a normative account of his own intellectual practices. The selection of Thales, then, serves the purpose of portraying philosophy as theoretical and as "universal, knowledge of the ultimate causes and principles of things, of what there is, quite generally."[21]

But in advocating this view of philosophy, Aristotle rejects another and older view, articulated by Hippias in the *Synagoge*. It is important that we understand how polemical Aristotle's articulation is, a point highlighted by Mansfeld.[22] At the core of the Aristotelian articulation of philosophy lies a suppression of an alternate—and unacknowledged because unnamed—articulation. By imposing a limit on when philosophy began—with Thales—Aristotle is simultaneously imposing a limit on what philosophy is and ought to be: that is to say, non-Hippian. There is thus a double process at work in the *Metaphysics*. To begin with, Aristotle chooses not to mention Hippias by name as the subject of his critique, effectively delegitimizing Hippias' status as a *sophos*. But Aristotle also rejects Hippias' intellectual position on the history and scope of philosophy. As opposed to Hippias, for whom philosophy is not unique to the Greeks nor sufficiently distinct to require separate treatment from the earliest poetic expressions, Aristotle chooses not to grant the status of philosophy to any of Thales' precursors.

This phenomenon is not limited to the *Metaphysics*, Aristotle, or even Hippias. Snell, Classen, Patzer, and Mansfeld have shown that Plato too drew on

---

[19] "Aristotle, by making a clear cut, prevents the origins of philosophy from disappearing in the remote legendary past of Greece or even of the Near East," Frede 2004:33.

[20] Frede 2004:15–16. In reality, there seems to have been a great deal of fluidity among the different types of *sophoi* and temporal continuity in their intellectual practices. For philosophical pluralism and fluidity in philosophical traditions before Plato, see Lloyd 2005:11: "there was no uniformity about what 'philosophy' is or should be in Greek thought before Plato ... Plato and Aristotle themselves began the reprocessing of earlier Greek thought in the light of their own—far from identical—images of philosophy."

[21] Frede 2004:23.

[22] "Aristotle's main point is polemical ... Aristotle explicitly rejects the view of those who want to find anticipations of Thales' statement that water is the *arche* of things in the old theologizing poets ... Aristotle, in other words, argues that Hippias' parallels are not conclusive," 1990:88–89.

Hippias' work, also without mentioning Hippias' name or explicitly acknowl-edging his source.[23] As already mentioned, Mansfeld has made the case that Protagoras and Gorgias engaged in rudimentary doxography. Their works would presumably also have been available to Plato and Aristotle. We might suspect, though with less certainty than in the case of Hippias, that the Platonic and Aristotelian suppression of alternate articulations of philosophy applied also to these two key sophistic figures.[24]

Except for the titillating suggestion of a comprehensive work authored by Hippias—thus predating Plato (ca. 427–347BCE)—on the origin and develop-ment of philosophy, the real significance of this discussion lies in the evidence of a competing articulation of the Greek wisdom tradition. Hippias' concep-tion of philosophy, according to this analysis, is lurking behind and informing the accounts of both Plato and Aristotle. We might say that Hippias comes to personify the presence of a competing, but ultimately suppressed tradition. It is of course tempting to ask what philosophy could have looked like if Hippias' view had won the day. Just as Aristotle's articulation of philosophy is inherently linked with his conceptualization of its beginning, so, presumably, is Hippias'. As enticing as the "what if" question of the Hippian articulation of philosophy is, however, it is too broad for the current project. Let it suffice to say that others have turned to the sophists to find a corrective and more tolerant view of philosophy than that found in Plato and Aristotle—with mixed results.[25]

During Hippias' lifetime, the debate about philosophy was still actively pursued, and no single position had yet prevailed. It is against this realization that we need to read Plato's and Aristotle's all but total omission of competing accounts—a strategy that has proven remarkably successful. In tandem with this omission, Plato and Aristotle also managed to characterize the sophists as an intellectually homogeneous group—and as one that was decisively alien to their own intellectual tradition. Perhaps the most enduring effect of the Platonic characterization of the sophists is precisely their unique status. This "other-ness," I argue, was established first by Plato and later developed by Xenophon

---

23 Snell 1944, Classen 1965, Patzer 1986, esp. chapters 2–3, and Mansfeld 1990, esp. 84–96.

24 "It is probable that the aims of Protagoras and certain that those of Gorgias were polemical. It is also certain that Gorgias' classification was not set out for its own sake but as part of a larger argument, and likely that the same would hold good for Protagoras' polemics," Mansfeld 1990:27.

25 Karl Popper, for example, saw in them the articulation of a "new faith of the open society, the faith in man, in equalitarian justice, and in human reason," Popper 1962:189. Eric Havelock, in turn, laments the fact that their world–view did not prevail. If it had, argues Havelock, modern Europe would have looked much different: "Had their doctrine been allowed to prevail and influ-ence the mind of Europe at a crucial stage in its development, who is to say what happier and sunnier societies would not have in time arisen on the plains of Gaul and Germany?" Havelock 1957:308.

and Aristotle, and it has been a feature of almost all consecutive discussions of the sophists up till the present time.[26]

Sophistic Distinctiveness

I will survey central criteria of sophistic otherness, in order to outline what stands in the way of assuming a fully integrated position for the sophists in the Greek wisdom tradition. I will start with the characteristics established by the Platonic tradition and move on to features that have been added over time by successive commentators, both ancient and modern. In some cases there exists a large body of scholarly literature critical of the Platonic portrayal. In these instances, I will mostly summarize those findings. In other instances, however, the Platonic verdict has largely gone unchallenged. I shall have more to say about those points later on. The first three criteria of sophistic distinctiveness fall into this category.

A certain group of practitioners of wisdom were singled out and labeled sophists. This classificatory designation clearly marks them off as a distinct category of *sophoi*. In the first chapter, I will examine the use of the term σοφιστής in antiquity and go on to argue that it is only in Plato and Aristotle that we find a consistent application of it to specific individuals. Elsewhere the term was in far wider use, and referred to a wider range of intellectual life. Yet, most modern treatments of fifth and fourth century BCE Greece use the term sophist in respect to the individuals so designated in Plato and Aristotle without acknowledging its wide—and contentious—application in antiquity. By perpetuating this use of the term sophist, then, we are perpetuating a Platonic category—in a way analogous to the hypothetical scenario of labeling Socrates a sophist because he is so characterized in Aristophanes' *Clouds*, without considering the wider implications of its comic and Aristophanic use.

We are so trapped in Platonic categories that it is almost impossible to discuss this group of thinkers without simultaneously reinforcing their unique status as championed by Plato. But since this is a connection that I am trying to

---

[26] Cf. Ford 1993:45: "Nevertheless, the Sophists even now seem to remain to the side of philosophy, for the common academic divisions of ancient philosophy tend to keep them in a kind of protective isolation." It is important to note that the sophists' otherness has been expressed not only in negative terms. There are also those who, like Untersteiner 1954 and Kerferd 1981, defend the sophists' intellectual seriousness and ascribe to it an equal value as that of, say, Plato and Aristotle. These scholars also assume that the sophists are qualitatively different from their predecessors and successors, but this time the difference conveys positive connotations. Consider, for example, the sympathetic treatment that the sophists receive by Untersteiner. He draws a sharp distinction between the *scientific* philosophy of the Presocratics and the *humanistic* philosophy of the sophists. Their teaching is described as, "the coming of humanism, which was destined to lead sophistic philosophy on to ground very different from that of the scientific philosophy which preceded it," xv.

question, what is the appropriate terminology to adopt to distinguish between the Platonically designed sophists, on the one hand, and the historical individuals, on the other? To add to this confusion, we should note that many individuals that we typically would not think of as sophists were frequently so labeled in antiquity. What terms can we employ that adequately capture and clearly differentiate these different groups?

Given that the label sophist is so ingrained, it seems impractical and unnecessarily counterintuitive to avoid it. I propose to sacrifice semantic precision for the sake of comprehensibility. The term sophist will be used with different significations, sometimes indicating anyone labeled σοφιστής in our primary texts, and sometimes referring strictly to the group of individuals so designated in Plato and onward, that is, Protagoras, Gorgias, Prodicus, Hippias, and the rest. The discussion in chapter one and elsewhere is intended to illustrate the semantic range of the term in antiquity and to demonstrate why it is problematic as a modern category to describe a set of specific individuals, given how dependent this grouping and its characterization are on the influential testimony of Plato.

More advisable, however, and to the extent possible, I will avoid group labels altogether and refer to each individual by his own name. To highlight the fluidity of categories in the Greek wisdom tradition and to emphasize the lack of intellectual specialization, I will occasionally use the term *sophos* (plural *sophoi*) as an unmarked designation to refer to individuals with a claim to wisdom (*sophia*). This term is common in Greek and embraces a wide variety of groups that we would hesitate to juxtapose, such as sages, lawgivers, religious experts, poets, and philosophers.

Another area in which the sophists' distinctiveness is claimed is that they are said to trade in wisdom. In fact, this association has become so strong that it works both ways; that is, anyone who is a sophist must teach for money, and anyone who teaches for money must be a sophist. Chapter two is devoted to exploring how this association of money and wisdom is part of a larger invective discourse with analogous features in old comedy and tragedy. In these genres charges of venality are frequently levied against *sophoi* in an attempt to undermine their position as authorities in wisdom by implying that they are motivated by greed. The Platonic characterization of the sophists as greedy peddlers of specious wisdom, I argue, needs to be understood less as a way to describe historical practices than as an attempt to undercut their intellectual integrity.

It is also regularly claimed that the sophists led an itinerant lifestyle and traveled all over Greece in search of employment. As opposed to their predecessors and contemporaries, their travels were not motivated by intellectual curiosity, only by the prospects of attracting students and of increasing their profits. Silvia Montiglio perfectly reproduces this essentially Platonic characterization when she establishes a contrast between the professional travels of the sophists and the intellectual journeys of Solon and Democritus:

> But unlike Solon or Democritus, the Sophists did not travel in order to acquire knowledge. Hardly any 'theory', any abstract curiosity or ethnographic interest motivated their travels. Rather, the Sophists traveled to sell their skill ... Travelling was part of their professional activity.[27]

However, an examination of the primary sources reveals that travel and wisdom were intrinsically linked in ancient Greece from at least the archaic period onward. In chapter four, I argue that travel was a fundamental aspect of the archaic Greek institutions of wisdom and of crucial importance to the circulation and dissemination of wisdom. In the institutional framework that made travel possible and gave cultural credibility to individual sages to crisscross the Greek world there are no clearly identifiable differences between the travels of the sophists and those of other practitioners of wisdom. Instead, they seem to undertake their travel for similar purposes and within established channels of communication. If anything, Socrates seems to be the odd man out with his insistence on remaining in Athens and rejection of (intellectual) travel.

Yet another persistent claim is that the sophists were predominantly concerned with rhetoric, not philosophy.[28] Both Schiappa and Thomas Cole have argued convincingly that the close association of rhetoric with the sophists is another Platonic and Aristotelian definitional imposition aimed at circumscribing sophistic intellectual practices and portraying them as subordinate to their own philosophical enterprises.[29] Schiappa writes that "the word *rhêtorikê* may have been coined by Plato in the process of composing the *Gorgias* around 385 BCE."[30] As Andrea Nightingale has pointed out, it was in the *Gorgias* that Plato first offered an exhaustive definition of philosophy and applied it to his own activities. She goes on to note that, "if Schiappa is right about *rhêtorikê*, then

---

[27] Montiglio 2000:92. Cf. Montiglio 2005.

[28] In the *Gorgias*, for example, Plato's main objective seems to be to separate philosophy from rhetoric, and to locate the activities of the sophists in the latter category: ταὐτό ... ἐστὶν σοφιστὴς καὶ ῥήτωρ, ἢ ἐγγύς τι καὶ παραπλήσιον (520a). For a discussion of the Platonic strategies at work in the *Gorgias*, see McCoy 2008, esp. 85–110. For modern proponents of the importance of rhetoric for the sophists, see e.g. Gomperz 1912 and Harrison 1964.

[29] "Plato felt the sophists' art of λόγος was in danger of being ubiquitous and hence in need of definitional constraint," Schiappa 1990:467. See also Schiappa 1991, and Cole 1991.

[30] Schiappa 1990:457. But see Pendrick's 1998 criticism of Schiappa's argument: "the significance that Schiappa attributes to Plato's supposed invention of the name and notion of rhetoric appears illusory, despite the formidable array of modern theorizing he summons in support of his contentions. The term ῥητορική itself certainly antedated its appearance in the *Gorgias*, and there is no reason to think that Plato either invented or redefined it in the way, and with the motives, Schiappa suggests," 22.

the first explicit and systematic definition of the art of rhetoric would go hand in hand with the first attempt to define philosophy. In attempting to define his own territory, as it seems, Plato had to define and delimit his rival's terrain."[31]

There are thus good reasons to question the contention that the sophists' intellectual activities were predominantly focused on rhetoric, especially given the negative assessment of rhetoric in comparison with philosophy found in both Plato and Aristotle. The workings of language was an area of interest that many of the sophists shared, but it was not restricted to what Plato labels rhetoric,[32] nor was it their exclusive interest,[33] and it had not gone unexplored by earlier practitioners of wisdom. In the *Helen* (2–3), for example, Isocrates compared the rhetorical writings of Gorgias and Protagoras to those of Zeno and Melissus,[34] who are traditionally included among the Presocratics; and Aristotle, in his lost work the *Sophist* (DK 29A10 = Diogenes Laertius 8.57) wrote that Empedocles invented rhetoric and Zeno of Elea dialectic.[35] G. B. Kerferd has shown how Heraclitus and Parmenides, both in different ways, struggled with the relationship between language and reality, and he has suggested that their arguments "provided the starting point for sophistic discussions of linguistic theories."[36]

As for the rhetorical features that we do find in the writings of the sophists, Mark Griffith has argued that, far from being novel in nature, they exhibit strong traditional characteristics:

> Such writers as Gorgias, Protagoras, and Euripides, though they certainly struck their contemporaries as doing something strange and (to many) shocking, were not for the most part introducing radically new techniques or attitudes, but rather exploiting, systematizing, and exaggerating possibilities that they found already well developed by their poetic predecessors.[37]

As we have already seen, however, it was not only in the poetic predecessors that models for the sophistic rhetorical techniques were found. There is no doubt that the focus on public oratory intensified in the fifth and fourth centuries BCE. But it was not exclusive to the group Plato labels sophists, nor can it be

---

[31] Nightingale 1995:72.

[32] For a discussion of the distinction that Plato establishes between philosophers and sophists through his elaboration of the nature of rhetoric, see McCoy 2008.

[33] This interest in the workings of language ranged from rhetoric, grammar, philosophy of language and linguistic theory to literary criticism. For examples and discussion, see Kerferd 1981:68–77 and Barney 2006:90–94.

[34] Lloyd 1979:81n112.

[35] For a discussion of the attribution of the discovery of dialectic to Zeno, see Kerferd 1981:59–67.

[36] Kerferd 1981:71.

[37] Griffith 1990:187.

used as a sufficient defining characteristic to describe the extent of their intellectual activities.

It is often claimed that the sophists falsely represent the content of their teaching—that they teach what appears to be X but is not X—thus actively deceiving their pupils. This is a position upheld by Plato, Xenophon, and Aristotle—and modern scholars, too. Aristotle gives the position a clear expression:

ἔστι γὰρ ἡ σοφιστικὴ φαινομένη σοφία οὖσα δ' οὔ, καὶ ὁ σοφιστὴς χρηματιστὴς ἀπὸ φαινομένης σοφίας ἀλλ' οὐκ οὔσης.

The sophistic art appears to be wisdom without being it, and the sophist is one who makes money from what appears to be, but is not, wisdom.[38]

In the *Metaphysics*, Aristotle adds that "dialectic is tentative regarding the things where philosophy is capable of knowledge, and the sophistic art is what appears to be philosophy but is not."[39] The seventh definition of sophist in the Platonic dialogue of the same name unequivocally underscores the Platonic position:

VISITOR: Imitation of the contrary-speech-producing, insincere and unknowing sort, of the appearance-making kind of copy-making, the word-juggling part of production that's marked off as human and not divine. Anyone who says that the sophist is of this "blood and family" will be saying, it seems, the complete truth.

THEAETETUS: Absolutely.

Trans. White[40]

Xenophon, in turn, takes a less convoluted stance and asserts that, "the sophists talk to deceive, write for their own profit, and benefit no one."[41]

This characterization of the sophists as charlatans and intellectual forgers will receive substantial attention in chapters three to six. These chapters contain an exploration of the traditional elements of the sophists' intellectual practices and highlight how deeply embedded they were in the Greek wisdom tradition.

---

[38] *Sophistical Refutations* 165a21; cf. 183b36–184b8 and *Nichomachean Ethics* 1164a30.
[39] 1004b25–26: ἔστι δὲ ἡ διαλεκτικὴ πειραστικὴ περὶ ὧν ἡ φιλοσοφία γνωριστική, ἡ δὲ σοφιστικὴ φαινομένη, οὖσα δ' οὔ.
[40] *Sophist* 268c–d.
[41] *Cynegeticus* 13.8: οἱ σοφισταὶ δ' ἐπὶ τῷ ἐξαπατᾶν λέγουσι καὶ γράφουσιν ἐπὶ τῷ ἑαυτῶν κέρδει, καὶ οὐδένα οὐδὲν ὠφελοῦσιν.

The sophists, it is also claimed, subscribed to extreme relativism and denied the existence of objective judgments.[42] The basis for this view is mainly to be found in Plato's treatment of Protagoras' *homo mensura* doctrine in the *Theaetetus*. Modern scholars, treating Protagoras as the intellectual spearhead of the sophistic movement, seem to have generalized this Platonic characterization and applied similar views to the sophists as a group.[43] But, as Richard Bett has shown, extreme relativism, strictly speaking, can be attributed only to Protagoras, and even in his case with great uncertainty. It is of course possible to attribute relativistic ideas to the sophists—for example, that what qualifies as a virtuous action depends on the context and circumstances under which it is undertaken—but such reasoning is in no way exclusive to them; if this is the criterion for relativism, we would have to include both Socrates and Aristotle in this group.[44] In other words, if by relativism is meant the rejection of objectivity, then it is misguided to attribute this position to any of the sophists, with the possible exception of Protagoras.[45] There is very little evidence to suggest that the sophists as a group shared relativistic ideas or that such philosophical inclinations would constitute a trademark of their thinking.

It is further claimed that the sophistic movement developed in response to specific Athenian social forces, and that the sophists spent most of their time in Athens. Kerferd articulates this point most succinctly: "Their coming was not simply something from without, but rather a development internal to the history of Athens."[46] Another traditional assumption emphasizes the sophists' democratic sensibilities—an assumption closely linked to the previous point,

---

[42] Bett 1989:140–141, points out that relativism as a term is modern coinage without original application to ancient philosophy. As for a definition, he states that relativism "is the thesis that *statements in a certain domain can be deemed correct or incorrect only relative to some framework*," 141. For a detailed discussion of this definition, see 141–145. See also Woodruff 1999:300.

[43] Cf. Bett 1989:139, esp. n1, who also provides a list of modern scholars who assume that the sophists subscribed to relativism.

[44] For examples, see Bett 1989:149.

[45] "There is but one Sophist, Protagoras, whom we have any reason to regard as a relativist in any deep or interesting sense. It is not entirely clear whether even he deserves this label," Bett 1989:139.

[46] Kerferd 1981:22. Cf. Kerferd 1981:15: "Nonetheless they all came to Athens and it is clear that Athens for some sixty years in the second half of the fifth century B.C. was the real centre of the sophistic movement." Guthrie 1971:40, expresses a similar view: "They were foreigners, provincials whose genius had outgrown the confines of their own minor cities ... At Athens, the centre of Hellenic culture at the height of its fame and power, 'the very headquarter of Greek wisdom' as Plato's Hippias calls it (*Protagoras* 337d), they could flourish." Romilly 1992:18, also stresses the importance of Athens and its lack of predecessors: "But the fact remains that it is in Athens that we find them all ... Were it not for Athens, we should probably not even know the name 'Sophists'. And even if we did, it would have no meaning or interest. Without doubt, the vogue for the Sophists only came about thanks to a catalyst which Periclean Athens alone could provide."

since Athens is strongly identified with its democratic form of government. Jacqueline de Romilly writes that:

> A priori, it is certainly true that the development of their teaching programme was linked with that of the Athenian democracy. The rhetorical and political training that they purveyed only made sense if the skill of public speaking truly did make it possible for individuals to play an effective role.[47]

Against this Athenocentric view of the sophistic movement, Robert Wallace has argued that Athens—and its democratic form of government—has been given too much importance in understanding the sophists:

> Virtually all the various characteristics of their teaching and careers are attested earlier than 450, and not in narrow association with Athens. These characteristics developed not simply as a result of or always in conjunction with democracy—though they certainly flourished under open democratic systems—but also for internal philosophical reasons. Even during the second half of the fifth century, most of those whom we regularly call sophists spent most of their time outside Athens.[48]

Rosalind Thomas, in her work on Herodotus, is also highly critical of the way scholars tend to over-emphasize the significance of Athens, both as the sole impetus for the intellectual movement in the second half of the fifth century (at the expense of, say, eastern Greece), but also as the undisputed center of all intellectual activity in general.[49]

There is an abundance of evidence of the sophists' activities outside of Athens, explored in chapters four and five. When Gorgias first visited Athens in 427 BCE, for example, he was around sixty years old and had presumably already made a reputation for himself.[50] To judge from Plato's characterization in the

---

[47] Romilly 1992:213. Havelock 1957:230, an even stronger proponent of the close ties on the part of the sophists with democratic ideals, states: "Beginning with the sociology attributed to Protagoras with its rationality, its humanity, its historical depth, continuing with the pragmatism which seeks to understand the common man's virtues and failings and to guide his decisions by a flexible calculus of what is good and useful, and ending with a theory of group discourse as a negotiation of opinion leading to agreed decisions, we are steadily invited to keep our eye not upon the authoritarian leader, but upon the average man as citizen of this society and a voter in his parliament." See also Reimar Müller: "There can be no doubt that the sophistic movement as such, without the notion of democracy, is unthinkable," quoted from Wallace 1998:205. Cf. Schiappa 1991:169–171.

[48] Wallace 1998:205.

[49] Thomas 2000:1–16, esp. 10.

[50] For sources on Gorgias' dates, see Guthrie 1971:269 and Kerferd 1981:44. For his visit to Athens as the chief-ambassador of Leontini, see Diodorus Siculus 12.53, 1–5 = DK 82A4.

dialogue *Protagoras,* many years had elapsed since Protagoras' last visit—years during which he was active elsewhere.[51] As is argued at greater length in chapters four and five, to claim that the sophists owed their existence to Athens overstates Athens' importance and ignores intellectual developments elsewhere in Greece.

What about the sophists' democratic experiences outside of Athens? Eric Robinson has recently argued that modern scholarship has put too much emphasis on Athens while not sufficiently exploring the contexts in which the sophists initially shaped their intellectual frameworks. He concludes that:

> the sophists and democracy were indeed deeply connected, if in some unexpected ways. Athens, as a congenial visiting ground and a rich source of customers, played a role in the story, but was not as important as the democratic communities whence the sophists came.[52]

But the evidence to support a specifically democratic political influence on the intellectual articulations of the sophists is scant and mainly circumstantial, and it seems to be assumed solely as a result of Athens' presumed role in shaping the sophistic movement. More attractive—and certainly more substantiated—is G. E. R. Lloyd's claim that the development of Greek scientific rationality *as a whole* was intrinsically linked with democratic ideology.[53] Lloyd is careful not to argue for a direct causal relationship between the emergence of democracy and rationality, but he clearly sees democratic ideology as fertile ground for the kinds of intellectual developments typically associated with rationality and philosophy.[54] From the point of view of Lloyd's thesis, with its emphasis on democratic ideology over realities,[55] it seems unnecessary and even problematic to separate different degrees of democratic influence among the various philosophers; it seems preferable to assume a suggestive analogy between the political developments that took place in the wake of the rise of the *polis* and the emergence of a rational and philosophical discourse in ancient Greece.[56]

---

[51] *Protagoras* 310e.

[52] Robinson 2007:22.

[53] Lloyd (1979, esp. 226–267 and 1990, esp. 60–65), drawing on the work of Jean-Pierre Vernant (1982), stresses the importance of the rise of the *polis*-structure—and its concomitant institution of (more or less) free speech and debate, political participation, and public scrutiny and accountability—for the development of scientific rationality in ancient Greece.

[54] Lloyd 1990:63: "the ideology of the democracy provided a powerful statement of one point that is fundamental for other areas of Greek self-conscious rationality, namely the principle that in the evaluation of an argument it is the argument that counts, not the authority." Cf. Lloyd 1990:64: "it might be conjectured that the possibility of radical questioning in the political sphere may have released inhibitions about such questioning in other domains."

[55] Lloyd 1990:62 and 65–67.

[56] Lloyd's thesis is not without its problems and has recently been subjected to criticism by Richard Seaford (2004:175–189), who sees the spread of coinage, not democratic ideology, as

Greek Conceptions of Wisdom

This list of alleged criteria of sophistic distinctiveness is of course not exhaustive, but it does, I hope, help shed light on the pervasiveness of the ways in which the sophists have been construed as qualitatively different from their predecessors and contemporaries. The notion of sophistic difference seems to undermine any attempt to argue for a reconsideration of the areas of intellectual overlaps. But such an argument finds strong support in our primary sources. To begin with, we have ample documentation indicating that Gorgias, Hippias, Prodicus, and Antiphon had an interest in physical speculation, while Hippias and Antiphon were accomplished mathematicians—both areas traditionally considered a dividing line between philosophers and sophists.[57] But more importantly, if we take as our starting point Greek conceptualizations of wisdom and wise men, our modern taxonomies often appear ill-suited to describe with any kind of accuracy the multiplicity of positions found in ancient Greece.

What precisely did the Greeks mean by wisdom (*sophia*), and whom did they look to as experts (*sophoi*)? Lloyd stresses the range of the term *sophia* in the classical period, where:

> you can be called σοφός in any one of the arts, painting or sculpting or flute-playing, in athletic skills, wrestling, or throwing the javelin or horsemanship, and in any of the crafts, not just in piloting a ship or healing the sick or farming but, at the limit, in cobbling or carpentry or cooking: all those examples can be illustrated from the Platonic corpus.[58]

Aristotle's classic account of the different developmental stages of wisdom has had a strong influence on modern scholars.[59] In his view, described in the first chapter of the *Metaphysics*, wisdom showed a steady progression in Greek culture from skill in particulars to skill in universals, eventually culminating in Aristotle's own scientific philosophy.[60] Kerferd has persuasively rejected this view on the grounds that the account too directly reflects Aristotle's own theories of philosophy and the development of wisdom, especially in the emphasis

---

a fundamental cultural transformation that contributed to the emergence of philosophy and tragedy.

[57] For the evidence, see Lloyd 1979:87n146 and n147.

[58] Lloyd 1987:83.

[59] See Kerferd 1976:17n2.

[60] Kerferd 1976:1–18 gives the following summary of this development: "1. skill in a particular craft, especially handicraft, 2. prudence or wisdom in general matters, especially practical and political wisdom, 3. scientific, theoretic or philosophic wisdom."

on the intellectual vector from particulars to universals.[61] In opposing this Aristotelian account, Kerferd notes that wisdom was initially connected with the poet, the seer, and the sage, and that their knowledge was not pertaining to a particular skill, "but knowledge about the gods, man and society, to which the 'wise man' claimed privileged access."[62] This knowledge, in turn, was divinely inspired—always pertaining to content; and the content in question was education—the turf *par excellence* of *sophoi*.[63]

In response to Aristotle's teleological vision, Kerferd argues for a single and unified notion of *sophia* and stresses the role of the wise man as educator.[64] Depending on context, *sophia* can come to take on particular meanings, but this should not invite us to see shifts in the overall meaning of the word itself; [65] rather, we must investigate the various meanings by paying particular attention to the context in which the word occurs.[66]

---

[61] "[T]his sequence is artificial and unhistorical, being essentially based on Aristotle and his attempt to schematize the history of thought before his own time within a framework illustrating his own view about the nature of philosophy, above all that it proceeds from the particular to the universal," Kerferd 1981:24.

[62] Kerferd 1981:24.

[63] "They are such not in virtue of techniques or special skills, but in virtue of the content of their thinking and teaching, their wisdom or Sophia," Kerferd 1976:28. Cf. Gernet (1981:357), who traces a similar genealogy of philosophy. He argues that philosophy owes much to the mystical sects of the archaic period, and when discussing the elusive figures connected with these sects (Abaris, Aristeas, Epimenides, Hermotimus, Pherecydes, and the rest) he writes: "What is the nature of this prerogative they proclaim and authorize for themselves? It has two elements, but is still one: these men are in special and direct contact with divinity, and this contact is manifested by the miraculous revelation they are granted." Later (361), Gernet discusses Empedocles and sees in his practices and traits "the relic of the 'king-magician,' one whose unique character and authority derive from his ability to control nature, from his infused science of divination, and from his miraculous feats of prehistoric 'medicine.'"

[64] Cf. Griffith 1990:188–189, who argues for a tripartite division of *sophia*: "(a) knowledge and factual accuracy (the *sophos*-poet knows how things were and are, tells them 'truly,' gets names, pedigrees, and events right, and is therefore valuable to the community as a repository of information); (b) moral and educational integrity (the *sophos* presents advice or instruction, or unambiguous examples of good and bad conduct, by which the community is supposed to be collectively and individually improved); (c) technical skill and aesthetic/emotional impact (the *sophos*' uncanny verbal, musical and histrionic powers can excite the ear and the eye as well as the mind, dazzle and delight an audience, and arouse in it irresistible feelings of wonder, sympathetic engagement, and emotional release—'tears and laughter,' 'pity and fear.'"

[65] Kerferd 1976:27: "No matter that in different contexts and for different writers the content of such wisdom may vary—of course it does. But these are not variations in the meaning of the term, nor do they justify us in attempting to trace 'stages' in the development of its meaning. So far as meaning is concerned there is throughout a single concept of 'wisdom.'"

[66] Kerferd 1976:23: "Thus it is no longer possible to maintain that words are receptacles containing fixed and defined meanings which it is the proper function of scholarship to identify as such. Rather they must be seen as acquiring and retaining particularised meanings only in particular linguistic and social contexts."

Built into any definition of *sophia* must be an understanding of its polyvalence and the competing (and sometimes mutually exclusive) conceptions that existed at different times and in different groups in Greek culture. A good example of such a contestation over *sophia* is Euripides' *Bacchae,* where Pentheus' vision and wisdom are repeatedly contrasted to those of Cadmus and Teiresias. Line 395, uttered by the chorus of Bacchae, perfectly captures the tension between the two camps, as the Bacchae challenge the position of Pentheus: τὸ σοφὸν δ' οὐ σοφία, "cleverness/wisdom is not wisdom." Here τὸ σοφόν is equated with the rejection of the gods as opposed to the true devotion of the Bacchae themselves. The approach adopted in this study is to avoid fixed, lexicographical definitions and instead expect multiple appropriations and contestations of the meaning and development of *sophia.* Fixed definitions run the danger of ignoring such cultural processes. In other words, rather than proceeding from the meaning of *sophia* to the successive establishment of the category of *sophos,* we would perhaps arrive at a better understanding if we turned this formula on its head and explored *sophia* precisely through the category of *sophos:* whoever could authoritatively claim a position as *sophos* would be an illustrative example of *sophia,* regardless of how well (or not) his expertise fits standard definitions of the term.[67]

Methodological Preliminaries

But what were the necessary requirements to claim a position as a *sophos*? Wits and personality, argues Lloyd.[68] As much as this statement is true and avoids reifying the concept of philosophy and philosopher, it nevertheless fails to take seriously the problem of authority, that is, the process of acquiring the cultural legitimacy necessary to claim a position of *sophos.* Authority, it seems to me, is ideally considered sociologically.

The crucial theoretical assumptions in my approach have to do with building into the analysis a critical understanding of the competitive and opposing claims to authority by the practitioners in the field of *sophia.* These claims often go unnoticed as such, since they are presented by the individual *sophoi* as disinterested and, thus, as universal. My approach draws on the cultural sociology of Pierre Bourdieu and places the locus of contestation in the internal dynamics of the field,

---

[67] Cf. Schiappa's (1995:38) discussion of a "nominalist approach" when defining philosophy: "those people or ideas that are self-identified as philosophical or are considered such by their peers are, presumptively, part of the history of philosophy. Such an approach avoids claims about who is 'really' a philosopher and who is not, and instead asks the question: Who are the people and what are the ideas that have tried explicitly to join the conversation known as philosophy? Apart from what philosophy may mean to us today, what has it meant to thinkers in other places and times?"

[68] "Anyone could set himself up as a philosopher or as a sophist or, come to that, as a doctor. You depended not on legally recognised qualifications ... nor even simply on accreditation ... What you had to rely on, largely, was your own wits and personality," Lloyd 1987:103.

a realm of social practices that has managed to carve out its own social space and to achieve relative autonomy vis-à-vis other fields.[69] Autonomy translates into cultural authority. The higher the degree of autonomy acquired by a field—the extent to which it can impose its own logic and rules on the players and resist the logic of other fields—the greater the authority of its practices. Internally, in turn, a similar struggle over legitimacy occurs among the participants, where each individual or institution attempts to present his or her own practices as most in line with the logic of the field and, therefore, as most legitimate. This internal jockeying for position creates a highly agonistic climate where contestation is endemic.[70] In the words of Loïc Wacquant, "a field is an arena of struggle, through which agents and institutions seek to preserve or overturn the existing distribution of capital ...; it is a *battlefield* wherein the bases of identity and hierarchy are endlessly disputed over."[71] The struggle over hierarchy often takes the form of a struggle over definitions and categories, over orthodoxy versus heterodoxy, in attempts to boost one's own position by describing it as orthodox and undermining the positions of others by categorizing them as heterodox.[72]

Bourdieu's notion of field has particular hermeneutic value for studying the social world of ancient Greece. We do not have a clearly differentiated social world in ancient Greece with distinctly separated fields of, say, politics, economy, religion, and philosophy, so the applicability of his concept will not be entirely straightforward. But even though the process of differentiation might not yet be fully advanced in this early period, the period under investigation, the development of higher degrees of separation among various social realms is nevertheless underway. Indeed, following Bourdieu, I would argue that the field of philosophy is among the first social realms to establish itself as a truly independent social universe, and that this development started to take place in the fifth century BCE.[73]

---

[69] For a good discussion of Bourdieu's use of field, see Wacquant 1998.

[70] To Bourdieu, this contestation has important political ramifications, since, to him, all intellectual positions are at the same time political: "Then we realize how overdetermined, both politically and academically, are the options selected as philosophically significant for the chosen theoretical line, on the strictly philosophical plane (which is doubtless supposed to be untainted by any political or academic considerations). There is no philosophical option—neither one that promotes intuition, for instance, nor, at the other extreme, one that favours judgement or concepts, nor yet one that gives precedence to the Transcendental Aesthetic over the Transcendental Analytic, or poetry over discursive language—which does not entail its concomitant academic and political options, and which does not owe to these secondary, more or less unconsciously assumed options, some of its deepest determinations," Bourdieu 1991:57.

[71] Wacquant 1998:222.

[72] In this context, it is useful to call to mind, as Bourdieu often does in his writing, that the literal meaning of the Greek word for "to categorize" (κατηγορεῖν) means "to accuse publicly."

[73] "The philosophical field is undoubtedly the first scholastic field to have constituted itself by achieving autonomy with respect to the developing political field and the religious field, in Greece in the 5th century BC," Bourdieu 2000:18.

For these reasons Bourdieu's notion of field can be a useful theoretical tool to analyze the spawning process of social differentiation and of rival claims to legitimacy and authority among ancient practitioners of wisdom. I put this theoretical insight to work in focusing on the internal contestation among *sophoi*, to illustrate, for example, how the term σοφιστής became critical in the struggle over legitimacy, and how accusations of teaching for pay took on a similar role. If this interpretation is valid, it becomes problematic for modern critics to adopt ancient categories (such as σοφιστής) confidently as if they were neutral designations, totally removed from their original, contentious context. In doing this we would effectively be taking sides in an ideologically driven battle over legitimacy, rather than examining the conditions under which the categories came to be attached to certain individuals, and the connotations that those categories conveyed.

The rehabilitation of the sophists championed in this study is of course not altogether new. In recent decades the intellectual balkanization of the sophists has been challenged in a number of influential contributions to the study of Greek culture. G. E. R. Lloyd, for example, has questioned the validity of the category of sophist and stressed the fluidity among the different categories of practitioners of wisdom.[74] Andrea Nightingale, while emphasizing the continuity in practices among the early practitioners of wisdom, has warned about the danger of adopting Platonic and Aristotelian terms when discussing the early practitioners of wisdom.[75] Robert Wallace, too, has pointed out that "[i]n fifth-century texts the distinction between sophist and philosopher was not made."[76] R. P. Martin, finally, has expanded on our understanding of the meaning and cultural significance of wisdom in early Greek society. In an ethnographic exploration of the Seven Sages, Martin has emphasized the non-verbal and gestural qualities of the wisdom distinct to the early sages.[77] His notion of the early

---

[74] "The category of sophist, in Plato himself, as well as elsewhere, is far from hard-edged, and there were important overlaps not only between sophists and natural philosophers but also and more especially between sophists and medical writers or lecturers," Lloyd 1987:93. Cf. Thomas 2000:21: "It is increasingly clear that there are few demarcations between the various groups who may be categorized by modern scholars as Presocratics, natural philosophers, sophists, doctors—even if you accept, for instance, the distinction that sophists share their wisdom for money, the interests and methods of prominent individual sophists, as conventionally labeled (e.g. Protagoras, Prodicus) are by no means entirely distinct from some of the *physiologoi* or natural philosophers or from certain writers in the Hippocratic Corpus."

[75] Nightingale 2000.

[76] Wallace 1998:205. Cf. Wallace 2007. See also Ostwald 1986:259n: "the Athenian public made no attempt to differentiate sophists from philosophers;" Schiappa 1995:45: "The distinctions familiar to us between 'sophistry' and 'philosophy' from Plato's and Aristotle's writings were by no means commonly known—let alone accepted—by most people during most of the fifth and fourth centuries BCE."

[77] Martin 1993.

sages as "performers of wisdom" offers a rich template from which to understand the Greek conceptualization of wisdom and the way in which these qualities appear—however refracted—in later practitioners of wisdom, including the sophists. While there is thus no shortage of contemporary scholarship to support a rehabilitation of the sophists—and it is precisely in dialogue with these works that I would like to position my own analysis—most of these works address the sophists only incidentally. There has not appeared since Kerferd's *Sophistic Movement* a monograph devoted entirely to exploring their role in the Greek wisdom tradition. The present study hopes to remedy this situation by providing such a full-length examination.

1

The Many and Conflicting Meanings of
Σοφιστής

MOST MODERN TREATMENTS OF THE SOPHISTS assert that there existed in fifth-
and fourth-century Greece a distinct group of individuals called sophists
(σοφισταί).[1] Such studies often mention in passing that the term had an earlier,
less pejorative undertone, but that by the end of the fifth century a new class of
people had emerged who appropriated the term for their practices.[2] Once this
group had established itself, the old, complimentary connotation fell out of use.
This new class of practitioners of wisdom is meticulously distinguished from
other groups, such as the Presocratics, Platonists, Aristotelians, medical writers,
and poets.[3] Although modern treatments occasionally disagree over who should
be included in and excluded from the different groups, they generally concur on
the establishment of taxonomies consisting of distinct types of individuals. But
it is far from clear that this classificatory system accurately expresses historical practices, or that the ancients consistently employed strict categories that
referred to clearly identifiable classes of people. It is equally unclear that the
historical emergence of the sophists once and for all fixed the semantic range

---

[1] See, for example, Guthrie 1971:3–26 and Romilly 1992:vii–xv. This balkanization of the sophists
    has been challenged, mainly through Lloyd's influential contributions to Greek philosophy (e.
    g. Lloyd 1979:81, esp. n112; 1987:92–93). See also Ford 1993; Wallace 1998 and 2007; Nightingale
    2000; Thomas 2000:10 and 21. For the most part, however, this challenge to the validity of
    "sophist" as a useful category has been voiced without reexamination of its use in antiquity.
    Ultimately, the decision to abandon "sophist" as an intellectual and historical category has to
    rest upon such an investigation. See introduction, esp. 9–10.
[2] E.g. Guthrie 1971:27–34. But see Edmunds 2006, who argues that no such narrowing of the use of
    σοφιστής had taken place in the fifth century, but only later, mainly through Plato's establish-
    ment of philosophy as a distinct and specialized activity.
[3] "Presocratic" is a modern coinage, notably adopted by Diels in his *Die Fragmente der Vorsokratiker*.
    Surprisingly, this neologism has become almost universally adopted and is frequently used along-
    side the term sophist, which, in contrast, was in general circulation in antiquity. The modern
    adoption of clear and consistent taxonomies can sometimes make us oblivious to a term's
    original polyvalence and contested status. For a more complete discussion of "Presocratic" as a
    historical category, see Laks 2006.

of the term σοφιστής, so that it thereafter referred only to one clearly defined group of people. Against this backdrop, is sophist still a meaningful category?

There is compelling evidence that the term σοφιστής was contested in antiquity, especially in the works of Plato and Isocrates. It is thus problematic for moderns to treat this term as if it were a neutral classification—thereby removing it from its original, contentious context. The use of σοφιστής is intertwined with the development of increasingly specialized practices within the field of *sophia* and the corollary struggles over the appropriation of the terms *philosophia* and *philosophos*.[4] If the term sophist occurred in a struggle over cultural and intellectual authority—where it was employed (mainly by Plato) to denigrate certain *sophoi* as less legitimate—then the uncritical adoption of Platonic terminology effectively runs the risk of taking sides in an ideologically driven battle over legitimacy.[5]

Plato, Xenophon, and Aristotle ultimately won the struggle over definition, and the pejorative designation of certain *sophoi* as sophists has become the "historical" truth. But this truth still does not support our embrace of the term as inevitable. Instead, we must seek to recreate the range of possible intellectual positions available at the time as well as the various points of contention among them; that is, our job is not to perpetuate the Platonic victory of classification, but rather to examine the conditions under which the term "sophist" came to be attached to certain individuals with derogatory connotations.[6]

For the moment, however, I hope to show only that the almost universal modern adoption of the definitions of "sophist" and "sophistry" advocated by the Platonic tradition has been instrumental in balkanizing a number of practitioners of wisdom as fundamentally different—frequently with a derogatory subtext.[7] By the Platonic tradition, I mean to imply two (not necessarily mutually exclusive) groups of writers: those who for the most part agree with Plato's characterization of the sophists, such as Xenophon and Aristotle; and those whose accounts of the sophists seem for the most part to be derived directly from the first group, such as Philostratus, Olympiodorus, and Themistius. In

---

[4] For a discussion of early contestations over *philosophia* and *philosophos*, see Ford 1993:41; Nightingale 1995, esp. chapter 1. See also Lloyd 2005, who points out that some of the earliest attested uses of *philosophia* and *philosophos* appear to carry derogatory connotations (12).

[5] Cf. Nehamas (1990:5), who, in respect to the contrasting views of Plato and Isocrates on philosophy, writes: "It is not my purpose here to argue that either Plato or Isocrates was correct in his conception of the nature of philosophy, especially since I believe, on independent grounds, that this is not a question that can ever be answered. Indeed, I might say that this is precisely the point I am trying to make in historical terms in this essay."

[6] My theoretical orientation owes much to the cultural sociology of Pierre Bourdieu. For the implications of his method to my analysis, see introduction, 19–21.

[7] There are good reasons to focus on the many areas of intellectual overlap and continuity among the various groups of *sophoi* rather than exclusively seeking to separate and compartmentalize them. This is the ambition with the discussion in chapters three to six.

contrast to the wide-ranging use of the term "sophist" in antiquity, the modern employment of the label seems to perpetuate a particular point of view at the expense of other applications. As a result, the historical validity of the term as an intellectual category is deeply problematic. To make this point more compelling, however, it is necessary first to examine in greater detail the ancient uses of the label "sophist." Next, we shall turn to Plato to scrutinize the intellectual genealogy he proposes for the sophists and the role he assigns them in the Greek wisdom tradition. In the final part of the chapter, we shall consider Isocrates' alternative understanding of the label "sophist." This exploration will help us appreciate the rival views of sophists in antiquity and simultaneously caution us against assuming a uniform meaning that consistently referred to a specific set of individuals.

The Ancient Use of Σοφιστής

Our starting point for the examination of the ancient use of σοφιστής will be the statement by Diogenes Laertius to the effect that originally the term sophist was used interchangeably with *sophos* (οἱ δὲ σοφοὶ καὶ σοφισταὶ ἐκαλοῦντο, 1.12).[8] Some scholars have used this statement as evidence that in early Greek society σοφιστής was indistinguishable from σοφός, and that only later, with the emergence of a novel group of practitioners of wisdom (Gorgias, Protagoras, and the rest), it took on a new, specialized meaning.[9] This "limited" meaning was from then on consistently applied to these figures, although the old, "indeterminate" sense was occasionally still in use.[10] However, it was the association with the new group of thinkers that gave it its pejorative ring, similar to the modern connotations of "sophistry" and other similar derivatives. According to this explanation, there is a precise shift from a general to a specific meaning, a process that seems to mirror the concomitant process of intellectual specialization in Greek society. But does this account hold up under scrutiny? Can we detect in our sources a shift in the application of the word σοφιστής that is coexistent with the figures traditionally referred to as the sophists?

Herodotus, a contemporary of many sophists but whose area of interest lay in past events, seems to express well the older, general meaning of the word.

8   Cf. Photius *Lexicon* 528 Naber: τὸ δὲ παλαιὸν σοφιστὴς ὁ σοφὸς ἐκαλεῖτο.
9   For this view, see Nestle 1942:249. Kerferd 1950:8, on the other hand, following Grote 1872, distinguishes between an originally more general use of σοφός and σοφία and the restricted application of σοφιστής.
10 The terms "limited" and "indeterminate" are Grant's, 1885, 1:110. On page 113 he writes: "We see, then, that the word 'Sophist,' having first had a merely general signification, denoting 'philosopher,' 'man of letters,' 'artist,' &c., acquired a special meaning after the middle of the fifth century, as the designation of a particular class of teachers. And then men began to talk of '*the* Sophists,'—referring to this class."

He refers to a number of different people as σοφισταί: Solon and the sages who visited Croesus at Sardis (1.29.1), Pythagoras (4.95.2), and Melampus and his followers, who are said to have introduced Dionysus to the Greeks (2.49.1). Indeed, σοφιστής is a fairly common attribute of the early Greek sages, especially of the Seven Sages. But it was in no way limited to this group. Starting out from Kerferd's classification of the earlier uses of the word σοφιστής (that is, with reference to figures that predated the sophists), we can see that in addition to the Seven Sages and early wise men it was frequently used to refer to poets, musicians, soothsayers and other religious experts, and Presocratic philosophers.[11] Kerferd concludes that, as opposed to the more open-ended application of σοφία and σοφός, "the term σοφιστής is confined to those who in one way or another function as the Sages, the exponents of knowledge in early communities."[12] Elsewhere he appears to link the notion of function as crucial to the sophists by emphasizing that their most distinguishable feature was professionalism.[13] Both George Grote and Alexander Grant had anticipated him in stressing function and professionalism: "they had nothing in common except their profession, as paid teachers," writes Grote, who, on the grounds that there was no doctrinal cohesion among the sophists, rejects the use of the descriptive term "*die Sophistik*" and instead restricts his discussion to a "community of profession."[14] Grant follows suit: "At first the word σοφιστής was used in an intermediate sense to denote any one 'who *by profession* practiced or exhibited some kind of wisdom or cleverness;' thus it was applicable to philosopher, artist, musician, and even poet."[15] According to this view, the sophists inherited the functional aspects of their predecessors and developed them towards a purer form of professionalism. This process is the crucial link between them: the sophists did not necessarily share in the content of their predecessors' teaching, but they extended their functional roles as exponents of wisdom. And it was the hyper-professionalism of the sophists that helped cause the term's subsequent depreciatory tinge.

Others have turned to the history of the word σοφιστής to find more specific predecessors to the sophists. Werner Jaeger, Wilhelm Nestle, and John Morrison, for example, conclude that the sophists were the inheritors of the early Greek poetic legacy, since Homer, Hesiod, Solon, and Simonides were all referred to by

---

[11] See Kerferd 1950.

[12] Kerferd 1950:8.

[13] Kerferd 1981:25. Cf. Grant 1885, 1:106.

[14] Grote 1872:53. He further elaborates this point by saying that it "is impossible therefore to predicate anything concerning doctrines, methods, or tendencies, common and peculiar to all the sophists. There were none such; nor has the abstract word, '*Die Sophistik*', any real meaning, except such qualities, whatever they may be, as are inseparable from the profession or occupation of public teaching," 53.

[15] Grant 1885, 1:106.

that name, and since the sophists all seemed to continue the educational vocation of the poets.[16] The reason for the shift of the word σοφιστής from the poets to the sophists—from poetry to prose—was that "the didactic function came to be more and more fulfilled through this medium."[17]

But all these conclusions rest on the assumption that there is a clear break in the use of the term σοφιστής in the second half of the fifth century BCE, when the sophists established themselves as a new kind of practitioner of wisdom, and that only the pre-sophistic uses are illustrative of its wider range of connotations. It is my contention that this is an artificial demarcation, and that the time limit imposed on the examples considered is problematic. Instead, I would like to reconsider the use of σοφιστής well into the second half of the fifth century and beyond, without making any a priori assumptions about its application. We must thus be open to the possibility that the sophists did not constitute the end stage of the semantic development of the word σοφιστής, but that it could continue to be used—even after the emergence of the "sophistic movement"—to refer to a broad group of people. More specifically, we shall focus on its continued use in respect to "philosophers," that is, to those practitioners of wisdom we traditionally refer to as Presocratics, Socratics, Aristotelians, etc.

Many of the so-called Presocratic philosophers were referred to as σοφισταί.[18] Diogenes of Apollonia (a contemporary of Herodotus), for example, labels the (Ionian) natural philosophers (φυσιόλογοι) sophists.[19] Xenophon (*Memorabilia* 1.1.11) calls those who engage in natural investigations and discussions about the cosmos by the same name, and elsewhere (*Memorabilia* 4.2.1) he mentions that Euthydemus had collected many works of the renowned poets and σοφισταί, presumably referring to the Presocratics.[20] Isocrates attests that Pericles studied with two sophists, Anaxagoras and Damon. Later he warns students not to get too caught up in the subtleties of the early sophists, and he mentions Empedocles, Ion, Alcmaeon, Parmenides, Melissus, and Gorgias as examples of this group.[21] Diodorus Siculus (12.39.2) also refers to Anaxagoras as Pericles' teacher and a σοφιστής, as does Athenaeus (5.220b), though without

---

[16] Jaeger 1965:296; Morrison 1949:57–59; Diogenes Laertius 1.12 (Homer and Hesiod); Isocrates *Antidosis* 313 and Herodotus 1.29 (Solon); Plato *Protagoras* 316c5–e5 (Homer, Hesiod, and Simonides). Nestle 1942:253–254, shares the same view, but he does not emphasize their shared epithet, rather their shared educational vocation.

[17] Guthrie 1971:30.

[18] I have found the discussions in the following works very useful for this section: Grote 1872:32–80; Grant 1885, 1:106–116; Nestle 1940:250–259; Kerferd 1950; Guthrie 1971:27–34; Imperio 1998:43–130; Edmunds 2006:414–425; Wallace 2007:215–237.

[19] Diogenes of Apollonia *apud* Simplicius *Physica* 151.20 = DK 64A4.

[20] See Kerferd 1950:8, who also understands this in reference to the Presocratics.

[21] Isocrates *Antidosis* 235 and 268.

mentioning Pericles. Finally, Plato (*Meno* 85b), in an apparent reference to the mathematicians, labels them σοφισταί.

The frequent application of the word σοφιστής continues in reference to figures who were contemporaries of the sophists, like Socrates and Isocrates, and in reference to figures who succeeded them, like Aeschines the Socratic and Aristotle. In Aristophanes' *Clouds* (360–361), the chorus professes that Prodicus and Socrates are the foremost of the astrological sophists (μετεωροσοφισταί). But it is not only Aristophanes who refers to Socrates as a sophist; Androtion[22] and the orator Aeschines (1.173)—only some fifty years after Socrates' death—also call him by that name.[23] A number of Socrates' disciples (the so-called Socratics) were categorized as sophists: Lysias thus designates Aeschines, Aristotle uses the term in reference to Aristippus, and Xenophon in reference to Antisthenes.[24] Isocrates is called a sophist by Plutarch (*Quaestiones Convivales* 1.1); and to judge from Isocrates' defensive attitude against his detractors in the *Antidosis*, it seems reasonable to assume that Plutarch had many predecessors in that practice.[25] Isocrates, in turn, delivers an attack against what seem to be Plato's *Laws* and *Republic* in *To Philip* (12), where he dismisses them as sophistic works.[26] Lysias also calls Plato a sophist.[27] Timon is less discriminating in his use of the term: he labels all philosophers—Plato and Aristotle included—sophists.[28] Finally, Timaeus in his abuse of Aristotle refers to him as a pedantic sophist (σοφιστὴς ὀψιμαθής).[29]

As is clear from this survey, the word σοφιστής was in use in reference to a wide category of *sophoi* both during and after Plato's lifetime. Its broad continuous application is an indication that Plato's restricted use of the term was neither in general use nor universally accepted.[30] It does not seem that the word

[22] Jacoby *FGrH* 324 F 69 = Aristides 46.311.

[23] See Nehamas 1990, who discusses the application of the label sophist to Socrates, and Plato's intense attempts to rid him of this epithet. See also Taylor 2006:157, who interestingly argues that Plato "presents Socrates, not merely by implication but avowedly, as sharing some of the characteristics which define a sophist." Plato does this to emphasize that Socrates' own profession merely to detect and eliminate false beliefs does not qualify him as a "systematic philosopher" but as "a magician, an individual with an unaccountable power of divining the truths and leading others to it, and by the same token no longer, by Platonic standards, a philosopher, but a very special, and very noble, sophist" (168). See Edmunds 2006 for a discussion of the various epithets associated with Socrates.

[24] Aristides 46.311; cf. Athenaeus 13.611d–612f (Lysias); Aristotle *Metaphysics* 996a (Aristippus); Xenophon *Symposium* 4.4 (Antisthenes).

[25] Isocrates *Antidosis* 166, 196, 213, and 231.

[26] Cf. Grote 1872:33; Sidgwick 1872:293; Grant 1885:112–113.

[27] Fr. 281 Baiter-Sauppe = Aristides 46.311.

[28] Timon *apud* Diogenes Laertius 9.65 and 112. Cf. Grote 1872:33.

[29] Timaeus *apud* Polybius 12.8.4 = *FGrH* 566 F 156.

[30] This is a sentiment already expressed by Grote 1872:35, although he does not discuss its post-Platonic use: "Moreover, Plato not only stole the name out of general circulation, in order to fasten it specially upon his opponents, the paid teachers, but also connected with it express discreditable attributes, which formed no part of its primitive and recognized meaning, and

went through a substantial change or crystallization in its definition after the emergence of the sophists. Indeed, in light of these other examples, a question is raised about Plato's generally privileged position as a witness for the meaning of σοφιστής.[31] This privileged position is further questioned when considering two crucial passages where Plato seems to advance a double, false genealogy of the sophists.

Plato's Sophistic Genealogy

Kerferd is illustrative of why we need to exert critical vigilance against adopting Plato's classification of the sophists. When talking about their most distinguishable feature, their professionalism, Kerferd refers to the testimony of Plato in the *Hippias Major* (282c-d),[32] where Socrates says that the sophists were the first to charge money for their services, and that none of the people of old (οἱ παλαιοὶ ἐκεῖνοι) thought fit to do that.[33] But Kerferd fails to notice the false genealogy of the sophists that Plato advances immediately preceding this passage in the *Hippias Major*. There Socrates asks Hippias why sages of old—as opposed to the sophists—refrained from participating in politics:

> τί ποτε τὸ αἴτιον ὅτι οἱ παλαιοὶ ἐκεῖνοι, ὧν ὀνόματα μεγάλα λέγεται ἐπὶ σοφίᾳ, Πιττακοῦ τε καὶ Βίαντος καὶ τῶν ἀμφὶ τὸν Μιλήσιον Θαλῆν καὶ ἔτι τῶν ὕστερον μέχρι Ἀναξαγόρου, ὡς ἢ πάντες ἢ οἱ πολλοὶ αὐτῶν φαίνονται ἀπεχόμενοι τῶν πολιτικῶν πράξεων;

> But, Hippias, whatever is the reason, why those men of old, whose names are called great with respect to wisdom—Pittacus, and Bias, and Milesian Thales and his followers—and also the later ones up to Anaxagoras—that all, or the majority of them, manifestly stayed away from politics?

> 281c

---

were altogether distinct from, though grafted upon, the vague sentiment of dislike associated with it."

[31] Although the word σοφιστής was still in wide application during and after Plato's lifetime and did not crystallize in its meaning at any given point in time, it nevertheless appears to have acquired a more pejorative tinge in its later use. But this is far from absolute: Xenophon, for example, in the *Cyropaedia* (3.1.14 and 38) relates the tragic fate of a sophist (σοφιστής) who was unjustly put to death by the Armenian king on charges of corrupting (διαφθείρειν) his son Tigranes. When he was about to die, the sophist sent after Tigranes and asked him not to feel any anger towards his father, since he was acting out of ignorance (ἄγνοια) and not malice (κακόνοια), and, since he was acting out of ignorance, he was acting against his own will. This story is surely meant to allude to the fate of Socrates, and it would be particularly odd if Xenophon chose to use a strictly pejorative epithet in such a context.

[32] For the authenticity of *Hippias Major*, see chapter two, 40n5.

[33] Kerferd 1981:25.

This account can be usefully compared to a passage in the *Protagoras,* where Plato has Protagoras say that, although he was the first to call himself a sophist, the sophistic art had earlier practitioners:

ἐγὼ δὲ τὴν σοφιστικὴν τέχνην φημὶ μὲν εἶναι παλαιάν, τοὺς δὲ μεταχειριζομένους αὐτὴν τῶν παλαιῶν ἀνδρῶν, φοβουμένους τὸ ἐπαχθὲς αὐτῆς, πρόσχημα ποιεῖσθαι καὶ προκαλύπτεσθαι, τοὺς μὲν ποίησιν, οἷον Ὅμηρόν τε καὶ Ἡσίοδον καὶ Σιμωνίδην, τοὺς δὲ αὖ τελετάς τε καὶ χρησμῳδίας, τοὺς ἀμφί τε Ὀρφέα καὶ Μουσαῖον· ἐνίους δέ τινας ᾔσθημαι καὶ γυμναστικήν, οἷον Ἴκκος τε ὁ Ταραντῖνος καὶ ὁ νῦν ἔτι ὢν οὐδενὸς ἥττων σοφιστὴς Ἡρόδικος ὁ Σηλυμβριανός, τὸ δὲ ἀρχαῖον Μεγαρεύς· μουσικὴν δὲ Ἀγαθοκλῆς τε ὁ ὑμέτερος πρόσχημα ἐποιήσατο, μέγας ὢν σοφιστής, καὶ Πυθοκλείδης ὁ Κεῖος καὶ ἄλλοι πολλοί.

But I claim that the sophistic art is old, and that those men of old who practiced it, because they feared the revulsion it evoked, veiled and disguised it, some as poetry, such as Homer, and Hesiod, and Simonides; others, in turn, as mystery rites and prophesies, such as Orpheus, and Musaeus, and their followers; I have perceived that some disguised it also as gymnastics, such as Iccus of Tarentum and Herodicus of Selymbria, originally from Megara, who, still being alive, is a sophist second to none; and your Agathocles, a great sophist, disguised it as music, as did Pythocleides of Ceos and many others.

316d–e

In the passage from the *Hippias Major* (281c), Plato singles out Pittacus, Bias, and Thales—all of whom were counted among the Seven Sages—and disassociates them from any political involvement. He does this in sharp contrast to Hippias, Gorgias, Prodicus, and Protagoras, who are all said to be able to combine effort-lessly a lucrative private profession with a successful public career. In other words, the Seven Sages are qualitatively different from the sophists precisely because of their abstention from politics.[34] In the *Protagoras,* this revision is taken one step further. There the functional predecessors and contemporaries of the sophists are listed, and they fall into four groups: poets (Homer, Hesiod, and Simonides), religious experts (Orpheus and Musaeus), gymnastic teachers (Iccus and Herodicus), and musicians (Agathocles, and Pythocleides). These groups closely correspond to the pre-sophistic use of σοφιστής as outlined by Kerferd; we have seen how σοφιστής frequently referred to poets, religious experts, and

---

[34] Harrison 1964:184 writes that this passage is "heavy with irony" and appears thus to dismiss it as a revisionist statement by Plato. Woodruff 1982:37 points out the factual inaccuracy of Socrates' statement and attributes it to Socrates' desire for "making a fool of Hippias."

musicians.[35] It thus makes good historical sense for Plato to stress their role as the predecessors of the sophists. What is significant in the pre-sophistic use of σοφιστής, however, is that it occurs most frequently in reference to early wise men in general and the Seven Sages in particular. And it is precisely this early association that Plato seeks to obfuscate in the *Hippias Major*, just as he reinforces the validity of the other group in the *Protagoras*.[36] Plato, in effect, accomplishes a double false genealogy of the sophists by suppressing the functional continuity of σοφιστής that goes back to the Seven Sages, while at the same time highlighting its earlier affiliation with poets, religious experts, and musicians. Plato is thus not necessarily a trustworthy witness of the meaning and application of σοφιστής because he has his own agenda to promote. That agenda, in turn, is predicated upon the dissociation of the sophists from the sage tradition and subsequent identification of them with poets, religious specialists, and musicians—to the degree that these three categories can be clearly separated. In addition, the difference established between sophists and older practitioners of wisdom in the *Hippias Major* hinges on the assertion that they teach for pay. The sophists' reputed professionalism, then, is integral to the Platonic characterization of the sophists and serves to reinforce their categorical distinction. With this reading, Kerferd's acceptance of Plato's testimony of the sophists' habit of teaching for pay as a factual statement becomes questionable. Plato's insistence on the sophists' monetary practices seems integral to establishing them as outsiders to the sage tradition. In fact, I would suggest that we understand the close association of the sophists with money as part of an invective discourse aimed at undercutting their authoritative position, and not as statements about actual historical practices.[37]

In the same spirit we should re-examine the historical validity of Plato's claim that Thales, Pittacus, and Bias shunned politics.[38] Herodotus tells how Thales advised the Ionians to set up a council (βουλευτήριον) common for all the Ionians to avert the impending Persian threat (1.170), and Diogenes Laertius mentions that he practiced politics before turning to the study of nature (1.23).

---

[35] For complete references, see Kerferd 1950:8.

[36] It is true that in the *Hippias Major* (281d–282a) Socrates asks Hippias if he thinks that the wisdom of the sages of old is inferior when compared to that of the sophists, and, if Bias should come to life again, would he not make himself a laughingstock compared to them. Hippias answers both questions in the affirmative. To this extent, Plato could be said to highlight the continuity between the sages and sophists rather than attempting to obfuscate it. But Hippias explains that he surpasses Bias in using his wisdom to make money by plying his trade both in the private and public. What makes him superior is precisely what makes him *different*. In 283b Socrates sums up Hippias' comments on the sages of old by remarking that "the definition of a wise man, then, is someone who can make the most money." In other words, Hippias' rejection of Bias reinforces the discontinuity that Plato is outlining and does not establish intellectual continuity.

[37] See chapter two for a full discussion of the issue of the sophists and teaching for pay.

[38] For a fuller discussion of the sage tradition, see Martin 1993. See also Nightingale 2000 and 2004.

Diogenes (1.25) goes on to say that Thales had proven himself a prudent advisor in political matters: he convinced the Milesians to reject Croesus' proposal for an alliance, thus saving the city after Cyrus' ascent to power. The traditional accounts surrounding Pittacus depict him as a politically active and respected figure: he held command in the war against Athens over Sigeum, and he is said to have collaborated with Alcaeus' brother to overthrow Melanchrus, the tyrant of Lesbos.[39] Later, he was elected *aisymnetes* (arbitrator with supreme command during a period of domestic crisis)[40] for ten years in his native Mytilene, during which time he is said to have brought about reform and introduced new laws. Alcaeus, a hostile—and contemporary—witness to Pittacus' power, accuses him of being a tyrant, but other sources assert that he indeed gave up his power after his allotted ten-year period of rule.[41] As for Bias, Herodotus (1.170) relates that after the Ionian defeat by the Persians he advised the Ionians to leave and go to Sardinia to found a new colony there to escape Persian rule. In other sources, Bias is consistently praised for his legal expertise. As early as Hipponax, Bias had become the touchstone against whom any successful speaker was measured, something the sixth-century BCE elegiac poet Demodocus seems to be alluding to in one fragment.[42] Plutarch tells us that Bias was sent as an ambassador from Priene to Samos during the war against the Milesians, and that he was held in great honor for his diplomatic accomplishments during that mission.[43] Finally, Diogenes Laertius, who provides the quotes from both Hipponax and Demodocus, illustrates Bias' effectiveness in court by relating how Bias, after successfully pleading his case, leaned against his grandson and died. Unaware of his fate, the opposing party delivered its speech, the jury voted, and Bias won a posthumous victory.[44]

It is against these consistent accounts that Plato asserts that Thales, Pittacus, and Bias avoided politics. Indeed, Alcaeus, Demodocus, Hipponax, and Herodotus are all earlier than Plato, and their picture is repeatedly mirrored in later authors. It is especially relevant that Aristotle deviates from Plato's revisionist portrayal of the apolitical sage. For examples, he refers to Pittacus as a ruler, lawgiver, and *aisymnetes*,[45] and in the *Nicomachean Ethics* he quotes Bias in

---

[39] For the ancient sources of the Sigean War, see Herodotus 5.95; Strabo 13.1.38; Diodorus Siculus 9.12; Diogenes Laertius 1.74. See also Page 1955:152–161; cf. Andrewes 1974:92–99.

[40] Aristotle explains the office of *aisymnetes* as elective tyranny (αἱρετὴ τυραννίς), *Politics* 1285a. For the meaning of αἰσυμνήτης and Mytilene's political situation, see Page 1955:149–161 and 239–240; Andrewes 1974:96–99; Romer 1982; Gagarin 1986:59–60.

[41] Alcaeus fr. 348 Lobel and Page; Aristotle *Politics* 1274b, 1285a; Diodorus Siculus 9.11–12; Strabo 13.1.38–39, 13.2.3; Diogenes Laertius 1.74–76.

[42] Hipponax fr. 123 West; Demodocus fr. 6 West. For Demodocus' date, see Campbell 1982:343.

[43] *Aetia Romana et Graeca* 296a.

[44] Plutarch *Quaestiones Graecae* 20; Diogenes Laertius 1.84.

[45] *Politics* 1274b, 1285a; *Nicomachean Ethics* 1167a; *Rhetoric* 1402b.

the context of the importance of justice for a ruler.[46] In Aristotle's mind, then, both Pittacus and Bias could be invoked as examples of politically significant historical figures.[47]

Plato's own contemporary Isocrates also provides a different version from the account in the *Protagoras* (317b6–7), according to which Protagoras was the first to call himself a sophist.[48] Among the Athenians, it was Solon, writes Isocrates, who first bore this title,[49] and he is thus in agreement with the typical pre-sophistic use of the word in linking it to the Seven Sages—precisely the association that I have argued Plato works so hard to obfuscate.[50] What makes his attribution of the title sophist to Solon the more intriguing, however, is Isocrates' assertion that it was due to Solon's rhetorical expertise (ἐπιμέλεια τῶν λόγων; ἄριστος ῥήτωρ) that he acquired this epithet, and that this skill is no longer held in honor among his contemporaries. But we have no more in our sources to corroborate Solon's position as a master orator and student of rhetoric than we have to support the Platonic claim of Bias and Pittacus' apolitical stance. It thus seems likely that Isocrates, far from innocently using σοφιστής in its old "indeterminate" sense, is consciously seeking to project back onto Solon intellectual interests and pursuits similar to his own.

---

[46] *Nichomachean Ethics* 1130a.

[47] In the case of Thales, however, Aristotle seems more receptive to Plato's characterization. Indeed, he retells the story of Thales' practical genius in the *Politics* (1259a) only to reinforce his position as a disinterested (and poor) philosopher. See also *Nichomachean Ethics* 1141b, where Thales is said to be engaged in knowledge that is useless (ἄχρηστα), since he does not pursue human goods (τὰ ἀνθρώπινα ἀγαθά). Perhaps this portrayal is related to Thales' generally privileged position in Greek culture. He is often invoked as the archetypical philosopher and is never poked fun at in old comedy (Dover 1968:xxxvi).

[48] In *Meno* 91e–92a, however, Socrates says that Protagoras was not the first sophist. Grant 1885:115 points out that Aristotle seems to juxtapose and distance Protagoras from the sophists in the *Nicomachean Ethics* 1164a23–26.

[49] One could of course object that there is a difference between being called a sophist by others, as in the case of Solon, and calling oneself a sophist, as in the case of Protagoras. Isocrates also limits his application of the term to the Athenians, whereas Plato considers its application throughout Greece. Still, the contrast between Isocrates and Plato is significant in two ways. First, even if Solon was an Athenian, he lived long before Protagoras. Isocrates thus gives the term a much older pedigree than that found in Plato. Second, and related to the first point, whereas the *Protagoras* passage states that there existed people even before Protagoras who should be considered sophists but who refrained from using the title out of fear of its pejorative connotations, Isocrates explicitly states that the Athenians considered the label *honorific*. Especially significant for my analysis is the term's association with the Seven Sages in Isocrates.

[50] *Antidosis* 313 and 235, where Solon is included among the Seven Sophists (οἱ ἑπτὰ σοφισταί); cf. 231–232. Hegel is a testament to the power and long-lasting effects of Plato's introduction of the apolitical sage/philosopher. In his *Lectures on the History of Philosophy* (1:52), he writes: "Thus the Greek philosophers held themselves far removed from the business of the State and were called by the people idlers, because they withdrew themselves within the world of thought." But cf. what he says on 157, where he describes the Seven Sages as men of affairs.

Given this alternative historical appropriation of the term "sophist" by Isocrates, it might be worthwhile to look closer at what role he assigns the sophists in his intellectual system. Such an investigation might help illuminate the competing—and often clashing—attempts at jockeying for position in the emerging field of intellectual production. Many scholars have focused on the wide discrepancies between Plato's and Isocrates' understanding of φιλοσοφία,[51] but few have extended their analyses to include the equally contradictory roles ascribed to the sophists. Some even quote Isocrates when discussing the "Platonic sophists" without pausing to question whether the label refers to the same persons.[52] Both Isocrates and Plato describe philosophy as much in terms of what it is not, as in terms of what it is. In this respect the sophists are of particular significance in both of their intellectual systems.

Isocrates' Sophists

In the *Antidosis*, Isocrates denies the label of philosophy to the study of astronomy and geometry, and he admonishes young men not to spend too much time in the pursuit of these disciplines, lest their minds (φύσιν) wither or run aground (ἐξοκείλασαν) on the theories of the old sophists (τῶν παλαιῶν σοφιστῶν).[53] From a Platonic perspective, this is an unusual connection, since for Plato geometry is generally treated as fundamental to philosophy,[54] whereas the sophists are usually located outside this tradition.[55] The shock comes when we hear who the Isocratean sophists are: Empedocles, Ion, Alcmaeon, Parmenides, Melissus, and Gorgias. But that is not all; Isocrates goes on to express discontent with what some call philosophy, and provides his own definition:

> I consider those to be wise who with the help of their judgment (ταῖς δόξαις) are able to reach generally for what is best, and I consider those to be philosophers (φιλοσόφους) who employ themselves with

---

[51] For the most recent and significant treatment of Plato's and Isocrates' differing views on φιλοσοφία, see Nightingale 1995 with bibliography. For philosophy as a contested term, see, in addition to Nightingale 1995, Ford 1993:45; Wardy 1996:94–96; and Ober 2004:26–27.

[52] For examples of such practice, see Guthrie 1971:36 and Blank 1985:2 and 4n15.

[53] *Antidosis* 266–268.

[54] For the link between geometry and philosophy, see, e.g. *Republic* 510c–511a, 526c–528e, and 533b–c. See also, e.g. Penner 1987:126–127n19; Kraut 1992b:6n24; and Mueller 1992:170–199.

[55] Xenophon (*Memorabilia* 1.1.11) also attributes physical speculation to the sophists—normally a distinguishing characteristic of the Presocratics—and appears less concerned than Plato to maintain the rigorous division between sophists and philosophers (cf. Sidgwick 1872:293). When talking about Socrates, Xenophon writes: "He did not discuss the nature of all things in the same manner as most of the others, nor did he examine the nature of the so-called cosmos of the sophists (ὁ καλούμενος ὑπὸ τῶν σοφιστῶν κόσμος) or the laws that govern the heavenly phenomena."

the studies from which they will most quickly acquire this practical wisdom (φρόνησιν).[56]

Next (*Antidosis* 275) Isocrates declares that what will create these wise men is the study of how to speak well (λέγειν εὖ) and of how to persuade one's hearers (πείθειν...τοὺς ἀκούοντας). Isocrates thus offers a complete reinterpretation of Platonic philosophy[57] where the focus is shifted from Plato's apolitical sage—who is now labeled a sophist—to the politically active and rhetorically astute figure of his own standing.[58] In the words of Henry Sidgwick:

> The testimony of Isocrates then comes to this: he attacks the Sophists in the same style as Plato: only Isocrates calls Sophists just those whom Plato and posterity call Philosophers, while the more honourable title of 'Philosophy' he reserves for his own special industry, the Art of Public Speaking.[59]

But who precisely are the Isocratean sophists?[60] We have already seen that, when explicitly defining whom he means by that label, he names Solon, Empedocles, Ion, Alcmaeon, Parmenides, Melissus, and Gorgias. In the *Helen* he also associates Protagoras, Gorgias, Zeno, and Melissus with the title, and it has been noted that he appears to refer to Plato's *Republic* and *Laws* as sophistical works in a dismissive remark in *To Philip* (12). With the exception of Protagoras and Gorgias, there is no overlap among the individuals Plato and Isocrates label sophists.[61] Ultimately, however, Plato's influence has proved more commanding and long-lasting in determining who should and who should not be designated σοφιστής.

---

[56] *Antidosis* 271.

[57] Isocrates is aware that his definition of φιλοσοφία deviates from what was typically associated with this term. In 272 he acknowledges that his opinions are so contrary to popular opinion (παράδοξα) that he is afraid to mention them, lest his audience respond with disapproving cries.

[58] Isocrates performs a similar equivocation of rhetoric with philosophy in *Against the Sophists* 17–18; cf. *Gorgias* 465c and 520a. For a discussion of the targets of Isocrates' invective in *Against the Sophists*, see Too 1995:161–164.

[59] Sidgwick 1872:293. Morrison 1958:218, expresses similar sentiments: "It is fascinating to observe how Isocrates has exactly reversed Plato's terminology, so that while the former's practical, purely professional training becomes philosophy, those who are concerned with *physis* are left with the name of sophist. 'Philosopher' and 'sophist' are labels now attached respectively to those teachers who do and those who do not subscribe to the speaker's view of the proper subjects for higher education."

[60] Isocrates uses the word thirty-one times: *Helen* 2 and 9; *To Philip* 12 and 29; *To Demonicus* 51; *Busiris* 43; *Panegyricus* 3 and 82; *To Nicocles* 13; *Panathenaicus* 5 and 18; *Antidosis* 2, 4, 148, 155, 157, 168, 194, 197, 203, 215, 220–221, 235, 237, 268, 285, and 313; *Against the Sophists* title, 14, and 19.

[61] There is some controversy over the remark that Zeno taught for money in *Alcibiades I* (119a4). If this dialogue is authentic, it would seem that Plato might have meant to designate him as a sophist. For a discussion of this passage, see Vlastos 1975:155–161, and chapter two, 44–45. For the authenticity of *Alcibiades I*, see Denyer 2001:14–26.

Whom, then, does Plato label sophist?[62] The list is short: Protagoras,[63] Gorgias,[64] Prodicus,[65] Hippias,[66] Euthydemus and Dionysodorus,[67] and Miccus.[68] In fact, many of the Isocratean sophists are treated as respectable philosophers in Plato.

In addition to the specific individuals that Isocrates classifies as sophists, he often uses the term in contrast to the poets, as a shorthand for practitioners of wisdom in general. This is how he employs σοφιστής in *To Demonicus* (51), where he admonishes his addressee to learn both what is best in the poets (τῶν ποιητῶν τὰ βέλτιστα) and the useful utterances of the other sophists (τῶν ἄλλων σοφιστῶν, εἴ τι χρήσιμον εἰρήκασιν); and he makes a similar bipartite division of the sources of wisdom between the poets (ποιηταί) and the sophists (σοφισταί) in the *Panegyricus* (82) and in *To Nicocles* (13).[69] In these examples, then, far from limiting its application to a defined and recognizable subgroup of practitioners of wisdom, Isocrates seems to use σοφιστής as an unmarked and inclusive term to refer to the wisdom tradition in a broad sense, presumably entailing everyone from the Seven Sages onward.[70]

In the *Antidosis* (168–170), Isocrates further clarifies his understanding of the relationship among rhetoric, sophistry, and philosophy. When elaborating on the reasons he is viewed with suspicion by his fellow Athenians, he notices that there is a general intolerance against rhetorical instruction (τὴν τῶν λόγων παιδείαν) in Athens, and that he thus runs the danger of suffering harm due to the common prejudice against the sophists (τῆς δὲ κοινῆς τῆς περὶ τοὺς σοφιστὰς διαβολῆς). But, he continues, he will give many reasons to prove that the prejudice against philosophy is unjust (φιλοσοφίαν ... ἀδίκως διαβεβλημένην) and that it should rather be embraced than hated.[71]

The first part of the argument is clear enough: the sophists, who teach rhetoric, have caused a general ill will against eloquence. Isocrates is not a sophist, but fears that the hostility against the sophists will be directed unfairly and

---

[62] This is not an attempt to treat exhaustively all the various contexts in which a figure occurs in conjunction with the labels "sophistry", "sophistic", etc. The present focus is simply to explore whom Plato explicitly labels a sophist.

[63] *Cratylus* 391c; *Protagoras* 311e, 313c, 314c, 314e, 317b, 317c, and 357e.

[64] *Meno* 95c; *Hippias Major* 282b.

[65] *Protagoras* 357e; *Symposium* 177b; *Laches* 197d; *Eryxias* 399c; *Euthydemus* 277e.

[66] *Protagoras* 314c, 349a, 357e; *Apology* 19e.

[67] *Euthydemus* 271c.

[68] *Lysis* 204a.

[69] The label seems to have an equally broad application in *Panegyricus* 3, where Isocrates remarks that he is aware that many who profess to be sophists (πολλοὶ τῶν προσποιησαμένων εἶναι σοφιστῶν) have eagerly taken up the topic that he is about to address.

[70] Solon is labeled sophist (*Antidosis* 313), and he is also mentioned as one of the seven sophists (*Antidosis* 235). Isocrates thus seems to have envisioned the Seven Sages, in general, and Solon, in particular, as the functional predecessors of the subsequent practitioners of wisdom.

[71] Cf. *To Philip* 29, where Isocrates reiterates how unjustified the opprobrium directed toward the sophists is (δυσχερείας τὰς περὶ τοὺς σοφιστάς).

indiscriminatingly against himself.[72] So far Isocrates' account seems to be in perfect harmony with Plato's *Apology,* where we hear of Socrates' unfair association with the sophists.[73] Indeed, in the *Apology,* Plato is very careful to point out the differences between the sophists and Socrates: as opposed to the sophists, Socrates never teaches for pay (31b–c), he is not a teacher (33a–b), and he possesses no wisdom (21b). To Plato, then, there is a fundamental difference between Socrates and the sophists, and Plato repeatedly has Socrates locate his own practices within the realm of philosophy (23d, 28e, 29c, 29d); the understood extension, of course, being that the sophists do not participate in this privileged field, but that their practices are un- or even anti-philosophical.

But it is precisely here that Isocrates deviates from the Platonic typology. Instead of maintaining the distinction between philosophy and sophistry, he seems to conflate the two by saying 1) that there is a common prejudice against the sophists, and 2) that the prejudice addressed against philosophy is unjustified. He uses a participial form of διαβάλλομαι twice within one paragraph to link semantically the prejudice directed at the sophists and philosophy, and so signifies that the same group of people is meant, only from two different perspectives: in the first instance they are labeled by the derogatory tag of their detractors (σοφιστής), while in the second instance they are given the privileged treatment by Isocrates as fellow *sophoi,* and their practices are thus referred to as belonging to the field of philosophy (φιλοσοφία).[74] Isocrates seems to suggest that the word sophist is used as a term of abuse against *all* those involved in philosophy, not exclusively with reference to a special subgroup of second-rate intellectuals, as is the practice in Plato.[75] When representing voices sympathetic to practitioners of wisdom, however, Isocrates uses the word φιλοσοφία to characterize their practices.

---

[72] Cf. *Panathenaicus* 5, where he complains that he is a victim of prejudiced misrepresentations at the hands of the discredited and worthless sophists (ὑπὸ μὲν τῶν σοφιστῶν τῶν ἀδοκίμων καὶ πονηρῶν διαβαλλόμενος).

[73] For the *Apology* as a subtext to Isocrates' *Antidosis,* see Nightingale 1995, especially chapter one.

[74] There is a similar conflation of sophistry and philosophy in Xenophon's *Memorabilia* (1.2.31), where we hear that Critias after coming to power as part of the Thirty passed a law against the teaching of rhetoric (λόγων τέχνην μὴ διδάσκειν) in an attempt to take revenge on Socrates for an old insult. Critias thereby sought, writes Xenophon, to impute the common censure against the philosophers to Socrates (τὸ κοινῇ τοῖς φιλοσόφοις ὑπὸ τῶν πολλῶν ἐπιτιμώμενον ἐπιφέρων αὐτῷ), and so misrepresented (διαβάλλων) him before the people. By predicating the common censure against the philosophers on the teaching of rhetoric Xenophon effectively obliterates the sharp distinction between sophists and philosophers, so carefully maintained in Plato (cf. Sidgwick 1872:291). Xenophon's choice of the verb διαβάλλω implies that the prejudice is undeserved, and this is similar to the Isocratean use.

[75] But even Plato acknowledges in the *Statesman* (299b) that σοφιστής could be used as a derogatory label against anyone undertaking clever speculations (σοφιζόμενος ὁτιοῦν) that go beyond the accepted norms. Cf. Sidgwick 1872:293.

These examples illustrate how contentious the words "philosopher" and "sophist" were. Both Plato and Isocrates sought to manipulate, appropriate, and even naturalize these terms so as to fit seamlessly into their own intellectual agendas.[76] In this context the label "sophist"—far from entailing certain unequivocal characteristics—is employed relative to "philosophy," frequently as an accusatory and derogatory designation. "Philosophy," on the other hand, is almost always reserved for the speaker's own intellectual position and penchants.

We have thus seen that there appears to have been no consensus in antiquity, either before or after the fourth century BCE, as to the precise nature and definition of σοφιστής,[77] or as to which individuals should be so labeled—and the same holds true for "philosophy," one might add. The sharp discrepancy between Plato's and Isocrates' views seems particularly helpful in expounding how contentious and multifaceted its application was, as Sidgwick observes:

> When two antagonists, with vocations so sharply contrasted as those of Plato and Isocrates were, both claim for themselves the name of Philosopher and endeavour each to fix on the other the odious appellation of Sophist, we may surely conclude that either term is in popular usage so vague as easily to comprehend both, and that the two are varyingly contrasted according to the temper of the speaker.[78]

We should thus be sufficiently warned neither to reify the term σοφιστής nor even to assume that it applies to specific individuals. It is true that Plato and Isocrates are in agreement that both Protagoras and Gorgias should be counted among the sophists, but the disagreement—particularly with regard to Solon, Empedocles, and Parmenides—is significant enough to underscore their widely different positions on sophistry and philosophy. I have focused on the difference between Plato and Isocrates in their understanding and application of "sophist" and "philosopher." One could of course argue that an exploration of how Xenophon and Aristotle use these terms might give more weight to the Platonic evidence in favor of Isocrates. But both Xenophon and Aristotle are heavily indebted to the Platonic position and add surprisingly little by way of

---

[76] Cf. Nehamas 1990:5, who has called attention to this agonistic process: "In the fourth century B.C. terms like 'philosophy,' 'dialectic,' and 'sophistry' do not seem to have had a widely agreed-upon application. On the contrary, different authors seem to have fought with one another with the purpose of appropriating the term 'philosophy,' each for his own practice and educational scheme." See also Nightingale 1995, esp. 13–60, for the conflicting views on philosophy in Plato and Isocrates.

[77] The present discussion is limited to the so-called "first sophistic." The situation is different in respect to the "second sophistic." For this intellectual current, see Whitmarsh 2005.

[78] Sidgwick 1872:293.

new or dissenting material on the sophists. One might equally complain over the lack of consideration of later evidence from, say, Philostratus and the rest, but here the difficulty is both the strong echoes of Plato, on the one hand, and the distance in time, on the other. What makes Isocrates so relevant is precisely his position as a contemporary of Plato—and one with a dissenting view on philosophy and sophistry.

In conjunction with his elaborate double attempt at disassociating the sophists from the tradition of the Seven Sages and the "legitimate" philosophical tradition, Plato remarks that the sophists were the first to charge money (*Hippias Major* 282c6). Given the contentious nature of Plato's history of philosophy just outlined, we need to reevaluate his statement of the sophists' habit of teaching for pay with this context in mind. To this we turn next.

2

Wisdom for Sale?

The Sophists and Money

Plato constantly accuses the sophists of teaching for money. For example, in the *Hippias Major* (282c–d) Socrates elaborates a distinction between the wise men of old, who did not think it right to charge fees, and the sophists of his own day, who all made huge profits from their instruction. This comparison is not incidental; it is absolutely integral to Plato's characterization of the sophists and their practices. But why is money so important as a distinguishing trait? In this chapter I will argue that it is not a descriptive term reflecting historical realities—that the sophists were the first to charge money for wisdom—but rather that the close association of the sophists with money is redolent of disparagement and bias, a fact that scholars have perhaps not paid sufficient attention to.[1] In what follows I will explore some possible connotations this connection carried in antiquity, and I will also develop reasons why Plato adopted it as basic to his portrayal of the sophists.

I will proceed by first considering the pervasiveness of the juxtaposition of the sophists and fees in the Platonic tradition,[2] and then turn to other genres and writers. Of particular significance are the attitudes represented in old comedy and Isocrates, since these sources, to varying degrees, are independent of Platonic influence. I will focus especially on the degree to which it is possible (or not) to detect a consistent attitude vis-à-vis the sophists in these non-Platonic writers that corroborates the traditional characterization of them as a distinct group of practitioners of wisdom set apart by the practice of teaching for pay. In the final section I will broaden my exploration to include other ancient juxtapositions of money and *sophia* to see if we can identify additional groups of *sophoi* that were criticized for charging money. Such groups could potentially be used

---

[1] Blank 1985:3 is an exception to this trend: "The testimonia referring to the fees, wealth, and mode of life of the sophists are tinged with both envy and disgust. They are extremely difficult to interpret, both in specific and in their general tendency."

[2] For a discussion of what is meant by the Platonic tradition, see chapter one, 22.

as parallels to our sophistic material to help us understand better the Platonic predilection for focusing on money and fees.

I will argue that teaching for pay was an inflammatory charge to which all *sophoi*, to one degree or another, were susceptible. It is important that we allow for a split between historical realities—about which we often know very little—and the way that those realities were expressed. A fee can be described as a gift or a bribe, but the practice of charging money can also go without comment. The language surrounding monetary transactions in antiquity is notoriously difficult to assess. Of particular sensitivity is the language surrounding *sophia* and the commodification of wisdom. Indeed, a favorite way to undermine the authority of a *sophos* (or public figures in general) was to suggest that they had monetary motivations and were driven by greed. We need to read the accusations—which is really what they are—against the sophists of exacting fees in light of these considerations.

Sophists and Money in the Platonic Tradition

First, then, let us consider what the Platonic tradition has to say about the sophists' practice of accepting money for instruction. Although, as David Blank concludes, Plato never explicitly has Socrates condemn the sophists for taking money,[3] the Platonic corpus is full of satirical diatribes against their pecuniary aspirations.[4] Few passages capture these sentiments as well as the beginning of the *Hippias Major* (282d–e), where Socrates remarks that Protagoras, Gorgias, and Prodicus all earned a lot of money from their wisdom (*sophia*). To which Hippias answers:

> Socrates, you know nothing of the beauties of this. For if you knew how much money I have made, you would be amazed. I will not bring up everything, but after coming once to Sicily I earned much more than one hundred-fifty minas in a short time, despite the fact that Protagoras was in town (he was famous and older than me); and from one really small place, Inycum, I made more than twenty minas. And after I went home with this money, I gave it to my father, so that he and the other citizens should be amazed and astonished. I dare say I think I made more money than any two sophists together.[5]

---

[3] Blank 1985:6.

[4] *Laches* 186c; *Meno* 91b; *Protagoras* 310d, 313c, 349a; *Gorgias* 519c–d; *Hippias Major* 281b–283b; *Sophist* 223a, 224c, 226a. Quoted from Corey 2002:189n4.

[5] There is little reason to doubt the authenticity of *Hippias Minor,* especially since it is mentioned by Aristotle in *Metaphysics* 1025a6–13 (see Friedländer 1964, part 2:146). With the *Hippias Major* it is a different story: it was first condemned as inauthentic in 1816 by Friedrich Ast, a student of Schleiermacher, who is known for disputing the authenticity of *Alcibiades I.* Few scholars would

Similar attitudes can be found in the *Sophist* (223b). There the visitor gives a definition of the expertise of the sophists. He describes it as belonging to the moneychanger's trade (νομισματοπωλικῆς), since it is a chase of rich and prominent young men (νέων πλουσίων καὶ ἐνδόξων γιγνομένη θήρα).[6] This juxtaposition of sophists and fees is ubiquitous in Plato. E. L. Harrison has collected some thirty passages where the two are mentioned in conjunction, and he argues that this association is essential to Plato's portrayal of the sophists:

> Indeed, it is no exaggeration to say that he is almost incapable of using the term sophist without at the same time making some explicit reference to this professionalism. And it comes as no surprise when this professionalism looms larger than any other element in each of the definitions of the sophist which appear in the dialogue of that name.[7]

It should be clear that if Plato is not outright condemning the sophists for taking fees, he is also not using a value neutral language when describing their practices. Far from it: they are regularly portrayed as more interested in procuring material rewards for their services than in worrying about the intellectual content or effect of their *sophia*. All this is in sharp contrast to his characterization of Socrates in the *Apology*, where Socrates' commitment to wisdom and the moral development of his fellow citizens has reduced him to all but total poverty. This hostile attitude towards the sophists is picked up and further elaborated by Xenophon and Aristotle. In the *Cynegeticus* (13.8–9), for example, Xenophon asserts that:

> The sophists speak to deceive and write for their own profit (κέρδει), and they never benefit anyone in any way. There neither was nor is any wise man (σοφός) among them, but each one of them is content to be called a sophist, which is a reproach, at least among prudent men (παρά γε εὖ φρονοῦσι). I thus recommend that you shun the precepts (παραγγέλματα) of the sophists, but that you do not dishonor the arguments (ἐνθυμήματα) of the philosophers. The sophists hunt young and

---

uphold the verdict of Ast today, when there seems to be a general consensus that it is a genuine Platonic dialogue. See Woodruff 1982:93–105 with bibliography, for a discussion of the issue of authenticity. But see also Kahn's (1985, esp. 267–273) review of Woodruff and his detailed argument for inauthenticity. For Schleiermacher's condemnation of *Alcibiades I,* see Denyer 2001:14–26.

6   I agree with Harrison 1964, when he remarks that, although this is a reference to "the eristical type of sophist ... it makes little difference whether he is a genuine successor of Protagoras or merely a degenerate Socratic: he is still a true sophist in the Platonic sense, i.e. he teaches rhetoric and makes money out of it," 191n46. Cf. 231d, where the first definition of the sophist is given: νέων καὶ πλουσίων ἔμμισθος θηρευτής, "hired hunter of wealthy young men."

7   Harrison 1964:191 and n44.

wealthy men (πλουσίους καὶ νέους θηρῶνται), while the philosophers are common (κοινοί) to and friends with all; they neither honor nor dishonor the fortunes of men.

The phrase πλουσίους καὶ νέους θηρῶνται echoes the line νέων πλουσίων ... θήρα of the *Sophist* quoted above, and the thematic content of the passage— that the sophists prioritize money over wisdom and are thus undeserving of serious intellectual consideration—is perfectly in line with Platonic sentiments. Aristotle makes the same connection in the *Sophistical Refutations* (165a22): "The sophist is a trafficker (χρηματιστής) in what seems to be, but is not, wisdom (σοφία)." In the *Memorabilia* (1.6.13), Xenophon employs a double strategy of first asserting and then condemning what he sees as an inherent connection between money and wisdom (the latter predicated on the former) among the sophists. But this time he adds an extra layer of opprobrium by expanding on the cultural implications associated with offering one's personal qualities for sale:

> Among us (παρ' ἡμῖν)[8] it is considered that there is a good and a shameful way to dispose of one's beauty and wisdom. If a man sells his beauty to any one who wants it, he is called a prostitute (πόρνον), but if he befriends someone he knows to be a noble and good lover (καλόν τε κἀγαθὸν ἐραστήν), he is thought of as prudent (σώφρονα). And in the same way we call those who sell their wisdom to anyone who wants it sophists, just as if they were prostitutes (ὥσπερ πόρνους),[9] whereas a man who befriends and teaches all the good he can (ὅτι ἂν ἔχῃ ἀγαθόν) to someone he knows to have a good natural disposition—he is considered to do what befits a good and noble citizen (καλῷ κἀγαθῷ πολίτῃ).

Here Xenophon establishes a thematic sequence consisting of wisdom, money, and prostitution, in which the interference of the intermediary phase—money— runs the danger of corrupting and even conflating the things of the mind with the sphere of the body.[10] This is, of course, exactly the opposite trajectory of what we are wont to see in Plato.[11] In the *Symposium* and the *Alcibiades I*, for example, love (ἔρως) is restricted to using the physical as an initial stepping stone only to climb the philosophical ladder and ultimately reject the body in favor of the mind, thus gradually transforming itself from a physical, sexual desire directed at a specific individual to a generic non-physical love of the

---

[8] For the meaning of παρ' ἡμῖν, see Morrison 1953 and Pendrick 2002:229.
[9] ὥσπερ πόρνους was deleted by Ruhnken and then Sauppe.
[10] For an exploration of the mind-body division in Plato, see Robinson 2000.
[11] This observation is indebted to Kurke's discussion (unpublished manuscript) of the philosophical trajectory from the body to the soul in the *Alcibiades I*.

beautiful.[12] By reversing this trajectory and by introducing the concept of intellectual promiscuity, Xenophon invites us to appreciate the contentiousness of his portrayal of the sophists. In this antagonistic depiction the mention of teaching for money is crucial in allowing the association of sophistic *sophia* with the body and, ultimately, with prostitution. Read in this way, teaching for pay takes on a more sinister facet than has previously been recognized, and it paves the way for the successive ubiquitous complaints of the speciousness of sophistic wisdom.

The fourth-century CE philosopher Themistius is a testament to the enduring relevance of the Platonic tradition. When trying to clear himself of accusations of being a sophist, he invokes Plato's definition in the *Sophist* (231d):

> According to the first in the list of arguments (καταλόγου τῶν λόγων) that Plato established with respect to the sophists, to be a sophist means charging the young and wealthy men (νέων καὶ πλουσίων) for any form of instruction (ἐφ' ὅτῳ δὴ σχήματι παιδείας).
>
> 23.289d

Themistius understands Plato's definition of sophist to include anyone who teaches for pay, regardless of the content of the instruction:

> But this is what I say: we shall consider receiving wages from the young men (νέων) for any instruction (ἐφ' ὅτῳ δὴ μαθήματι), whether it be serious or frivolous, as sophistical (σοφιστικόν), if we are to follow the argument [of Plato].[13]
>
> 23.290b

In Themistius' mind, then, the sole criterion for distinguishing a sophist hinges on whether he charges money for instruction. Considerations of intellectual content (e.g. rhetoric vs. dialectic; relativism vs. idealism) are of less relevance than this formal characteristic. To Themistius, just as to Socrates in the passage from Xenophon's *Memorabilia* quoted above (1.6.13), the pecuniary focus of the sophists inevitably disqualifies them from being considered serious philosophers and consigns them to the sphere of the body. Themistius is careful to

---

[12] See Ferrari 1992 for a fuller account of the role of ἔρως in Plato.

[13] In reaching the conclusion that anyone who teaches for pay is a sophist, Themistius refers to Plato's *Protagoras* (316d–317a), where the athletic trainers Iccus from Taras and Herodicus from Selymbria are outed as sophists, since this was their true identity, despite their attempts to hide under the veil of athletics out of fear of public hatred. Themistius goes on to say that Plato so designated them because they made money off of young men (ὅτι ἐχρηματίζοντο ἀπὸ τῶν νέων). But this is not the emphasis of Protagoras' speech. He focuses instead on his ability to educate men better than their own relatives and acquaintances. The issue of remuneration is ignored by Plato's *Protagoras*.

highlight the difference between himself, who improves both the body and the mind of his students, and the sophists, whose focus is exclusively on the body:

> But if he should care for the body (σαρκός) while plotting against the mind (τῇ διανοίᾳ), he would be a sophist and impostor (ἀλαζών).

23.290c

The sixth century CE Platonic commentator Olympiodorus brings the significance of the theme of teaching for pay into focus in his comments on a passage in Plato's *Alcibiades I*. At 119a4 Socrates says that Pythodorus and Callias became wise by associating with Zeno, and that each paid him a hundred minas (ἑκάτερος Ζήνωνι ἑκατὸν μνᾶς τελέσας). "Why," writes Olympiodorus, "did Zeno exact a fee, if he was a philosopher?" He goes on to speculate about possible reasons: to accustom his students to despise money, or to assist the poor by taking from the rich. The assumption seems to be that philosophy is incompatible with teaching for money, and Olympiodorus consequently concludes that Zeno "pretended to take money without taking it," (91–92 Westerink). But why is Olympiodorus so hesitant to accept this portrayal of Zeno in the *Alcibiades I*? Gregory Vlastos is very helpful in clarifying what such a portrayal would entail: "To so represent him [Zeno] is to portray him unmistakably as a professional sophist."[14] Olympiodorus presumably reached similar conclusions, that is, that teaching wisdom for pay is shorthand for sophist, and that is the reason for his consternation.[15] In accounting for this portrayal, Vlastos faced a dilemma. He either had to accept the depiction of Zeno as a sophist by Plato—which would question Zeno's traditional inclusion in the canon of the Presocratic philosophers—or else he had to reject the *Alcibiades I* as inauthentic:

> Now if this is what Zeno had been in fact, how could we account for the portrait in the *Parmenides*? Do we not know Plato's veneration for Parmenides, his scorn for sophists as hucksters of pseudo-wisdom and pseudo-virtue? Even if we were to think of that portrayal as pure invention, this would not mitigate the difficulty: even in a fictional setting, why should Plato have cast a *sophist* in the role he gives Zeno there— that of Parmenides' faithful disciple and intimate friend, erstwhile boy-love, now travelling-companion and fellow-guest in the home of an upper-class Athenian? On just these grounds, I submit, the historical veracity of this text in the *Alcibiades I* would be highly suspect.[16]

---

[14] Vlastos 1975:155.

[15] Zeno is never explicitly called a sophist in Plato. Isocrates (*Helen* 2) calls him a sophist along with Protagoras, Gorgias, and Melissus.

[16] Vlastos 1975:156.

A little later Vlastos revisits the issue of the dialogue's inauthenticity and writes:

> Can the case against the reliability of this particular *testimonium* be made to rest on more specific grounds? It can: First and foremost among these I would place the clash of this Zeno-sophist of our text with the figure portrayed elsewhere by Plato as Parmenides' right-hand man.[17]

But there is a case to be made that the two portrayals of Zeno in the *Alcibiades I* and *Parmenides* are not necessarily incompatible.[18] To begin with, in the *Parmenides* 128b–e Zeno says that he wrote his book in a youthful competitive spirit and that it was later published through unauthorized copying. This seems to imply that to Plato Zeno's work was predominantly eristic in nature and had more affinities with the sophists than with philosophers. In *Phaedrus* 261b–e it is presumably Zeno who is intended by the epithet "the Eleatic Palamedes" whose rhetorical skill is such that "his listeners will perceive the same things to be both similar and dissimilar, both one and many, both at rest and also in motion" (trans. Gill and Ryan). This portrayal reinforces the picture from the *Parmenides* that to Plato Zeno's work was predominantly eristic in character, and it does not seem entirely unreasonable to think that Plato regarded him as a sophist. The question remains why Vlastos would find the Zeno-sophist portrayal incompatible with his characterization as "Parmenides' right-hand man."

Nevertheless, as representatives of the Platonic tradition, both Olympiodorus and Vlastos found it puzzling, even impossible, to accept as sincere the designation of Zeno as teaching for pay by Plato, and so they devised different strategies to circumvent this dilemma: Olympiodorus postulated hidden motivations for Zeno's behavior, while Vlastos challenged the Platonic authorship. To both, however, teaching for pay had become synonymous with being a sophist, even though Plato himself never explicitly made that connection or used the word sophist in connection with Zeno.

Thus far we have seen that there is a remarkable unity of attitudes in the representations of the sophists in the Platonic tradition. This tradition exhibits a thematic emphasis on money over wisdom, on body over mind, in stark opposition to the Platonic valorization of the intellect. More than anything, though, the lasting effect, as exemplified by Xenophon, Themistius, Olympiodorus, and Vlastos, is that the definition of "sophist" became based on a formal characteristic rather than on intellectual content. Next we shall turn to old comedy and Isocrates to see to what extent this unanimity of attitudes is reflected there as well.

---

[17] Vlastos 1975:156.
[18] I owe this point to one of *CP*'s anonymous readers (cf. Tell 2009).

Sophists and Money in Old Comedy and Isocrates

In his influential article "Socratics Versus Sophists on Payment for Teaching," David Blank undertakes to "summarize 'popular' complaints about the sophists' accumulation of wealth."[19] He concludes that, "the Athenians seem to have thought that the sophists charged outrageous fees."[20] According to Blank, there is sufficient evidence in non-Platonic authors and genres—mainly old comedy—to support the claim that complaints directed at the sophists go well beyond Platonic criticism, and that Plato's hostile characterization of them simply reflects these pre-existing, negative popular attitudes.

Before accepting Blank's conclusions, however, let us review the *testimonia* that he uses in support of his argument. We are especially interested in any sources that fall outside the Platonic tradition, since they would testify to popular discontent with the sophists that is independent of Plato.[21] To what extent can we justifiably talk about resentment of the sophists for venality outside the Platonic tradition?[22]

In surveying Blank's *testimonia* for popular discontent with the sophists, I have chosen to divide the material into five sections. We shall first treat Plato's predecessors and contemporaries in old comedy (1) and Isocrates (2). Next, we shall consider the evidence found in Philostratus (3). Finally, we shall deal with two groups (4–5) of predominantly later sources that offer *testimonia* regarding the one hundred mina fees of Zeno, comments on Protagoras and Gorgias, and miscellaneous remarks about the sophists and fees.

Following Nestle,[23] Blank quotes liberally from the comic fragments to illustrate attacks on the sophists' avaricious practices. But his treatment is often problematic. For example, when referring to Eupolis' Κόλακες, he translates fragment 175 (K-A) as: "neither fire nor spear nor sword could keep sophists from coming to dinner" (1985:5), though there is no equivalent for the word sophists in the Greek (οὐ πῦρ οὐδὲ σίδηρος / οὐδὲ χαλκὸς ἀπείργει / μὴ φοιτᾶν

---

[19] Blank 1985.

[20] Blank 1985:1 and 3. See also his useful compilation of relevant *testimonia* (25–49); cf. Nestle 1942:455–476.

[21] Blank's reconstruction of popular discontent with Protagoras, Prodicus, Hippias, and Thrasymachus is based exclusively on Plato and thus needs no comment. As for Eupolis' attack on Protagoras in Κόλακες (fr. 157 K-A) for being "the *aliterios* who speaks nonsense about the heavenly phenomena while eating the things from the ground," this has nothing to do with Protagoras' fees or monetary ambitions; it pokes fun at the discrepancy between his unworldly intellectual pursuits and earthly desires. For a discussion on how to translate *aliterios*, see Storey 2003:185–187.

[22] The following survey will be based on the sources Blank has collected in his 1985 paper "Socratics Versus Sophists on Payment for Teaching." I have occasionally left out or included an additional item to Blank's list. For the most part, however, I have attempted to adhere closely to his sources.

[23] Nestle 1942, esp. 455–476.

ἐπὶ δεῖπνον). Storey offers a different interpretation of this passage, one where the sophists have no place at all: "I suspect it comes from the *parodos,* when the chorus of *kolakes* enters. The chorus would be describing their own abilities."[24] Blank assigns Protagoras as the speaker of fragment 172 (K-A), although there is no evidence to support the view that the chorus consisted of sophists or indeed had anything to do with sophistical practices.[25] Storey has recently argued that such associations are mistaken: "these *kolakes* do not sound the least bit sophistic in fr. 172; they are expert spongers, and it is that picture that Eupolis is exploiting here."[26] Blank also incorrectly represents Plato Comicus as criticizing the sophists' greed,[27] when his remark is in fact limited only to Antipon's φιλαργυρία.[28] He further writes (1985:5) that in Ἀστράτευτοι ἢ Ἀνδρογύνοι (fr. 36, K-A) Eupolis "referred to the sophists who spent their time 'in the nicely shaded walks of the god Akedemos.'" But here, too, Blank seems to be mistaken:[29] "the associations of the Academy c. 420 are surely those of athletics rather than intellectuals."[30] Finally, Blank's assertion (1985:5) that the chorus of Eupolis' Αἶγες was "comprised of goats representing sophists," seems equally unwarranted.[31]

All in all, Blank's use of old comedy as evidence of popular discontent with the sophists is unconvincing. There appears to be little evidence to support the claim that they were systematically attacked in old comedy. As Carey observes, Aristophanes' rivals appear to have shown little interest in the sophists as individuals:[32]

---

[24] Storey 2003:191.

[25] Blank 1985:6. Storey translates the fragment in the following way (2003:17): "We shall now describe to you the life which the spongers lead. Hear first that we are clever men in every way. First we have a slave attending us, mostly someone else's, but a little bit mine as well. I have two good cloaks and putting on one or the other I head off to the Agora. When I see some fellow there, not too bright but very rich, I am all over him at once. Whatever this rich man utters, I praise to the skies and I stand there struck, pretending to enjoy his words. Then we go our various ways to dine off another man's bread. There the sponger must come out with many witty things immediately or be chucked out the door. I know that's what happened to Akestor (used to be a slave); he made a really bad joke, and the slave took him outside with a collar round his neck, and handed him right over to Oineus."

[26] Storey 2003:192.

[27] "The sophists' reputation for greed grew along with their bank balances. Plato the comic poet mentions *their* greed (φιλαργυρία)," 5. My emphasis.

[28] Plato Comicus *Peisandros* 110 (K-A) = [Plutarch] *Lives of the Ten Orators* 833c: κεκωμῴδηται δὲ (sc. Ἀντιφῶν) εἰς φιλαργυρίαν ὑπὸ Πλάτωνος ἐν Πεισάνδρῳ.

[29] Nestle 1942:459, too, thinks that the mention of Academus is meant to refer to a crowd of philosophers and sophists.

[30] Storey 2003:78.

[31] See Storey's discussion of the play, 2003:67–74.

[32] There is considerably more interest devoted to Socrates' person in old comedy. For references and discussions, see, for example, Dover 1968; Patzer 1994; Imperio 1998; Carey 2000; Whitehorne 2002; and Edmunds 2006.

Perhaps one of the most surprising aspects of the fragments of Old Comedy is the paucity of references to some of the most illustrious thinkers of the late fifth century. Gorgias, Prodikos, Hippias, and Thrasymachos are ignored in the fragments of Aristophanes' rivals ... But in contrast to the presence of Sokrates in the fragments of old comedy the silence is so striking that one is inclined to suppose that relatively little attention was paid to the major sophists as individuals.[33]

Far from singling out a distinct group of people as sophists, old comedy seems to use σοφιστής as a derogatory epithet applied to a broad category of intellectuals. The sophists "are presented more as an example of a familiar social nuisance (or in the case of Sokrates as an example of unworldly folly) than as a new and sinister corrupting force."[34]

Isocrates also offers numerous *testimonia* regarding the sophists and money. What makes him a critical source is his contentious relationship with Plato. They disagreed about the role and content of education, and the wide discrepancies in their understanding of *philosophia* are well documented in modern scholarship.[35] Isocrates, then, just like the authors of old comedy, has the potential of offering us a view of the sophists that is independent of Platonic manipulation.

In the *Antidosis* (220) he asserts that the income of a sophist is contingent upon the moral development of his students: the better the student, the larger the earnings. He describes the successful students as "noble, honorable and wise and held in great esteem by their fellow citizens" (καλοὶ κἀγαθοὶ καὶ φρόνιμοι ... καὶ παρὰ τοῖς πολίταις εὐδοκιμοῦντες). This characterization strikes a different tone from what we find in the Platonic dialogues, where the very possibility of teaching someone to be καλὸς κἀγαθός for a fee is questioned. In the same speech (155–156), in an effort to downplay the rumored gains of the sophists, Isocrates mentions that Gorgias—in his view the most successful of the sophists—left behind only a thousand staters despite his dedication to money-making. At the beginning of the *Helen* (2–3), Isocrates identifies particular individuals as sophists. He speaks disparagingly of their intellectual activities and criticizes them for "caring for nothing else but to make money off of the youth" (χρηματίζεσθαι παρὰ τῶν νεωτέρων, *Helen* 6). But the individuals that Isocrates singles out as sophists in the *Helen* significantly differ from the Platonic equivalent: Isocrates names Protagoras, Gorgias, Zeno, and Melissus.[36] Elsewhere he

---

[33] Carey 2000:427. Protagoras is mentioned by Eupolis in *Kolakes,* frs. 157–158 (K-A).
[34] Carey 2000:430.
[35] For Plato's and Isocrates' contention over *philosophia,* see discussion in introduction n3, and chapter one n4–5, n51, and n76.
[36] For a list of the Platonic sophists, see chapter one, 34.

also refers to Solon, Empedocles, Ion, Alcmaeon, and Parmenides as sophists,[37] and he alludes to Plato's *Republic* and *Laws* as sophistical works in a remark in *To Philip* (12).[38]

Most of the Isocratean sophists are treated as respectable philosophers in Plato. In contrast to Plato, Isocrates does not seem to see the issue of teaching for pay as a necessary corollary of the use of the word sophist; only twice does he mention particular individuals as sophists and remark on their habit of teaching for pay. When he discusses sophists and their fees elsewhere, he never identifies particular individuals. In *Against the Sophists*, for example, he complains about those who set themselves up as teachers of the young. They are, he writes, themselves in need of instruction and should thus pay rather than accept fees.[39]

As opposed to the unsympathetic treatment of the sophists in the Platonic tradition—a treatment that seems motivated by their portrayal as greedy peddlers of specious wisdom—Isocrates offers a more nuanced critique. In *Against the Sophists* (4) he points to the discrepancy between their practice of charging fees while publicly downplaying the importance of money:

> They say that they have no need for money, dismissively referring to wealth as worthless silver and gold (ἀργυρίδιον καὶ χρυσίδιον τὸν πλοῦτον ἀποκαλοῦντες), but in their desire for a small profit they promise to make their students all but immortal (μικροῦ δὲ κέρδους ὀρεγόμενοι μόνον οὐκ ἀθανάτους ὑπισχνοῦνται τοὺς συνόντας ποιήσειν).

In Isocrates there is a distinction between what the sophists say and what they do: their official position is to dismiss the value of money—presumably in line with dominant social norms—while privately pursuing monetary gains. What upsets Isocrates is that they deviate from their publicly stated position. In contrast to Plato's one-dimensional picture of sophistic greed, Isocrates acknowledges two points about teaching for pay: one that the sophists themselves publicly promote (disregard for money), and one that attracts Isocrates' censure (greed). Far from openly announcing their fees, the Isocratean sophists are careful, at least rhetorically, not to violate the propriety of the social norms by presenting themselves as engaged in money-grabbing practices. They do not publicly endorse the practice of offering instruction for money, nor do

---

[37] Isocrates uses the word thirty-three times: *Helen* 2 and 9; *To Philip* 12–13 and 29; *To Demonicus* 51; *Busiris* 43; *Panegyricus* 3 and 82; *To Nicocles* 13; *Panathenaicus* 5 and 18; *Antidosis* 2, 4, 148, 155, 157, 168, 194, 197, 203, 215, 220–221, 235, 237, 268, 285, and 313; *Against the Sophists* title, 14, and 19; *fragments* 8 and 17.

[38] See chapter one for a fuller discussion of the differences between Plato's and Isocrates' sophists.

[39] 13.13; cf. 13.7 and 13.9. See Too 1995:156–161, for a discussion of the stratification of the targets of Isocrates' invective.

they describe their relationship with students as an economic rapport between producer and consumer.

Isocrates himself offers an instructive example of how to negotiate the tension between charging fees and avoiding public opprobrium for greed.[40] As Yun Lee Too has shown, "he prefers to present the teacher-student relationship as an extension of a friendship (*philia*) or a guest-host relationship (*xenia*)."[41] Too goes on to point out that Isocrates frequently refers to his own teaching in terms of public service, and that he characterizes the advice that he offers in his writings as gifts.[42] In other words, Isocrates carefully embeds any discussion of what could be described as economic transactions in the language of friendship and reciprocity. The fees, together with the instruction itself, are represented as disinterested gifts presented out of a sense of gratitude (χάρις),[43] not as a contractual compensation for rendered services. By adopting the language of friendship and guest-host relationship, Isocrates skillfully resists seeming to commodify his *sophia* and simultaneously ensures that his practices appear decorous and safely situated within the social practices of the elite.

Isocrates' self-presentation offers us an interpretive model by which to understand the complicated and often contentious language surrounding teaching for pay. He is preoccupied with making sure that no one mistakes his students' fees as merely fees, but that they be understood as motivated by gratitude and reciprocity. It seems clear, given this emphasis, that there were others who disputed his characterization and accused him of banausic professionalism.[44] Many *sophoi* developed similar rhetorical strategies of representing their practices as embedded in networks of gratitude and civic service.[45] These rhetorical justifications were motivated by the frequent invectives against the

---

[40] He is reported not to have charged Athenian citizens, only students from abroad (see Forbes 1942:20, and Too 1995:109). This claim seems to be based on Isocrates' remark in *Antidosis* 39, where he states that all his wealth has come from abroad (ἐμοὶ δὲ τὰς εὐπορίας ... ἔξωθεν ἁπάσας γεγενημένας).

[41] "In several works he insists that by offering counsel to certain individuals he is continuing the friendship which he had with their fathers (cf. *Epistle* 5.1; *Epistle* 6.1). He specifically asks the addressees of *Epistle* 6 to consider the epistle as *xenia*, as a token of guest-friendship (4)," Too 1995:110. For the importance and relevance of the institution of *xenia* in general, see Herman 1987.

[42] Too 1995:109–111. "In the prefaces to *To Demonicus* and *To Nicocles* Isokrates characterises the advice he gives to his addressees as a gift (*dōron, To Demonicus* 2; *dōrean, To Nicocles* 2)," 111.

[43] For the importance of χάρις in Isocrates, see Too 1995:109. For χάρις in the orators, see Ober 1989:226–230 and 236 with bibliography.

[44] For an exhaustive discussion of *banausia*, see Nightingale 1995:56–59, esp. n93. See also Nightingale 2004:123–127.

[45] See Kurke 1991:85–107 for Pindar's employment of the language of ξενία and χάρις in respect to his patrons and audience.

monetary—and thus moral—integrity of *sophoi*.[46] What makes this a particularly difficult subject to address, however, is our almost complete lack of knowledge about the historical realities regarding teaching for pay in the ancient world.[47]

We will explore invectives against *sophoi* for venality in the next section. For now, I would like to round up the discussion about Isocrates by noting that he does not consistently single out specific individuals whom he labels sophists and accuses of teaching for pay. When he does identify particular individuals as sophists, however, they are at a strong variance with the Platonic sophists. He often leaves the objects of his invective vague and unspecific, as in *Against the Sophists*. This has led scholars to ask who the subjects of his attacks are.[48] Too has suggested that this vagueness is motivated by the genre of invective:

> Invective, as a discourse, produces stereotypes and so it has a tendency to efface the distinctive differences between the individuals it targets. It tends to lump its victims together into broad, readily identifiable classes, transforming them into something 'other' to be dismissed.[49]

In *Against the Sophists*, Isocrates appears to be using the sophists as foil for the articulation of his own intellectual position. He lumps them together as an amorphous group that he can attack with impunity. This practice resembles closely Carey's description of old comedy's utilization of the label sophist in respect to a broad type of *sophoi* as "an example of a familiar social nuisance"[50]— an indistinct group of people onto whom a number of unattractive qualities can be projected and subsequently criticized.

Next we shall consider Philostratus, who provides numerous *testimonia* on sophistic instruction for pay. He mentions the fees of Protagoras, Gorgias, Prodicus, and Hippias, but in so doing he seems largely to be rehearsing Platonic sentiments. For example, just as he relates that Protagoras was the first to converse for a fee (μισθοῦ διαλέγεσθαι πρῶτος εὗρε), he mentions Plato and alludes to a passage from the *Protagoras*.[51] In this passage Socrates describes

---

[46] The most obvious example of such attacks is perhaps Aristophanes' treatment of Socrates in the *Clouds* and the defense mounted by the Platonic tradition; cf. Owen's (1986) illuminating discussion of "Philosophical Invective."

[47] When it comes to Plato and Aristotle, for example—who both accuse the sophists of taking fees— we have only vague ideas of how they financed their schools: "Very little is known about the financial aspect of either school. Plato accepted gifts of money from Dion, Dionysios, and others (*Epistle* 13). There is similar evidence that support from Alexander the Great was one of the means by which Aristotle's school was able to carry on some of its more elaborate research," Lynch 1972:83. See Forbes 1942 for a general discussion of the evidence of teaching for pay in antiquity.

[48] For Isocrates' invective in *Against the Sophists*, see Too 1995:161–164.

[49] Too 1995:160–161.

[50] Carey 2000:430.

[51] *Lives of the Sophists* 1.10.

how Protagoras refers to himself as a sophist and as being so confident in his ability as a teacher of excellence (ἀρετή) that he was the first to deem it right to charge a fee for this (πρῶτος τούτου μισθὸν ἀξιώσας ἄρνυσθαι).[52] When talking about Gorgias' high fees for teaching Polus, on the other hand, Philostratus quotes directly from the *Gorgias* (467b), where Polus is featured as Socrates' interlocutor.[53]

In the introduction to the *Lives of the Sophists* (482–483), Philostratus describes how Prodicus went from city to city with his Heracles fable and gave a paid lecture (ἔμμισθον ἐπίδειξιν), and he adds that he "charmed the cities like an Orpheus" (θέλγων αὐτὰ τὸν Ὀρφέως ... τρόπον), a phrase that appears to be borrowed from Plato's description of Protagoras in *Protagoras* 315a (κηλῶν τῇ φωνῇ ὥσπερ Ὀρφεύς). His description of Prodicus' habit of "searching out the young nobles (εὐπατρίδας) and those from wealthy homes" echoes Plato's definition of the sophist as "a paid hunter of wealthy young men" in *Sophist* 231d.[54] Finally, when addressing Hippias' desire for money, he mentions Hippias' visit to Inycum in Sicily, narrated in *Hippias Major* 282e, and adds that Plato mocked its citizens.[55] It seems safe to say, then, that Philostratus offers little evidence about the practice of teaching for money of Protagoras, Gorgias, Prodicus, and Hippias that can justifiably be classified as independent of Plato. His discussion of the sophists' fees appears deeply informed by the Platonic dialogues, which he often paraphrases or directly quotes.

Finally, we need to consider two clusters of evidence: one that deals with the one hundred mina fees and one that contains miscellaneous remarks about teaching for pay. In 1975 Vlastos protested against what he saw as the uncritical scholarly acceptance of five ancient *testimonia* claiming that Zeno, Protagoras, and Gorgias charged one hundred mina fees.[56] Vlastos contrasted these references with earlier sources (mainly Plato and Isocrates) and concluded that the one hundred mina fee was a fantastic sum "fished up" by later writers.[57] Kerferd, writing in 1981, adopted a more agnostic stance, and acknowledged that we know close to nothing about the actual circumstances regarding the fees, such as the length of the course or number of students.[58] The *testimonia* look suspiciously standardized, and their lateness and uniform agreement on the one hundred mina fee detract from their validity as compelling sources on the sophists' fees. But to try, as did Vlastos, to establish actual historical amounts based

---

[52] *Protagoras* 349a.
[53] *Lives of the Sophists* 1.13.
[54] *Lives of the Sophists* 1.12.
[55] *Lives of the Sophists* 1.11.
[56] Vlastos 1975:159, esp. n114. Zeno: *Alcibiades I* (119a). Protagoras: Diogenes Laertius 9.52; scholion to Plato, *Republic* 600c Greene. Gorgias: Diodorus Siculus 12.53.2; Suda [Gorgias].
[57] Vlastos 1975:160.
[58] Kerferd 1981:27.

on Plato and Isocrates seems equally misguided. The sum probably originates from Plato's *Alcibiades I.* As evidence for teaching for pay, however, this group of *testimonia* offers little of value.

There is finally a group of miscellaneous references to the sophists and teaching for pay. Diogenes Laertius (9.50) records that Protagoras and Prodicus declaimed speeches (λόγους ἀναγινώσκοντες) for which they charged fees. The very next sentence begins with a reference to Plato's *Protagoras*, so it seems reasonable to suspect that Diogenes is drawing on Plato, perhaps having the *Cratylus* (384b2–6) in mind, where we hear of Prodicus' variously priced lectures. Diogenes also relates an anecdote (9.56) of how Protagoras quibbled with a student over a fee.[59] In this group of *testimonia* we find Themistius' description of how Protagoras, Gorgias, and Prodicus used to advertise their wisdom as just another thing for sale.[60] We have already explored Themistius' indebtedness to Plato. Finally, Athenaeus (3.113d–e) mentions in an off-hand remark that Blepsias made more from his erudition than both Protagoras and Gorgias. These miscellaneous remarks do not amount to much in terms of offering independent evidence of the sophists' practice of teaching for pay. Blank's argument for the existence of popular discontent with the sophists' fees—a discontent that Plato taps into, but does not articulate—seems unsupported. Many of the later sources seem simply to recycle the negative sentiments of the Platonic tradition, while Plato's predecessors and contemporaries diverge in significant ways from his depiction of the sophists.

Plato's testimony, in turn, is not a value-neutral description of historical realities, as it has often been treated, but a polemical and disparaging portrayal. It should perhaps be understood better as an example of what Owen has labeled "philosophical invective." We are familiar enough with how invectives operate in genres such as iambic poetry, comedy, and oratory—where misrepresentation of or all out disregard for the facts is to be expected—but personal abuse in philosophical writing has rarely been studied.[61] In the final section we shall shift our focus from philosophical texts to attacks on *sophoi* in other genres. We shall be careful to note any analogies between the treatment of *sophoi* in these genres and the Platonic characterization of the sophists.

---

59 This story was also retold by Roman authors. For discussion and references, see Forbes 1942:18, esp. n45.

60 23.286b–c; cf. 289c–d.

61 "[I]f we had been considering the orators and not the philosophers it would have seemed no more than a commonplace that there are stock forms of abuse in fourth-century invective, conventional slanders which can be employed with little or no care for the facts," Owen 1986:357. See Worman's (2008) recent exploration of how the language of insult operates in Greek literature, which has chapters devoted to Plato, Aristotle, and Theophrastus.

Money and *Sophia*

Lloyd has called attention to how the author of the *Sacred Disease* charges his rivals with fraud (2.1–10) and of being desirous of gain (βίου δεόμενοι, 4.17).[62] The epithets used to describe opponents are μάγοι (quacks/wizards), καθαρταί (purifiers), ἀγύρται (charlatans/beggar priests), and ἀλαζόνες (impostors).[63] In discussing this passage, Lloyd emphasizes the discrepancy between the vigor of the attacks and the self-assurance on the part of the author, on the one hand, and the actual differences of treatment promoted by the author and his opponents, on the other:

> [T]he testimony of *On the Sacred Disease* would tend to run counter to any thesis to the effect that the undermining of magical beliefs follows an increase in the control that could be exercised over the areas of experience to which the beliefs in question related. It is striking that our chief critical text deals with a topic—epilepsy—where the author himself, so far from having any effective means of treating the disease, was—*we* should have said—just as helpless as the charlatans he attacked.[64]

The author directs charges of greed against fellow medical practitioners,[65] and to these charges he attaches accusations of quackery and charlatanism. Based on our knowledge of the medical practices and treatments, however, there is a sharp discrepancy between the "argumentative weaponry"—where differences are stressed—and the actual "empirical content"—where significant overlaps existed.[66] On the empirical level the differences seem far less absolute than the rhetorical posturing would lead a reader to believe.[67] The chief thrust of the rhetorical argumentation is devoted to undermining rival views. This strategy was presumably a two-way street: just as the author of the *Sacred Disease* accused his opponents of fraud and greed, so they would retort with similar

---

[62] Lloyd 1979:16–17. For practitioners of medicine as *sophoi* and members of the Greek wisdom tradition, see e.g. Lloyd 1979 and Thomas 2000. There is a strong link between wisdom and healing in figures such as Epimenides, Empedocles, and Alcmaeon. For examples of doctors as *sophoi* in Plato, see, for instance, *Lysis* 210a, *Euthydemus* 280a, *Theages* 123d–e, and *Epinomis* 976a. All references to the *Sacred Disease* are from the edition of Jones 1923.

[63] We need to be careful not to maintain or assign exact meanings to these terms of abuse. They are generally employed in reference to anyone singled out for strong censure. Cf. Lloyd's (1979:56) comments regarding the practice of accusing one's rivals of practicing magic or of being magicians in the Hippocratic corpus: "The connotations and denotations of these terms are not fixed (any more than those of 'charlatan', ἀλαζών, were); rather they are used of what particular writers happen to disapprove of."

[64] Lloyd 1979:49.

[65] As to the identity of those opponents, see Lloyd 1979:37–39.

[66] The formulations are those of Lloyd 1979:125.

[67] For examples of overlaps, see Lloyd 1979:39–45.

accusations.[68] The allegation of greed in the *Sacred Disease*, then, seems closely linked to the larger rhetorical strategy of undermining the authority of the opponents, and the invectives of quackery work in tandem with this challenge. The accusation of greed seems to yield little information about the historical practices of doctors. Instead, it is part of a stock repertoire of invective directed at an opponent in an attempt to undermine his claim to *sophia*. This is a theme familiar from comedy, where attacks against *sophoi* for greed are also frequent.

Aristophanes' portrayal of Socrates and his disciples in the *Clouds* closely mirrors the Platonic treatment of the sophists. Socrates and his followers are said to teach success in speech if they receive pay (ἀργύριον ἤν τις διδῷ, 98), and this monetary arrangement is referred to three more times in the course of the play (245–246, 876, and 1146).[69] But this is not the only exchange of wisdom for money ridiculed in comedy, and the charge is not limited to Socrates and his followers. We see similar caricatures aimed at seers in the *Birds* (958–991) and the *Peace* (1045–1126). In these plays diviners appear on stage claiming to possess useful divine knowledge, but we soon learn that they are more interested in procuring gifts for themselves in return for their prophesies.[70] This arrangement of wisdom (*sophia*) for money or gifts is similar to the exchange between Strepsiades and Socrates in the *Clouds* as well as the sophistic practices portrayed in the Platonic tradition.

Seers in particular seem to be portrayed as possessing qualities that are usually associated with the sophists.[71] The connection between *sophia* and divination was strong in antiquity. Seers held a prominent position in the Greek wisdom tradition and were often referred to as both σοφοί[72] and

---

[68] For evidence of the animosity between practitioners of temple medicine and doctors, see Lloyd 1979:46.

[69] Socrates (*Apology* 19b–c) refers to Aristophanes' representation of him in the *Clouds* as slander (διαβολή).

[70] Aristophanes stages a χρησμολόγος in the *Birds* and a μάντις in the *Peace*. "A μάντις is one who interprets divine signs: a χρησμολόγος is one who has a store of oracles," Platnauer 1964:154. See also Mikalson 1991:92 and n118 for bibliographical references; and Flower 2008:58–65 for the differences among seers, priests, and oracle-singers.

[71] Cf. Flower 2008:147. This is, of course, not to ignore the similarities (more commonly noted among scholars) between seers and poets: "Now poets and seers were closely related, as both were dependent on kings, were inspired, led itinerant lives, were often represented as blind, and pretended to possess supernatural knowledge," Bremmer 1996:102. On seers, see Burkert 1983 and 1985; Roth 1984; Smith 1989; Mikalson 1991; Dillery 2005; and Flower 2008.

[72] Teiresias: *Bacchae* 178–179, *Oedipus Rex* 484; cf. Calchas: *Iphigeneia in Tauris* 662 and *Ajax* 783, and seers in general in *Rhesus* 65–66. For a discussion of the early Greek wisdom tradition, see Guthrie 1971, esp. 27–32, and Kerferd 1976.

    The necessity to split Teiresias' competence in the *Bacchae* into two (as does Mikalson 1991:95 and 147)—one pertaining to mantic expertise and one pertaining to traditional qualities of the wise man—is thus unnecessary; the figure of the seer was *ipso facto* a wise man.

σοφισταί.[73] They also exhibit similar social practices as the sophists. Like them, many led an itinerant lifestyle and interacted almost exclusively with the elite. In his exploration of the social position of the seers in ancient Greece, Jan Bremmer has noted that those who figure in our sources "belonged to the highest aristocracy."[74] Mark Griffith likewise has called attention to tragedy's portrayal of Teiresias "as a long-standing and integral member of the Theban political community" who never interacts with "lower-class characters."[75] In the *Republic* (364b–c), Plato offers an unflattering portrayal of how seers (ἀγύρται δὲ καὶ μάντεις) come to the doors of the rich (ἐπὶ πλουσίων θύρας) to persuade them that they possess a god-given power (δύναμις) that, at little expense (μετὰ σμικρῶν δαπανῶν), they can put at the disposal of their wealthy patrons.[76] This description bears strong resemblances to the Platonic account of the sophists' gravitation towards the houses of the wealthy.[77]

But similarities between sophists and seers are not limited to formal characteristics. Grube detected a significant intellectual indebtedness to the sophistic movement in the Euripidean portrayal of Teiresias in the *Bacchae*, and he posited that there were other such "theological sophists" active in fifth-century Athens:

> There must have been many seers and prophets in fifth-century Athens, theological sophists who clung to the orthodox belief in gods with all but human forms and personality, but who were intelligent enough to know that they must make some concessions to rationalism.[78]

Building on Grube, Paul Roth has explored the intellectual indebtedness of fifth- and fourth-century seers to their surrounding intellectual environment, and he has persuasively argued for strong overlaps.[79] Just like sophists, then, seers are represented as practitioners of wisdom eager to sell their *sophia* to anyone interested in paying for it, and their avarice is viciously criticized. The treatment of the Theban seer Teiresias in tragedy is exemplary of this development—a treat-

---

[73] Herodotus 2.49; Aristophanes *Clouds* 331–334; Dio Chrysostom 32.39. References quoted from Kerferd 1950:8. For the sophistic qualities of Teiresias in the *Bacchae*, see Roth 1984 and Smith 1989.

[74] Bremmer 1996:97. Cf. 1996:100. For the elite status of many seers, see Flower 2008, esp. 5–6 and 47.

[75] Griffith forthcoming.

[76] Cf. *Laws* 909b, where Plato accuses religious experts of being willing to use their expertise to wreak havoc on individuals, homes, and cities for the sake of money (χρημάτων χάριν). For a discussion of the Greek conception of magic and the use of the terms ἀγυρτής and μάντις in Plato's *Republic*, see Graf 1997, esp. 20–29.

[77] For example, Callias' house in the *Protagoras* and Callicles' in the *Gorgias*. Plutarch (*Pericles* 36.3) also chronicles Pericles' association with known sophists, especially Protagoras.

[78] Grube 1961:404, quoted from Roth 1984:60n4.

[79] Roth 1984.

ment we will explore next to illuminate the typological characteristics of the censure against seers.[80]

Teiresias is repeatedly referred to as σοφός[81] and is welcomed on stage as a well-disposed and potentially salutary figure. When he first appears in *Oedipus Rex* (300), for example, he is heralded by Oedipus as possessing omniscient powers and as being the sole savior of the state, the one on whom they were all depending (ἐν σοὶ γὰρ ἐσμέν, 314). After Teiresias' initial refusal to share his divinely inspired information (φάτιν, 323), Oedipus gently prods him by pointing out that his unwillingness to share his knowledge is not a grateful gesture vis-à-vis the city that nurtured him (οὔτε προσφιλῆ πόλει / τῇδ', ἥ σ' ἔθρεψε, 322–323). Oedipus' strategy consists in emphasizing the bonds of kinship and mutual dependency that exist between them to compel the seer to volunteer his information. When Teiresias finally speaks out and reveals that it is Oedipus who is the murderer of Laius, Oedipus quickly discards any remaining notions of affinity and accuses Teiresias of conspiring against him with Creon. He goes on to add that Teiresias has eyes only for profits but is blind in respect to his art (ἐν τοῖς κέρδεσιν / μόνον δέδορκε, τὴν τέχνην δ' ἔφυ τυφλός, 388–389). There is thus a complete reversal of the initially cordial reception: Teiresias goes from being a savior to an impostor and quack (μάγος and ἀγύρτης, 387–378).[82] In connection with this emotional turnaround, Oedipus introduces the accusation of greed.

In *Antigone,* Creon directs a similar accusation of venality at Teiresias. Initially (993), however, Creon stresses that he has always in the past followed Teiresias' advice, and that he can testify to the benefits of doing this from personal experience (ἔχω πεπονθὼς μαρτυρεῖν ὀνήσιμα, 995). When it becomes clear to Creon that the advice that Teiresias gives—that he allow a proper burial for Polynices—goes against his own creed, he lashes out at him (1035–1036) and complains that he has been bought and sold and exported long ago (ἐξημπόλημαι κἀκπεφόρτισμαι πάλαι) by the race of seers; and a little later, in line 1055, he exclaims that the whole breed of seers is money-loving (τὸ μαντικὸν γὰρ πᾶν φιλάργυρον γένος). Just as in the passage from *Oedipus Rex*, the charge of greed is triggered by the failure of reciprocity: only when Teiresias fails to deliver what Oedipus and Creon have reasons to expect from a trusted and valuable advisor do they resort to attacking his credibility by accusing him of greed. The same pattern is repeated in the *Bacchae* (255–257), where Pentheus accuses Teiresias

---

[80] For Teiresias in Greek tragedy, see Flower 2008:204–208.

[81] For references, see n72.

[82] It is of particular interest that Oedipus chooses to call Teiresias an ἀγύρτης and μάγος here. The author of *The Sacred Disease* uses the same words to attack all who assert that the sacred disease is divine (he adds καθαρταί and ἀλαζόνες to the list), and Plato employs ἀγύρτης in the *Republic* (364b–c) to brand seers as greedy peddlers of fraudulent religion.

of having introduced the worship of Dionysus to give himself more opportunities to observe the birds and to charge fees for interpreting burnt offerings.[83]

Teiresias, then, is introduced as a privileged advisor to the rulers. He is revered for his wisdom and is thought of as well-disposed to the leaders and the community he serves. In *Oedipus Rex* and *Antigone* he is invited to help bring resolution to the affliction that is currently weighing down on the *polis*. When Teiresias provides information that is perceived as unfavorable to the ruler and the *polis* at large, the offended party retorts by invalidating his *sophia* by charging him with greed. By implication, if his answer complies with the expectations of his interlocutors and is seen as beneficial, no such charge would be levied against him. What is so titillating about the initial encounters between Teiresias and Creon in *Antigone,* and Teiresias and Oedipus in *Oedipus Rex* is that it offers a glimpse of what an ideal interaction might look like.[84]

To judge from his cordial reception, we can infer that Teiresias' advice was well-received in the past, and that his socially elevated position depends on his previously successful guidance. As opposed to comedy, tragedy does not convey an exclusively negative picture of seers as butts of abuse, but tends instead to focus on the breakdown in reciprocity, when cordiality turns into invective. What motivates this charge, then, is not the historical realities—all seers were greedy and all too willing to sell their wisdom for money—but the rhetorical strategy of attacking one's opponent's weakest point. The allegation of greed and bribery accomplishes precisely that: it undercuts the authoritative position of the *sophos* by implying that he has ulterior motives.

I suggest that we use the findings from the *Sacred Disease,* comedy, and tragedy as an analogy to the charges against the sophists of teaching for pay in the Platonic tradition. There are important overlaps and thematic continuities in the way the accusations of venality are treated in these authors and genres. First, the charge often occurs as part of a more general invective discourse, coupled with abusive and derisive epithets such as ἀλαζών, ἀγύρτης, and μάγος.[85] Second, its force is mainly destructive, aiming to undermine the authoritative claims of the opponents. Finally, it does not seem to be motivated by an ambi-

---

83   Already in the *Odyssey* (2.186), Eurymachus scolds Halitherses for his interpretation of a bird portent, and charges him with trying to procure gifts for his own household.

84   See Flower 2008:188–210, who outlines what a successful consultation between diviner and client would have looked like.

85   Plato's treatment of the sophists deviates from this pattern, since he avoids the epithets ἀλαζών, ἀγύρτης, and μάγος in conjunction with his criticism of their practice of charging money. But his satirical portrayal of them as hunters of the young (*Sophist* 221–223) and as retailers in wisdom (*Protagoras* 313d) leaves little doubt that his remarks belong to an abusive context (for more examples, see discussion above: 40–41); Plato seems to be more concerned in his choice of epithets with emphasizing the trend towards unchecked commodification of wisdom among the sophists—a fact that Xenophon's likening them to prostitutes perfectly illustrates (*Memorabilia* 1.6.13).

tion to establish actual historical differences in social practices; rather it is an expression of what Lloyd calls the "argumentative weaponry" of the accusers.

In political oratory, charges of bribery are legion, but few would mistake rhetoric for reality in this context.[86] We need to allow for a similar split in the representation of seers in comedy and tragedy and, by extension, of the sophists in the Platonic tradition. Our knowledge about the factual details regarding fees and monetary rewards for instruction is very scant, but the treatment of Teiresias offers us an interpretive framework for understanding the shift from a potentially unproblematic interaction to an aggressive emphasis on money and intellectual fraud.[87] Although Plato's characterization of the sophists (or the comic treatment of seers) shows no interest in this shift of attitude but focuses exclusively on invective, the motivation for the abusive treatment remains comparable: to deflate the intellectual credentials of the opponents and, concomitantly, to boost one's own claims to *sophia*.

---

[86] For discussions of bribery and the many inflated charges found there, see, e.g. Perlman 1976; MacDowell 1983; Harvey 1985; and Taylor 2001a and 2001b..

[87] The practice of charging money seems to have been common among poets, artists, and doctors. For references and discussion, see Kerferd 1981:25 and Lloyd 1987:92n152.

3

Sophoi and Concord

IN THIS CHAPTER we shall examine the theme of concord (ὁμόνοια), which figures so prominently in the sources on the sophists. The aim is to advance our understanding of this concept beyond Kerferd's pessimistic verdict: "It is ... a matter for regret that it is simply not possible to recover the history of the term in fifth-century thought."[1] The discourse on concord offers an ideal case study to explore the intellectual continuities discussed up to this point. It links the sophists to contemporary and earlier practitioners of wisdom, dating all the way back to the Seven Sages. Better understanding these continuities, in turn, will allow us to appreciate how integrated the sophists were in the Greek wisdom tradition, and also offer a corrective view to the Platonic insistence on the sophists' unique status.

We shall approach this topic by surveying the sources on the sophists to see in what contexts their calls to ὁμόνοια appear. We shall then consider the historical uses of the term beyond the sophists, broadening our exploration by moving away from an exclusive consideration of the word ὁμόνοια to a broader investigation of the theme of concord. This broader scope will direct us to the practices of the early lawgivers and sages, but we shall also consider in this context poetic and choral expressions of concord and equality. By exploring concord thematically, we can recover practices and preoccupations shared by a diverse group of *sophoi*. In the process, we shall see how the sophists were the inheritors of an intellectual discourse that traces its origins back to the beginning of the Greek wisdom tradition.

The History of the Discourse on Concord

Let us start with a short review of the actual fragments preserved to us from Gorgias, Thrasymachus, and Antiphon. Gorgias addressed the Greeks at Olympia

---

[1] Kerferd 1981:149.

during the Olympic Games on the matter of ὁμόνοια in 408 BCE.[2] The reason for his address, we are told, was the presence of discord (στάσις) among the Greeks:

> For seeing that Greece was distracted by factions (στασιάζουσαν γὰρ τὴν Ἑλλάδα) he became a counselor of concord (ὁμονοίας) to them, turning them against the barbarians and convincing them to make as prizes of their weapons not each others' cities, but the land of the barbarians.[3]

He is also reported to have given a speech at Delphi during the Pythian Games as well as a funeral oration at Athens. Philostratus gives the following account of his speech at Athens:

> Although he goaded the Athenians on against the Medes and the Persians and championed the same idea as in his *Olympic Speech*, he did not discuss concord (ὑπὲρ ὁμονοίας) with the Greeks at all, since he addressed the Athenians, who were desirous of rule (ἀρχῆς ἐρῶντας), which they could not obtain unless by resorting to drastic measures. But he kept praising victories over the Medes, pointing out to them that "victories over barbarians call for festive hymns, whereas victories over the Greeks call for lamentations."[4]

Thrasymachus laments the terrible political climate of his day in his speech *On the Constitution*:

> The past is enough: we are at war instead of peace and through dangers we have come to the present situation, where we long for yesterday and fear tomorrow. Instead of concord we have ended up with mutual hostility and turmoil (ἀντὶ δ' ὁμονοίας εἰς ἔχθραν καὶ ταραχὰς πρὸς ἀλλήλους ἀφικέσθαι).[5]

Antiphon is credited with writing a work *On Concord* (Περὶ Ὁμονοίας),[6] to which Diels and Kranz attribute a number of fragments.[7] The case of Antiphon poses a particular problem.[8] Nowhere in this work does the word ὁμόνοια appear, and the content has invited scholars to posit a unique use of concord, a use that pertains

---

2 Romilly 1972:228n5, argues for the year 392: "408 used to be suggested but that hypothesis has been, apparently correctly, abandoned," but Flower 2000:92 gives good grounds for keeping 408.
3 Philostratus *Lives of the Sophists* 1.9.4 = DK 82A1.
4 Philostratus *Lives of the Sophists* 1.9.5 = DK 82A1.
5 Dionysius of Halicarnassus *De Demosthene* 3 = DK 85B1.
6 Hermogenes *Id. (Peri ideon)* 2.11.116 = DK 87A2.
7 DK 87B44a–71.
8 See Pendrick's (2002) discussion and bibliography of Antiphon's Περὶ Ὁμονοίας, esp. 39–46.

to an inner, psychological, sense of concord. Hans Kramer has shown convincingly, however, that, whenever ὁμόνοια occurs in any Greek author before Plato, it is almost always contrasted with discord (στάσις), and this reinforces the idea that concord is a fundamentally political concept.[9] There is thus no evidence for it ever to have been used in an ethical sense before Plato, and there is no reason to assume a psychological, non-political meaning in Antiphon.[10]

It is not clear when ὁμόνοια was first used by any Greek author.[11] Kramer argues that it was coined sometime after the 450s BCE as a response to the growing political turmoil in the Greek city-states. In such a period of factionalism, says Kramer, it is easy to understand that wise men persuaded their cities to practice concord among each other, and the sophists were the first to do so.[12] In promoting this belief, however, Kramer had to dismiss several sources that point to an earlier use of the word. Plutarch preserves an account about Heraclitus who, it is said, was invited by his citizens to speak on the topic of concord:[13]

> Are not those who communicate the critical points figuratively (συμβολικῶς) without speech especially praised and admired? So Heraclitus, when the citizens demanded that he speak his mind on concord (περὶ ὁμονοίας), went up to the *bema* and took a cup filled with cold water. After sprinkling it with barley–meal and stirring it with a mint-sprig, he drank it and went away. Thus he showed them that being content with what one has and not wanting extravagant things maintains the city-states in a state of peace and concord (ἐν εἰρήνῃ καὶ ὁμονοίᾳ διατηρεῖ τὰς πόλεις).[14]

The same story is told by Themistius,[15] but he never mentions concord. Instead he tells us that Ephesus was under siege at that time and hanging onto life by a thread, and that Heraclitus was thus recommending a rationing of food. This siege is not mentioned by Plutarch, however, and some have argued that

---

[9] For examples of the subsequent transition of ὁμόνοια from a predominantly political to psychological force, see Plato *Republic* 352a and *Definitions* 413b. See also Pendrick 2002:41–42, esp. n76.

[10] Kramer 1915:54–59. For a fuller discussion of the political significance of ὁμόνοια, see Schmid-Stählin 1940:164, esp. n17. See Schofield 1991:128–129, for a discussion of the development of the term ὁμόνοια from Plato to the Stoics.

[11] The first known instance of it being used is probably in 411 BCE in Thrasymachus (DK 85B1); cf. Romilly 1992:226–227; and Huffman 2005:200–201.

[12] Kramer 1915:13–14. Cf. Moulakis 1973:20.

[13] Kramer 1915:15n7.

[14] Plutarch *De Garrulitate* 511b–c = DK 22A3b.

[15] Περὶ ἀρετῆς 40 = DK 22A3b.

he confused the historical circumstances.[16] Such confusion would disqualify Plutarch as a trustworthy source for the use of ὁμόνοια before the 450s BCE.

Pseudo-Aristotle also mentions concord before quoting Heraclitus in the spurious De Mundo,[17] but the author does not explicitly attribute this word to Heraclitus. Romilly has argued that we should not understand the mention of concord as being part of Heraclitus' philosophical discourse. We should rather see it as part of Pseudo-Aristotle's context and thus reject any connection to Heraclitus.[18]

The so-called Themistocles decree contains the participle ὁμονοοῦντες,[19] but the authenticity of this decree is hotly disputed, and it is possible that its actual date is not 480, as the content would indicate, but that it rather dates back to shortly before 348, as some stylistic features point to.[20]

Finally, we have preserved in Diodorus Siculus an oracular response of Delphi to Lycurgus, the shadowy lawgiver of Sparta:

> There are two roads that lie most apart from each other,
> One leads to the honorable house of freedom (ἐλευθερίας),
> But the other to the house of slavery (δουλείας), which is shunned by
>   mortals.
> It is possible to travel the former road through manliness
> And lovely concord (διά τ' ἀνδροσύνης ἐρατῆς θ' ὁμονοίας);
> Be sure you lead your people on this path;
> But the latter goes through hateful strife and impotent delusion
>   (διὰ στυγερῆς ἔριδος καὶ ἀνάλκιδος ἄτης);
> Be sure to be most on your guard against this one.[21]

The authenticity of this oracle has been the subject of much debate. Romilly argues that there are good reasons to reject it as a reliable historical document, especially to support an early use of ὁμόνοια.[22]

---

[16] See Kramer 1915:15n7. Cf. Romilly 1972:202–203.

[17] 5.396b7 = DK 22B10.

[18] Romilly 1972:202.

[19] Meiggs-Lewis 1969, 23:44.

[20] Andocides confirms the historicity of this decree in On the Mysteries (107), where he draws a parallel between the amnesty of Patroclides in 403 BCE and an amnesty made in the face of the Persian invasion of Greece. He refers to the result of both these amnesties as ὁμόνοια among the Athenians. The problem with this account, however, is the numerous historical errors committed by Andocides, such as not distinguishing between Marathon and Salamis. For a discussion on this with bibliography, see Meiggs-Lewis 1969:48–52; Romilly 1972:203–205; and Moulakis 1973:19. This inscription had not yet been published when Kramer wrote (it was first published in SEG 18 [1962] 153), and it was thus not considered by him.

[21] Diodorus Siculus 7.12.2.

[22] Romilly 1972:207. For a full discussion and bibliography of the various criticisms raised against this oracle, see Romilly 1972:205–209.

Except for these four sources, the earliest instances of ὁμόνοια are found in the late fifth century.[23] There is no way to confirm that the word was not used before that time. We can only note that in the texts that have come down to us it is not to be found in earlier authors.[24] Following Kramer, Romilly traces the emergence of the discourse on concord to a defense against the imminent disintegration of the city-state, which she dates to the end of the fifth century BCE, and she explains the occurrence of concord in the four texts quoted above as instances where discourses were borrowed from a later time and projected back onto an earlier context.[25] She allows for the possibility that there was an earlier use that we simply do not have preserved in our sources, and this she finds more plausibly to have existed in earlier textual traditions on Sparta.[26]

Scholars have noted and commented on the importance of concord for the sophists. Kramer, for example, writes that since they were well versed in every branch of knowledge, they were naturally turned to for help to solve the aggravated political situation that existed in many city-states towards the end of the fifth century BCE; and their response was a universal call for concord.[27] Romilly, likewise, attributes to them a profound investment in the needs of social life; and this investment translates into a commitment to a stable social and political situation of the city-states.[28] Guthrie, in turn, who emphasizes the sophists' democratic sensibilities, saw their preoccupation with concord as a natural expression of their egalitarian ethos.[29] Common to most modern interpretations, however, is the inclination to understand the word at face value, often reading into it a real, historical call to concord motivated by an imminent political crisis that threatened the community as a whole.[30] But this way of understanding the word—since it assumes a transparent meaning of concord—tends to pay less attention to the cultural context in which the word was used.

Few scholars have for example considered the connection between the sophists and the theme of concord from a perspective that predates the threat to the city-state during the end of the Peloponnesian War, and even fewer have sought to locate it in city-states other than Athens. This we shall attempt next, without reopening the question of the first dateable occurrence of ὁμόνοια. We shall instead focus on the broader connection between concord and wisdom,

---

23 Kramer 1915:13; Moulakis 1973:19.
24 Moulakis 1973:20.
25 Romilly 1972:200–201.
26 Romilly 1972:206.
27 Kramer 1915:13.
28 Romilly 1972:200.
29 Guthrie 1971:150.
30 Huffman 2005:200, exemplifies this position: "The concept of *homonoia* or concord among citizens is thus born from the need to defend the city against imminent disintegration, because of the strife between democrats and oligarchs."

specifically as expressed by philosophers, sages, mediators, lawgivers, poets, priests, magicians, and other groups invested with the authority of *sophia*. Our starting point will be a short survey of how the concept of concord was employed and by what authors.[31]

The concept of concord figures prominently in early texts, but the word ὁμόνοια itself does not occur until later. Instead we find words from the root ὁμοφρον-, as in the *Iliad, Odyssey, Homeric Hymns*, and Hesiod.[32] Herodotus never uses the word,[33] nor does it occur in classical Greek poetry but is limited to prose texts.[34] In reviewing the material on ὁμόνοια, I have found it convenient to divide it into four groups: occurrences that relate to the reconciliation after the regimes of the Four Hundred and the Thirty in Athens; discussions of internal unity and war against the barbarians; treatises on Sparta and the Spartan form of government; and philosophical or political discussions of the significance of concord.

Thucydides uses the word twice. It is first employed (8.75) in the oaths sworn by the Athenian soldiers at Samos in 411 BCE in the attempts of Thrasybulus and Thrasyllus to reconcile the democrats and oligarchs in face of the recent coup of the Four Hundred in Athens. The second use (8.93) relates to the same year, when Athenian hoplites in Piraeus were engaged in building a wall at Eetionia. Since they suspected that it would only serve to help the Four Hundred receive a Spartan fleet, they tore it down and marched on the city to overthrow the Four Hundred. Before reaching the city, however, they were won over by people sent out by the Four Hundred and agreed to hold an assembly on the theme of concord.

Aristotle uses the word with reference to the situation in 403, when the Spartan king Pausanias had facilitated reconciliation between the factions in Athens that had been for and against the rule of the Thirty. The terms of the agreement stipulated that the Thirty repay Sparta separately what they had borrowed for the war, but the Athenians decided to repay the loans from the public funds, since they thought that this was the necessary first step for reconciliation (ἡγούμενοι τοῦτο πρῶτον ἄρχειν δεῖν τῆς ὁμονοίας).[35] This action receives strong approval from Aristotle.[36] Both Isocrates and Demosthenes

---

[31]   This is not an attempt to exhaust every occurrence of ὁμόνοια, only to suggest a rough outline to determine in what sorts of contexts the word was discussed. I have found the work of Kramer extremely helpful for this purpose, and I have repeatedly drawn on his conclusions. His is the fullest treatment of ὁμόνοια and its meaning in Greek literature to date. See also Ferguson 1958:118–132; Romilly 1972; Moulakis 1973; Romer 1982; and Huffman 2005:182–224.

[32]   Kramer 1915:8–14.

[33]   Kramer 1915:12.

[34]   Moulakis 1973:19.

[35]   *Constitution of Athens* 40.3. Cf. Xenophon *Hellenica* 2.4.38.

[36]   *Constitution of Athens* 40.2–3.

mention this decision to repay the loans from public money, and they also ascribe it to a desire to promote ὁμόνοια.[37] The events that played out at the end of the fifth century that led up to the amnesty of 403 were later referred to as a praiseworthy example of how internal dissension was turned into concord by the courage and wisdom of the democrats who led the opposition against the Thirty from Piraeus.[38] In this set of examples ὁμόνοια becomes almost synonymous with the reconciliation that took place after the Thirty; this has motivated a number of scholars to conclude that the word arose in response to the fierce factionalism prevalent during the Peloponnesian War.[39] It is interesting to note, however, that Aristotle brings an economic dimension to his use of ὁμόνοια: the decision to repay the debt to Sparta from the public funds initiated the process of concord. The alternative, as Aristotle says in his appraisal of this action, would have been a total redistribution of land by the democrats after they seized power.[40] Economic moderation is a theme that reoccurs with some frequency in our sources on concord, and we will have occasion to revisit it at greater length later in this chapter.

Another important context for ὁμόνοια is the call to unified action on the part of the Greeks against the barbarians.[41] We have already observed that Gorgias in his *Olympic Speech* encouraged the Greeks to maintain concord among themselves while waging a collective war against the Persians. Lysias also delivered an *Olympic Speech,* whose synopsis and beginning are preserved in Dionysius of Halicarnassus.[42] In 388,[43] Lysias stood before the collected Greeks at Olympia and encouraged them to dethrone Dionysius, the tyrant of Syracuse, and to liberate Sicily, before Dionysius could join arms with the King of Persia and attack mainland Greece. In the preserved fragment, the word ὁμόνοια itself does not occur. Instead, Lysias pleads that the Greeks put off their wars against each other and, being of a single mind (τῇ δ᾽ αὐτῇ γνώμῃ χρωμένους), cling to their safety. The wording, at least in the short preserved fragment we possess, is not the same as in Gorgias, but the similarity between the two speeches in name, content (the Greeks must unite against an exterior enemy to survive), and occasion (delivered at the Olympic games), all suggest that Lysias was well aware of his predecessor's call to concord.

---

[37] Isocrates *Areopagiticus* 69; Demosthenes *Against Leptines* 12.

[38] Lysias *Funeral Oration* 63; *Subverting the Democracy* 20; Isocrates *Against Callimachus* 44–46; Andocides *On the Mysteries* 106 and 140.

[39] Kramer 1915:23; Moulakis 1973:20.

[40] *Constitution of Athens* 40.3.

[41] Cf. Kramer 1915:38–45.

[42] Dionysius of Halicarnassus *Lysias* 30.

[43] Dionysius himself does not give us a date for the speech, but Diodorus Siculus 14.107.1 and 14.109.1 mentions that Lysias held his address at the ninety-eighth Olympiad (388 BCE).

In the beginning of the speech, Lysias tells the story of how Heracles founded the Olympic Games and instituted two kinds of competition, one athletic and one intellectual. The reason why Heracles did this, Lysias goes on to explain, was because of the beneficial effects it would have on the Greeks:

> ἡγήσατο γὰρ τὸν ἐνθάδε σύλλογον ἀρχὴν γενήσεσθαι τοῖς Ἕλλησι τῆς πρὸς ἀλλήλους φιλίας.

> For he thought that the assembly here would be a beginning for the Greeks of mutual friendship.[44]

Lysias stresses the unifying force of the Olympic Games (and all other Panhellenic games, one may surmise) and, given the result of his call—the audience indeed looted the tents of Dionysius at the games—it seems reasonable to assume that he spoke to well-rooted conceptions of unity and common Greek identity that were cultivated through the institution of the Panhellenic games. That is precisely what makes them the perfect arena for his address of internal unity and external aggression. Herodotus (8.26) gives another example of the unifying force of the Olympic Games. After the battle at Thermopylae, some Arcadians approached the Persians in search of food and employment, and when asked what the Greeks were up to, they responded that they were celebrating the Olympic Games. When asked what the prize (κείμενον) was over which they were competing, they answered that it was a wreath of olive leaves. Upon hearing this, one of the Persians cried out in distress that they had to face men who do not compete for money but honor (οἳ οὐ περὶ χρημάτων τὸν ἀγῶνα ποιεῦνται ἀλλὰ περὶ ἀρετῆς). Herodotus, in addressing a Greek audience, skillfully uses the Persian bewilderment to comment on the formative experience that the celebration of the Olympic Games entails, an experience that in Herodotus' narrative is so peculiarly Greek so as to be unintelligible to non-Greeks.[45] The conclusion—that Greeks value honor higher than money—leaves little doubt as to the moral messages of the passage: the superiority of the Greek way of life, fostered and promoted at the Panhellenic centers.[46]

---

[44] Dionysius of Halicarnassus *Lysias* 30 = speech no. 33, Lysias OCT (Carey).

[45] Aristophanes' *Lysistrata*, performed in 411, presents us with additional evidence of the bonds of common identity fostered at the Panhellenic sites. In lines 1128–1134, a character reproaches the Spartan and Athenian delegates by declaring:
> You who at Olympia, at Thermopylae, and at Delphi—how many other places could I mention if I were to speak at great length?—purify the altars, like kinsmen, with a single sprinkling of lustral water, are destroying Greek men and Greek cities, though enemies are at hand with a barbarian army.

[46] To place further stress on the constitutive experience of the games, one could mention how important a task it was for the Olympic officials to prevent *barbaroi* from competing at the games; cf. Herodotus 5.22.2. See also Hall 1997:64.

Isocrates expresses similar ideas in *Panegyricus* 3, where he says that he has come as a counselor on the war against the barbarians and on concord among the Athenians. He proceeds by acknowledging that he is aware that many sophists have addressed this theme before him (οὐκ ἀγνοῶν ὅτι πολλοὶ τῶν προσποιησαμένων εἶναι σοφιστῶν ἐπὶ τοῦτον τὸν λόγον ὥρμησαν). Later in the same speech, he explains his rationale for counseling the Athenians to wage an external war while practicing concord among themselves:

> For neither is it possible to have a secure peace (εἰρήνην ... βεβαίαν), unless we fight the barbarians jointly, nor for the Greeks to practice concord (ὁμονοῆσαι τοὺς Ἕλληνας), until we get our spoils from the same people and face dangers against the same people.[47]

Isocrates reiterated this theme in a number of speeches throughout his life. When the Athenians and Spartans persevered in their hostilities, he sought the help of other potentates to promote his policy ideas: Jason, the tyrant of Pherae;[48] Dionysius, the tyrant of Sicily;[49] Archidamus, the son of Agesilaus;[50] and finally Philip, the king of Macedon.[51] Demosthenes, too, adopted the theme of concord among the Greeks and aggression against the Persian king.[52]

Michael Flower has sought to trace the origin of such Panhellenic appeals back to the period right after the Persian invasion of Greece and to the policies of Cimon.[53] Such a reorientation would push panhellenism as an idea some seventy years farther back in time than previously thought—many argue that Gorgias was the first to promote it[54]—and it would also shed new light on the sophists' role in this discourse: instead of originators they are to be seen as one installment in a long tradition that began after the Persian invasions of Greece and ended with the final conquest of Persia by Alexander the Great.

Flower draws mainly on Herodotus as a source to substantiate the existence of a Panhellenic discourse earlier than Gorgias' *Olympic Speech*.[55] In Book 5.49.3–9, for example, Herodotus describes how Aristagoras during the Ionian Revolt

---

[47] Isocrates *Panegyricus* 173.
[48] Isocrates *To Philip* 119.
[49] Isocrates *To Philip* 81.
[50] Isocrates *Epistle* 9.
[51] Isocrates *To Philip*.
[52] *On the Navy-Boards* 14. See also *Against Philip* 38.
[53] Flower 2000. The aspect of Panhellenism he is interested in pursuing is "the idea that the various Greek city-states could solve their political disputes and simultaneously enrich themselves by uniting in common cause and conquering all or part of the Persian empire," 65–66.
[54] Flower 2000:66, esp. n6–8.
[55] Flower also refers to the new Simonides papyrus on the Battle of Plataea. This poem was probably performed in the 470's, and it seems to raise the idea of a Greek invasion of Persia. It has further been suggested that this poem was a Spartan commission, which would support the view that the impetus for Panhellenism is not to be attributed exclusively to the ideological

went to Sparta to persuade King Cleomenes to attack Persia. This proposition is historically implausible but, as Flower says, it reveals "the thought patterns and agenda of Herodotus' own times," and can help illuminate the concerns discussed in the latter half of the fifth century.[56] If his interpretation is correct, Herodotus adapted the theme of a Persian invasion, relevant to a contemporary audience, and projected it back onto older events. Such displacement is at work in Book 6.84, for example, when Scythian representatives approach Cleomenes to discuss an attack on Persia in revenge for Darius' attack on Scythia; and this theme is even put into the mouth of Xerxes (7.11) in discussing an invasion of Greece. The options, he says, are either for the Persians to conquer Greece first or to be subjugated by the Greeks. Especially relevant for our discussion of concord is a remark made by some Thebans to Mardonius in Book 9.2 as he was marching on Athens:

> κατὰ μὲν γὰρ τὸ ἰσχυρὸν Ἕλληνας ὁμοφρονέοντας, οἵ περ καὶ πάρος ταὐτὰ ἐγίνωσκον, χαλεπὰ εἶναι περιγίνεσθαι καὶ ἅπασι ἀνθρώποισι.

> As far as the strength of the Greeks is concerned, if they, who actually were united in the past, practiced concord, it would be difficult even for all men to overcome them.

Similar sentiments are expressed in Book 5.3 regarding the Thracians:

> εἰ δὲ ὑπ᾽ ἑνὸς ἄρχοιτο ἢ φρονέοι κατὰ τὠυτό, ἄμαχόν τ᾽ ἂν εἴη καὶ πολλῷ κράτιστον πάντων ἐθνέων κατὰ γνώμην τὴν ἐμήν

> If they were ruled by one man or were united, they would, in my opinion, be invincible and by far the most powerful people.

But, Herodotus adds, the Thracians are indeed incapable of such unity and are therefore weak (ἀσθενέες). This theme is also touched upon in Book 8.75, when Themistocles secretly sends a messenger over to the Persian fleet to urge them to attack the Greeks, since they, not practicing concord (οὔτε γὰρ ἀλλήλοισι ὁμοφρονέουσι), would put up no resistance. Finally, in Book 8.3, Herodotus gives the reason why the Athenians did not clash over the command of the fleet in 480; they were concerned about the survival of Greece (μέγα πεποιημένοι περιεῖναι τὴν Ἑλλάδα) and realized that, if they were to quarrel over the command, Greece would surely be lost. Herodotus approves of their reasoning with the comment that:

---

framework of the Delian League and the Athenian empire. For the Simonides papyrus, see West 1989–1992:118–122 and 1993; and Flower 2000:66–69, which includes bibliography on this topic.

[56] Flower 2000:69–73. For the idea that no Greek would have thought that an attack on Susa would have been feasible, see 70–71, esp. n28–29, and 76.

στάσις γὰρ ἔμφυλος πολέμου ὁμοφρονέοντος τοσούτῳ κάκιόν ἐστι ὅσῳ
πόλεμος εἰρήνης

For a civil war is worse than a war of common consent by just as much
as war is worse than peace.

In the *Histories* we can detect a clear preoccupation with the idea of invading
Persia, a preoccupation addressed to a contemporary audience. Further, the
theme of internal concord is intrinsically linked to external aggression. War is
even described as bringing about concord (πολέμου ὁμοφρονέοντος). *Stasis*, on
the other hand, generates weakness. This typology fits well with our findings on
ὁμόνοια. There, too, we see the juxtaposition of *stasis* and concord, debilitation
and prosperity. Although it is possible to discern thematic similarities between
the two contexts, Herodotus never uses the word ὁμόνοια, instead favoring
ὁμοφρονέειν and other periphrastic locutions, such as φρονέειν κατὰ τὼυτό.

If the appeals to concord in Herodotus address contemporary concerns
rather than chronicling historical realities, whose concerns were they and with
whom did they originate? Flower argues persuasively that they date back to the
policies championed by Cimon:[57] "There is only one person whom we know of
whose policy was Panhellenic in the sense of waging incessant war on the possessions of the king of Persia and who was simultaneously well-disposed towards
cooperating with Sparta, and that was Cimon, the son of Miltiades."[58] This was
a theme that gained traction under Cimon and regained popularity during the
deteriorating conditions during the second half of the Peloponnesian War.

Yet another significant context for the language of ὁμόνοια is discussions
centering on the city and lifestyle of the Spartans.[59] Already in the sources
on the elusive lawgiver Lycurgus we find an oracular response by the Pythia
on this theme, quoted earlier (Diodorus Siculus 7.12.2). This theme recurs in
a number of sources and authors. Isocrates, for example, in the *Archidamus*
(65–67), a speech placed in the mouth of the Spartan king, tells how the allies
who defected from the Spartans have lost the concord (ὁμόνοια) they formerly
held under Spartan rule and now experience civil strife (στάσις) in its stead. The
situation has become so bad among the allies that the rich would rather throw
their property into the ocean than assist the needy, and the needy would be less
inclined to earn money for themselves than to seize the wealth of the rich.[60]
Isocrates touches on the importance of economic redistribution—for the rich to

---

[57] Flower 2000, esp. 77–84.
[58] Flower 2000:77.
[59] Cf. Kramer 1915:31–37.
[60] *Archidamus* 67: οἱ μὲν κεκτημένοι τὰς οὐσίας ἥδιον ἂν εἰς τὴν θάλατταν τὰ σφέτερ' αὑτῶν
ἐκβάλοιεν ἢ τοῖς δεομένοις ἐπαρκέσειαν, οἱ δὲ καταδεέστερον πράττοντες οὐδ' ἂν εὑρεῖν δέξαιντο
μᾶλλον ἢ τὰ τῶν ἐχόντων ἀφελέσθαι.

assist the needy—as a precondition for concord; once this agreement is broken, concord is also lost. We shall return later to this relationship and see how it is featured in our sources.

In the *Panathenaicus* (177), Isocrates again focuses on the elevated status concord held in Sparta. He writes that after the Dorian invasion the members of the third tribe, the Lacedaemonians, were engaged in civil strife like none of the other Greeks (στασιάσαι ... ὡς οὐδένας ἄλλους τῶν Ἑλλήνων). After the oligarchs got control, however, they set up a constitution that produced total concord among them. They instituted radical equality among themselves and excluded the rest of the population from having a share in it.[61] Isocrates condemns this setup and compares it to the ways of pirates.[62] He then falls into a dialogue with one of his former pupils, the panegyrist of the Lacedaemonians, who returns to the theme of concord and elaborates on the positive effects it has on Spartan society:

> In Sparta, no one could show an example of civil discord or murders or lawless exiles (οὔτε στάσιν οὔτε σφαγὰς οὔτε φυγὰς ἀνόμους γεγενημένας), nor seizure of money or disgrace done against women and children, nor a change in the constitution or cancellation of debts or redistribution of land or any other of the irreparable evils.[63]

Xenophon also discusses concord in relation to Sparta, and puts it into the mouth of Pericles, the son of Pericles, to complain about the degenerate ways of the Athenians. Pericles asks when the Athenians will learn from the Spartans and adopt their observance of concord (ὁμονοήσουσιν). As things stand, he says, the Athenians' lack of concord has enabled evil and cowardice to take root in the city, and much enmity and mutual hatred exists among the citizens.[64] Polybius reports that Ephorus discussed Sparta (6.45.1) and says that he highly praised the political prudence of Lycurgus:

> δυεῖν γὰρ ὄντων, δι' ὧν σῴζεται πολίτευμα πᾶν, τῆς πρὸς τοὺς πολεμίους ἀνδρείας καὶ τῆς πρὸς σφᾶς αὐτοὺς ὁμονοίας, ἀνῃρηκότα τὴν πλεονεξίαν ἅμα ταύτῃ συνανῃρηκέναι πᾶσαν ἐμφύλιον διαφορὰν καὶ στάσιν· ᾗ καὶ Λακεδαιμονίους, ἐκτὸς ὄντας τῶν κακῶν τούτων, κάλλιστα τῶν Ἑλλήνων τὰ πρὸς σφᾶς αὐτοὺς πολιτεύεσθαι καὶ συμφρονεῖν ταὐτά.

---

[61] *Panathenaicus* 178–179.

[62] *Panathenaicus* 226.

[63] *Panathenaicus* 259.

[64] *Memorabilia* 3.5.16–17: ἐξ ὧν πολλὴ μὲν ἀτηρία καὶ κακία τῇ πόλει ἐμφύεται, πολλὴ δὲ ἔχθρα καὶ μῖσος ἀλλήλων τοῖς πολίταις ἐγγίγνεται.

For, since there are two things through which every state is saved—
valor against the enemy and concord among the citizens—[Lycurgus],
when he removed greed also removed all civil disagreements and strife.
That is why the Lacedaemonians, being free from these evils, govern
themselves best of the Greeks and live in concord.[65]

Strabo (10.4.16) also quotes Ephorus as discussing concord, but includes the
passage in his treatment of Crete. Since the account is so close to the one in
Polybius, however, it seems reasonable to assume that it is derived from the
same source (presumably Ephorus' *Histories*). Strabo (10.4.17) makes it clear that
Ephorus thought that most Spartan institutions originated in Crete and that the
two states were fundamentally similar. Polybius (6.46.10) protests that Ephorus
actually describes Crete and Sparta in identical language, despite their many
differences, and that it is almost impossible to know which one he is talking
about unless paying close attention to proper names.[66] It is not surprising, then,
if Strabo, perhaps mistakenly, included the discussion of concord in his treatment of Crete rather than Sparta. We will thus include Strabo's Ephorus quotation as another illustrative example of the close thematic connection between
concord and Sparta. Ephorus makes the point that for concord to prevail, dissension, which is fueled by greed and luxury, must first be removed.[67]

Polybius himself also praises Lycurgus for instituting concord in Sparta:

δοκεῖ δή μοι Λυκοῦργος πρὸς μὲν τὸ σφίσιν ὁμονοεῖν τοὺς πολίτας
καὶ πρὸς τὸ τὴν Λακωνικὴν τηρεῖν ἀσφαλῶς, ἔτι δὲ τὴν ἐλευθερίαν
διαφυλάττειν τῇ Σπάρτῃ βεβαίως, οὕτως νενομοθετηκέναι καὶ
προνενοῆσθαι καλῶς ὥστε θειοτέραν τὴν ἐπίνοιαν ἢ κατ' ἄνθρωπον
αὐτοῦ νομίζειν

I think that Lycurgus was so successful as a lawgiver and displayed
such forethought—both with respect to the citizens practicing concord
among themselves and in the steadfast protection of the Laconian

---

[66] Ephorus was not alone in that practice. Polybius (6.45.1) expresses outrage that some of the most
learned Greek authors—Ephorus, Xenophon, Callisthenes, and Plato—claim that the Cretan and
Spartan constitutions are identical. Cf. Herodotus 1.65, who writes that Lycurgus brought the
Spartan constitution from Crete; and Aristotle *Politics* 1271b20 and 1271b22–4, who writes that
the Cretan and Spartan constitutions are similar, and that the Spartan constitution is modeled
on the Cretan. For a discussion of the similarities between the Cretan and Spartan forms of
government, see Perlman 2005, esp. 300–308.
[67] Strabo 10.4.16: τὴν μὲν οὖν ὁμόνοιαν διχοστασίας αἰρομένης ἀπαντᾶν, ἢ γίνεται διὰ πλεονεξίαν
καὶ τρυφήν.

land, and also in the firm guard over Sparta's freedom—that one could consider his thought to be divine rather than human.[68]

In the next paragraph he explains the preconditions for Spartan concord: equal possession of property (ἡ μὲν γὰρ περὶ τὰς κτήσεις ἰσότης) and a simple and common diet.

Plutarch relates how Lycurgus went to Crete and studied under Thaletas who, says Plutarch, disguised himself as a lyric poet, but really was an accomplished lawgiver.[69] His poems were exhortations to obedience (εὐπείθεια) and concord (ὁμόνοια); all who listened to them grew milder in their temperaments and moved away from their earlier enmity (κακοθυμία) and lived instead together in pursuit of the good (τὰ καλά).[70]

In this set of examples, we again encounter the connection between economic distribution and concord. Only when greed and luxury (πλεονεξία καὶ τρύφη) are removed is it possible to achieve harmony. In practical terms this is reflected in equal possession of property and dietary regulations, all of which was accomplished under the auspices of Lycurgus' legislative reforms. But equally strong is the link between legislative reforms and the practical realization of concord, which places concord within the domain of the capable sage and lawgiver. The traditions surrounding Lycurgus—about whom we know close to nothing for certain[71]—link him with both the Delphic oracle, where he was supposed to have received divine sanctification for his laws, and with Thaletas, under whose guidance he studied. Aristotle refers to Thaletas in his discussion of early lawgivers and mentions that some say that he was the pupil of Onomacritus, the first person to be skilled in legislation, and that both Lycurgus and Zaleucus studied under him in Crete.[72] Thaletas was also supposed to have been advised by the Delphic oracle to visit Sparta and to purify it from a plague with his music,[73] to which we shall return later. We shall also have more to say about the relationship between concord and legislative expertise.

The last and fourth set of examples of concord sort under the rubric of philosophical and political treatises, since they all occur in theoretical discussions on society and government.

---

[68] Polybius 6.48.2

[69] Aristotle (*Politics* 1274a28–30) also mentions their affiliation, but he does not specify Thaletas' status as either a lawgiver or poet.

[70] Plutarch *Lycurgus* 4.1–2. For concord as a theme in poetic and choral expressions, see discussion below.

[71] On Lycurgus, see Tigerstedt 1965–1978; Szegedy-Maszak 1978; Manfredini and Piccirilli 1980; and Hölkeskamp 1992.

[72] *Politics* 1274a25–30. It is important to note, however, that Aristotle himself did not subscribe to these opinions; he thought that the story was inconsistent with chronology (ἀσκεπτότερον τῶν χρόνων), 1274a30–31.

[73] Willets 1982:236. See also Campbell 1988:320–329.

Democritus is our first source:

ὅταν οἱ δυνάμενοι τοῖς μὴ ἔχουσι καὶ προτελεῖν τολμέωσι καὶ ὑπουργεῖν καὶ χαρίζεσθαι, ἐν τούτῳ ἤδη καὶ τὸ οἰκτίρειν ἔνεστι καὶ μὴ ἐρήμους εἶναι καὶ τὸ ἑταίρους γίγνεσθαι, καὶ τὸ ἀμύνειν ἀλλήλοισι καὶ τοὺς πολιήτας ὁμονόους εἶναι καὶ ἄλλα ἀγαθά, ἄσσα οὐδεὶς ἂν δύναιτο καταλέξαι.

When the powerful dare to lend money to the have-nots and assist them and show them favors, in that is already pity, and cancellation of loneliness, and creation of friendship and mutual protection, and concord among the citizens, and so many other good things that no one could list them all.[74]

When concord is achieved, Democritus says, the *polis* can truly perform extraordinary deeds:

ἀπὸ ὁμονοίης τὰ μεγάλα ἔργα καὶ ταῖς πόλεσι τοὺς πολέμους δυνατὸν κατεργάζεσθαι, ἄλλως δ᾽ οὔ

It is possible to accomplish the greatest deeds through concord, even wars for city-states, but not in any other way.[75]

Archytas expresses similar sentiments regarding concord and its impact on society:

στάσιν μὲν ἔπαυσεν, ὁμόνοιαν δὲ αὔξησεν λογισμὸς εὑρεθείς· πλεονεξία τε γὰρ οὐκ ἔστι τούτου γενομένου καὶ ἰσότας ἔστιν· τούτῳ γὰρ περὶ τῶν συναλλαγμάτων διαλλασσόμεθα. διὰ τοῦτον οὖν οἱ πένητες λαμβάνοντι παρὰ τῶν δυναμένων, οἵ τε πλούσιοι διδόντι τοῖς δεομένοις, πιστεύοντες ἀμφότεροι διὰ τούτω τὸ ἴσον ἔξειν.

Correct reckoning, once discovered, stops civil strife, and increases concord. For greed does not exist when correct reckoning has come into being and equality exists. For with it we are reconciled with respect to our transactions. Through it, then, the poor receive from the rich, and the wealthy give to those who need, and both parts believe that they will have equal rights through this.[76]

---

[74] DK 68B255.
[75] DK 68B250.
[76] DK 47B3, 7–12. For a thorough discussion of Archytas and fragment 3, see Huffman 2005, esp. 183–224.

Archytas contrasts concord with civil strife, which prevents the smooth operation of society. Democritus likewise describes the detrimental effects of civil strife in fragment 249:

> στάσις ἐμφύλιος ἐς ἑκάτερα κακόν· καὶ γὰρ νικέουσι καὶ ἡσσωμένοις. ὁμοίη φθορή.

> Civil strife is an evil on each side; both for the victors and losers. The destruction is equal.

Archytas affirms that correct reckoning (λογισμός), presumably his own Pythagorean philosophy,[77] has the capacity to remove civil strife and enhance concord. This seems to be one of the most efficacious qualities of his wisdom, at least as far as society is concerned. Democritus describes both the benefits of concord and the destructive effects of civil strife, but he does not explicitly elaborate on his own role in promoting the one and avoiding the other. It would seem reasonable to assume, however, that his reflections on στάσις and ὁμόνοια are anchored, one way or another, in his own philosophy, although that relation is not clearly fleshed out in the preserved fragments.

Xenophon ascribes to Socrates a discussion of the social effects of concord:

> ἀλλὰ μὴν καὶ ὁμόνοιά γε μέγιστόν τε ἀγαθὸν δοκεῖ ταῖς πόλεσιν εἶναι καὶ πλειστάκις ἐν αὐταῖς αἵ τε γερουσίαι καὶ οἱ ἄριστοι ἄνδρες παρακελεύονται τοῖς πολίταις ὁμονοεῖν, καὶ πανταχοῦ ἐν τῇ Ἑλλάδι νόμος κεῖται τοὺς πολίτας ὀμνύναι ὁμονοήσειν, καὶ πανταχοῦ ὀμνύουσι τὸν ὅρκον τοῦτον· οἶμαι δ' ἐγὼ ταῦτα γίγνεσθαι οὐχ ὅπως τοὺς αὐτοὺς χοροὺς κρίνωσιν οἱ πολῖται, οὐδ' ὅπως τοὺς αὐτοὺς αὐλητὰς ἐπαινῶσιν, οὐδ' ὅπως τοὺς αὐτοὺς ποιητὰς αἱρῶνται, οὐδ' ἵνα τοῖς αὐτοῖς ἥδωνται, ἀλλ' ἵνα τοῖς νόμοις πείθωνται. τούτοις γὰρ τῶν πολιτῶν ἐμμενόντων, αἱ πόλεις ἰσχυρόταταί τε καὶ εὐδαιμονέσταται γίγνονται· ἄνευ δὲ ὁμονοίας οὔτ' ἂν πόλις εὖ πολιτευθείη οὔτ' οἶκος καλῶς οἰκηθείη

> Yet truly concord seems to be the greatest good for the city-states and very often in them the senates and the best men exhort the citizens

---

[77] What does λογισμός mean? It is frequently used to mean "the exercise of reason in rational inference and thought," Irwin 1985:422. Huffman (2005:203) adds that it "is used in a wide range of Greek authors to refer to the rational part of a human being as opposed to the passions … It is what distinguishes human beings from animals, which live just by impressions (Aristotle *Metaphysics* 980b28), and adults from children, who from the beginning have spirit (θυμός) but may never partake of *logismos*." As to the precise meaning of λογισμός in fragment 3, Huffman (205–206) writes: "We have every reason to suppose, then, that Archytas saw *logismos* as including both of the proportions commonly applied to politics in the later tradition, the arithmetic and the geometric, and it is also conceivable that he thought other sorts of proportions were applicable as well."

to be of one mind, and everywhere in Greece there is a law that the citizens should swear an oath to be of one mind. And I think that this is so, not so that the citizens should choose the same choruses, nor so that they should praise the same flutists, nor so that they should pick the same poets, nor in order that they may take pleasure in the same things, but in order that they may obey the laws. For when the citizens abide by them, the city-states are strongest and most prosperous; but without concord neither could a city-state be well governed nor could a household be well managed.[78]

It is of particular interest that Socrates' interlocutor here is the sophist Hippias of Elis, since he is one of the sophists whose preserved work bears no trace of the use of the word concord. This passage allows us to link him to this discourse.[79] It is also significant that Socrates and Hippias in the preceding paragraph discuss Sparta and the lawful behavior that Lycurgus accomplished by enacting his legislative reform. This situates their discussion of concord within the framework of lawgiving and constitutional reform, just as was the case with the narratives around Lycurgus. The interconnectedness of concord and economic distribution—as stressed by Aristotle, Isocrates, Demosthenes, Democritus, and Archytas[80]—lends additional support to the legislative context for this discourse.

All four examples above discuss concord as a phenomenon common to the whole of Greece (αἱ πόλεις, πανταχοῦ ἐν τῇ Ἑλλάδι, etc.) and assume that its implementation is a concern for every community. The Panhellenic point of view these texts espouse, that is, that civil strife is a universal threat and concord a benefit to every *polis*, belies the understanding of concord as an exclusively Athenian concern, emerging first in the late fifth century BCE. Our sources clearly characterize concord as a preoccupation for all Greek *poleis* without precise historical framework.

The discussion up to this point has introduced a variety of authors who discuss the merits of concord in a variety of contexts. This range of contexts is another reason why we might question how Athenian this theme was. Should we not allow for the possibility that it had applications elsewhere (Olympia, for example, or Sparta)? Further, by pursuing a strictly philological investigation concerned exclusively with the employment of a single word and ignoring the

---

[78] *Memorabilia* 4.4.16.

[79] I am not contending that Xenophon described a historical encounter between Socrates and Hippias in which they discussed concord; only that to Xenophon's mind—and to his readers', too, one may surmise—it seemed like a germane topic for Socrates to discuss with Hippias. For a general statement about my treatment of the sources, see the Appendix.

[80] Aristotle (*Constitution of Athens* 40.3), Isocrates (*Archidamus* 67 and 69), Demosthenes (*Against Leptines* 12), Democritus (DK 68B255), and Archytas (DK 47B3, 7–12).

broader thematic typology, do we not run the danger of divesting concord of the force and meaning that it had acquired over time? In what follows we shall attempt to outline what such a broader typology might entail, and we shall pay particular attention to the sophists' historical predecessors in promoting concord.

The Thematic Typology of Concord

In their discussion on concord Schmid and Stählin note that it was no new theme to Greek thought, but a topic that had long been relevant to wise men.[81] They give as an example the actions of Thales, who urged the Ionian city-states to establish a council (βουλευτήριον) common for all the Ionians in an attempt to unite them in the face of the Persian threat.[82] But this is far from the only occurrence of political intervention performed by *sophoi*. Upon closer scrutiny, we shall find this to be a common theme.

Apart from his suggestion of creating a common council for all the Ionians, Thales is also said to have given excellent political advice to his city. He aborted Croesus' attempt to create a political alliance between Miletus and the Lydians, and this proved the city's salvation when Cyrus was victorious.[83] Herodotus (1.170) relates how Bias of Priene, at the onslaught of the Persians, advised the Ionians at a pan-Ionic gathering to go together to Sardinia and found a new city for all the Ionians (πόλιν μίαν κτίζειν πάντων Ἰώνων). Empedocles' father seems to have been an important figure in turning Acragas into a democracy after the expulsion of the tyrant Thrasydaeus, and when, after the father's death, despotic tendencies once again arose:

εἶτα τὸν Ἐμπεδοκλέα πεῖσαι τοὺς Ἀκραγαντίνους παύσασθαι μὲν τῶν στάσεων, ἰσότητα δὲ πολιτικὴν ἀσκεῖν.

Then Empedocles persuaded the people of Acragas to end their discords and practice political equality.[84]

Diogenes Laertius relates another incident where Empedocles spoke against the public funding of a memorial of one of the city's most famous physicians, and he did so "discoursing about equality" (περὶ ἰσότητος διαλεχθείς).[85] We also hear that he broke up an oligarchic assembly called the Thousand in favor of the

---

[81]   Schmid-Stählin 1940:163.
[82]   Herodotus 1.170.
[83]   Diogenes Laertius 1.25 = DK 11A1.
[84]   Diogenes Laertius 8.72 = DK 31A1; cf. Diodorus Siculus 11.53. See also Wright 1981:6–14.
[85]   Diogenes Laertius 8.65 = DK 31A1.

democracy, and that he saved the people of Selinus from pestilence by bringing two neighboring rivers to cleanse their city.[86]

In these examples, both Thales and Empedocles are represented as promoting the well-being of their *poleis* by directly intervening in the political issues of the day. Thales first sought to unify all the Ionians against the Persians, and he then encouraged Miletus to resist the invitations from the Lydians. This amounts to an external as well as internal solidification of Miletus. Empedocles' goal, likewise, seems to have been to prevent civil discord, and this he did by speaking out against the factionalism practiced by the citizens and by promoting reconciliation among the various groups. Empedocles' intervention (παύσασθαι μὲν τῶν στάσεων) echoes the words of Archytas (στάσιν μὲν ἔπαυσεν), who affirmed the potentially salutary power of his "correct reckoning." This echo is also carried over into Empedocles' discussion on equality (ἰσότης);[87] Archytas also refers to equality (τὸ ἴσον, ἰσότας) as the actualized ideal when the citizens practice concord. This theme is also evident in Democritus, who says that equality is best in everything (καλὸν ἐν παντὶ τὸ ἴσον),[88] and Phaleas of Chalcedon who, according to Aristotle, had much to say about equality:[89]

δοκεῖ γάρ τισι τὸ περὶ τὰς οὐσίας εἶναι μέγιστον τετάχθαι καλῶς· περὶ γὰρ τούτων ποιεῖσθαί φασι τὰς στάσεις πάντας. διὸ Φαλέας ὁ Χαλκηδόνιος τοῦτ' εἰσήνεγκε πρῶτος· φησὶ γὰρ δεῖν ἴσας εἶναι τὰς κτήσεις τῶν πολιτῶν.

For some people think that it is the most important thing for wealth to be well arranged; for they say that everyone makes their discords around this. Thus Phaleas of Chalcedon was the first to introduce this. For he says that the citizens should have equal possessions.[90]

In connection to this passage, Aristotle mentions that the equalization of property (ἡ τῆς οὐσίας ὁμαλότης) was an important theme even for some of the older generation of *sophoi*, and he goes on to mention the legislation of Solon

---

[86] Diogenes Laertius 8.66 and 70 = DK 31A1. There is also a tradition that he aided another city by counteracting winds with leather hides (Diogenes Laertius 8.60). For a discussion of how elements of magic and ritual in the sources on Empedocles fit (or not) with his philosophy, see Kingsley 1995.

[87] We should note that Empedocles assigns an important role to equality in his work on physics (DK 31B17, 20 and 27), where both Love (Φιλότης) and the four roots are modified by the adjective ἴσος.

[88] DK 68B102.

[89] For the importance of the concept of equality in early Greek thought, see Vlastos 1947. See also Vlastos 1981:184–185n78; and Huffman 2005:211–215.

[90] Aristotle *Politics* 1266a36–40. See Balot 2001a for Aristotle's discussion of Phaleas of Chalcedon.

as an example of this.[91] In fragment 4 (West), Solon says that his *polis* is being destroyed, not by the gods, but by the greed of its citizens (αὐτοὶ δὲ φθείρειν μεγάλην πόλιν ἀφραδίῃσιν ἀστοὶ βούλονται χρήμασι πειθόμενοι, 5–6).[92] The reason for this, he continues, is that they do not know how to check their insatiable greed (κατέχειν κόρον, 9) or to enjoy the present happiness in the peace of the feast (παρούσας εὐφροσύνας κοσμεῖν δαιτὸς ἐν ἡσυχίῃ, 9–10). This leads to slavery which, in turn, stirs up civil strife and war from its sleep (ἢ [δουλοσύνη] στάσιν ἔμφυλον πόλεμόν θ' εὕδοντ' ἐπεγείρει, 19). Such a development has disastrous consequences for the city with killings, people sold into slavery, and other evils. The remedy to all this is good order (Εὐνομίη, 32).[93] It ends greed (παύει κόρον, 34), civil strife (παύει δ' ἔργα διχοστασίης, 37), and the anger of painful strife (παύει δ' ἀργαλέης ἔριδος χόλον, 38).

The poetry of Solon resonates remarkably well with our sources on concord. Solon's emphasis on greed as a socially destructive force (also in 6.3 τίκτει γὰρ κόρος ὕβριν; and 13.71 πλούτου δ' οὐδὲν τέρμα πεφασμένον ἀνδράσι κεῖται) is echoed in our sources on Lycurgus (πλεονεξία καὶ τρυφή), Archytas (πλεονεξία), and Democritus (πλεονεξία). Aristotle, too, is sympathetic to this line of thinking and discusses the detrimental effect of greed at some length in the *Politics*. There, however, he underlines that equalization of property can only have a limited effect on preventing citizens from engaging in civil conflicts. The real problem is not social inequality, but greed:

ἡ πονηρία τῶν ἀνθρώπων ἄπληστον, καὶ τὸ πρῶτον μὲν ἱκανὸν διωβελία μόνον, ὅταν δ' ἤδη τοῦτ' ᾖ πάτριον, ἀεὶ δέονται τοῦ πλείονος, ἕως εἰς ἄπειρον ἔλθωσιν. ἄπειρος γὰρ ἡ τῆς ἐπιθυμίας φύσις, ἧς πρὸς τὴν ἀναπλήρωσιν οἱ πολλοὶ ζῶσιν. τῶν οὖν τοιούτων ἀρχή, μᾶλλον τοῦ τὰς οὐσίας ὁμαλίζειν, τὸ τοὺς μὲν ἐπιεικεῖς τῇ φύσει τοιούτους παρασκευάζειν ὥστε μὴ βούλεσθαι πλεονεκτεῖν, τοὺς δὲ φαύλους ὥστε μὴ δύνασθαι·

The baseness of men is insatiable; first two obols was enough, but now, when it is the norm, they always want more without end. For the nature of desire is limitless, and the majority of people live for the purpose of fulfilling it. The beginning of reform, then, rather than equalizing property, consists in accustoming the upper classes not to want to be greedy, and the lower classes not to be able to.[94]

---

[91] Aristotle *Politics* 1266b14–23.
[92] For Solon 4, see Irwin 2005, esp. 91–111.
[93] For Εὐνομίη, see, most recently, Irwin 2005:183–193, with bibliography.
[94] *Politics* 1267b1–9. For the significance of greed as a theme in antiquity, see Balot 2001b and Huffman 2005:206–211.

Our sources thus seem to agree about the ubiquitous and detrimental effects of greed and on the importance of checking this impulse.

Civil strife (στάσις) is portrayed as the direct result of unchecked greed. Note the verbal echo between Solon (στάσιν ἔμφυλον) and Democritus (ἐμφύλιος στάσις). Civil strife is consistently described as the antithesis to concord. In Solon, this is expressed through Εὐνομίη and ἡσυχίη. It was the citizens' incapacity to enjoy happiness in festive peace (ἡσυχίη) that started civil strife, and this sentiment is repeated in 4c (West), where Solon exhorts the rich to moderation (ὑμεῖς δ᾽ ἡσυχάσαντες ἐνὶ φρεσὶ καρτερὸν ἦτορ, 1). In Solon, ἡσυχίη is characterized as the opposite of στάσις, and to achieve this goal one must practice Εὐνομίη, which ends civil strife (παύει δ᾽ ἔργα διχοστασίης).[95] By the time of Euripides, this promise to bring a society from the brink of civil war to harmony had become such an axiom that he could write that removal of civil strife was the activity *par excellence* of the wise man, and that they deserved a good reward for their services:

ἄνδρας χρὴ σοφούς τε κἀγαθοὺς
φύλλοις στέφεσθαι, χὥστις ἡγεῖται πόλει
κάλλιστα σώφρων καὶ δίκαιος ὢν ἀνήρ,
ὅστις τε μύθοις ἔργ᾽ ἀπαλλάσσει κακὰ
μάχας τ᾽ ἀφαιρῶν καὶ στάσεις· τοιαῦτα γὰρ
πόλει τε πάσῃ πᾶσί θ᾽ Ἕλλησιν καλά.

Wise and noble men should be crowned with leaves,
both he who leads the city best, being a prudent and just man,
and he who removes evil actions with his words and takes away
battles and civil strifes. For such things are good both for every
city and for all Greeks.[96]

Solon, then, uses εὐνομίη and ἡσυχίη much in the same sense as we have seen ὁμόνοια being used by others. Democritus and Archytas, in turn, employ ἴσον almost interchangeably with ὁμόνοια. Phaleas of Chalcedon champions the notion of equal property as a means of avoiding civil strife, and such policy is attributed to Lycurgus by Polybius, who writes that the precondition for the Lacedaemonian concord was equality of property. We have also seen similar sentiments regarding equalization of property expressed in Aristotle, Isocrates,

---

[95] This connection is also established by Aristotle, who mentions that Solon was chosen as a mediator (διαλλακτής), since civil strife was severe (ἰσχυρᾶς δὲ τῆς στάσεως οὔσης), and that he exhorted the rich not to be greedy (παραινῶν τοῖς πλουσίοις μὴ πλεονεκτεῖν), *Constitution of Athens* 5.2–3.

[96] Euripides fr. 282, 23–28 (*Autolykos*) TGF. For a discussion on this fragment, see Marcovich 1978:20, and Kyle 1987:128.

Demosthenes, Democritus, Archytas, and Xenophon, and Aristotle saw this as fundamental to Solon's legislative reform.

The connection that Aristotle makes between Solon and equalization of property alerts us to another feature of concord: it is through the introduction of new laws that both Lycurgus and Solon removed στάσις and promoted concord (ὁμόνοια and εὐνομίη). But legislative expertise seems to be a feature that sets Lycurgus and Solon apart from other promoters of concord, such as the Presocratic philosophers and the sophists. We shall turn to these two groups of *sophoi* later to explore traces of legal expertise in their source material. Before doing this, however, there is another aspect of the fluidity of traditions we have not explored. We have considerable evidence of musical and choral interventions by poets that led to the suspension of civil discord and promotion of harmony. We shall next consider this tradition.

Poetic Appeals to Concord

Terpander's successful involvement at Sparta is chronicled in the *Suda*:

ὅτι οἱ Λακεδαιμόνιοι στασιάζοντες μετεπέμψαντο ἐκ Λέσβου τὸν μουσικὸν Τέρπανδρον, ὃς ἥρμοσεν αὐτῶν τὰς ψυχὰς καὶ τὴν στάσιν ἔπαυσεν.

When afflicted by civic turmoil, the Spartans summoned from Lesbos the musician Terpander, who brought harmony to their souls and ended their civil strife.[97]

---

[97] *Suda* M 701 = Terpander test. 9 Campbell. Diodorus Siculus 8.28 (test. 15 Gostoli) specifies that it was by playing a song on his lyre that Terpander restored harmony to the Spartans (καὶ δή τι μέλος Τέρπανδρος ἐντέχνως κιθαρίσας αὐτοὺς πάλιν συνήρμοσε), and he goes on to refer to this piece as "the song of harmony" (τῆς ἁρμονίας τῇ ᾠδῇ). Demetrius of Phaleron (test. 12 Gostoli) writes that the Spartans benefited greatly in terms of concord and the preservation of laws (καὶ πρὸς ὁμόνοιαν καὶ πρὸς τὴν τῶν νόμων φυλακήν) from listening to the Lesbian singer (without specifying his name). When they heard him, they ceased their internal rivalry and strife (παύσασθαι τῆς φιλονεικίας). Aristides 46.189 (test. 20 Gostoli) attributes Terpander with having established concord among the Spartans (τοὺς Λακεδαιμονίους ὁμονοεῖν ἐποίησεν). Philodemus (test. 14a Gostoli) relates how Terpander by singing in the *syssitia* checked the Spartans from engaging in discord ([ἐν τοῖ]ς φιλιτείοις ἄιδω[ν | τῆς τα]ραχῆς ἔπαυσε τοὺς [Λα|κεδαι]μον[ίο]υς). Later (test. 14b Gostoli) Philodemus expresses skepticism about the generally accepted account that Terpander was summoned in accordance with an oracle to put an end to the Spartans' civil discord (πρ[ὸ]ς κατάπαυσιν | ἐμφυλίου στά[σ]εως). For how could irrational songs (ἄλογα μέλη) put an end to rational discord (λογικὴν διαφοράν)? Finally, Philodemus (test. 14c Gostoli) narrates that Terpander delighted (ἔτερπεν) the Spartans during the contests (ἐπ[ὶ τῶν] ἀγώνων), which led them to lay aside their civic conflict (ἀποτεθεῖσθαι τὴν στά|σιν). Even if Philodemus' main object in discussing Terpander is to attack the Damonian position of music's power to instill justice in men—as has been argued by Anderson 1966:147–176—he nevertheless reinforces the strong link between *sophia* (this time musical), cancellation of *stasis*, and implementation of concord.

Aelian writes that, in addition to Terpander, the Spartans had also summoned Thaletas, Tyrtaeus, Nymphaeus, and Alcman in times of need.[98] Boethius testifies that Terpander and Arion from Methymna rescued the Lesbians and Ionians from severe illness through their song.[99] Plutarch relates that Lycurgus persuaded Thaletas, one of the wise men of Crete, to come to Sparta. Plutarch goes on to say that Thaletas, although he was hiding under the cloak of lyric poetry, was really an excellent lawgiver. His songs were exhortations (λόγοι ... ἀνακλητικοί) to obedience and concord (εὐπειθείαν καὶ ὁμόνοιαν), and upon hearing them the Spartans joined in zeal for the good (συνῳκειοῦντο τῷ ζήλῳ τῶν καλῶν) and stopped their usual ill-will (κακοθυμίας) towards each other.[100] Finally, Philodemus mentions the account given by Diogenes of Babylon (second century BCE), that Stesichorus put himself in the middle (καταστὰς ἐν μέσοις) of two warring factions drawn up for battle.[101] He sang them a hortatory song ([ᾖσέ τι παρα]κλητικόν), through which he reconciled and restored them to peace ([εἰς ἡσυχ]ίαν αὐτοὺς μετέσ[τησεν]).[102]

In this poetic material we are again reminded of the thematic relationship between civil strife and good governance by the astute interventions of *sophoi.*[103] The poets act in their capacity as *sophoi* and their effects on the citizens are described as analogous to those of the lawgivers.[104] The material on Terpander,

---

[98] Aelian *Varia Historia* 12.50 = Terpander test. 7 Campbell.

[99] Boethius *De musica* 1.1 = test. 22 Gostoli: *Terpander atque Arion Methymnaeus Lesbios atque Iones gravissimis morbis cantus eripuere praesidio.* In Herodotus (1.23–24), Arion's poetic performance saves him miraculously from being killed by the rogue Corinthian crew. Though Herodotus does not explicitly explain the sudden appearance of the dolphin as a result of Arion's song, he introduces the story as a θῶμα μέγιστον. Arion's subsequent dedication at Taenarum further establishes the connection between his performance and the divinely mediated escape. For Herodotus' account of Arion, see Gray 2001 with bibliography.

[100] *Lycurgus* 4 = Thaletas test. 6 Campbell.

[101] Diogenes Babylonius fr. 281c *PMG* = Philodemus *De musica* 1.30.31. It is not clear who the conflicting parties are. Kemke suggests the emendation [ἀστῶ]ν, "citizens," in which case it might refer to the Locrians. See Campbell 1991, 3:40.

[102] The emendation ἡσυχία in the material on Stesichorus fits well with Solon's use of ἡσυχίη in fragment 4 and 4c (quoted in the main text). Pindar appears to be using the word in a similar way, almost equivalent to how ὁμόνοια is employed in other authors. See, for example, *Olympian* 4.16, *Pythian* 1.70, and *Pythian* 4.296.

[103] In this context, we might recall that poets were traditionally referred to as *sophoi.* For discussion and examples, see Kerferd 1981:24; Lloyd 1987:83; and Griffith 1990.

[104] Cf. Plutarch *Agis* 10.3, who writes that Terpander, Thaletas, and Pherecydes, despite being foreigners, were held in honor at Sparta since they pursued the same ideas as Lycurgus in their songs and philosophies. We might speculate about the relationship between νόμος as law and νόμος as musical strain or "pattern of melody" (Anderson 1966:54). Terpander is repeatedly described as an innovator in music (e.g. Terpander test. 12–17 Campbell) and as introducing new νόμοι (e.g. Terpander test. 3 and 18–20 Campbell). Thaletas is also attributed with having brought about musical reforms in Sparta and introduced musical novelties (Pseudo-Plutarch *De musica* 9.1134b–c = Thaletas test. 7 Campbell; Thaletas test. 9–10 Campbell). Plutarch *Lycurgus* 4 states that Thaletas prepared the groundwork for Lycurgus' legislative reforms by exposing

Thaletas, and Stesichorus, then, should caution us against adopting a narrow view on the Greek wisdom tradition. In this material, there are no clear demarcations that separate practitioners of wisdom along the lines of philosophy, poetry, and law. I agree with Nightingale that philosophy as a distinct discipline was first fully developed by Plato; it would be anachronistic to apply his definitions and categories to the earlier *sophoi*.[105] Now having considered this poetic material, we shall return to the Presocratics and the sophists to investigate the extent to which the source material exhibits any signs of legal expertise on their part.

Legal Expertise and Wisdom

First, let us look at the material surrounding the sophists. It is reported that Gorgias was sent as the chief ambassador (ἀρχιπρεσβευτής) by his own city to Athens to ask for help, since the people of Leontini at that time were involved in a war with the Syracusans.[106] Protagoras, we are told, wrote the laws for the new colony Thurii that was founded in 444/3 BCE (Θουρίοις νόμους γράψαι).[107] Hippias of Elis is said to have made quite a name for himself on diplomatic missions throughout Greece and was apparently even granted several honorary citizenships. Philostratus writes that he went on more embassies on behalf of Elis than any other Greek (πλεῖστα δὲ Ἑλλήνων πρεσβεύσας ὑπὲρ τῆς Ἤλιδος) and that he maintained his reputation (δόξαν) while fulfilling his missions. He also made a lot of money (χρήματα πλεῖστα ἐξέλεξε) and was enrolled in the tribes of both large and small *poleis* (φυλαῖς ἐνεγράφη πόλεων μικρῶν τε καὶ μειζόνων).[108] When asked by Socrates in the *Hippias Major* why he has been away from Athens so long, he answers:

Οὐ γὰρ σχολή, ὦ Σώκρατες. ἡ γὰρ Ἦλις ὅταν τι δέηται διαπράξασθαι πρός τινα τῶν πόλεων, ἀεὶ ἐπὶ πρῶτον ἐμὲ ἔρχεται τῶν πολιτῶν αἱρουμένη πρεσβευτήν, ἡγουμένη δικαστὴν καὶ ἄγγελον ἱκανώτατον εἶναι τῶν λόγων οἳ ἂν παρὰ τῶν πόλεων ἑκάστων λέγωνται. πολλάκις μὲν οὖν καὶ εἰς ἄλλας πόλεις ἐπρέσβευσα, πλεῖστα δὲ καὶ περὶ πλείστων

---

the Spartans to his music and thus softening their ways and making them more prone to practicing concord. Terpander, too, accomplished social changes through his music similar to the legislative reforms of Solon, Lycurgus, and Pittacus. Clement of Alexandria (*Stromateis* 1.16.78.5 = Terpander test. 8 Campbell) writes that Terpander set the Spartans' laws to music (τοὺς Λακεδαιμονίων νόμους ἐμελοποίησε Τέρπανδρος). There seems to be a slippage between the musical and legislative use of νόμος in the material on the early sages and poets. Perhaps this is indicative of their overlaps in *sophia*.

[105] Nightingale 1995, esp. 13–59.

[106] Diodorus Siculus 7.53 = DK 82A4.

[107] Heraclides Ponticus apud Diogenes Laertius 9.50 = DK 80A1.

[108] Philostratus *Lives of the Sophists* 1.11 = DK 86A2.

καὶ μεγίστων εἰς τὴν Λακεδαίμονα· διὸ δή, ὃ σὺ ἐρωτᾷς, οὐ θαμίζω εἰς τούσδε τοὺς τόπους.

I have not had time, Socrates. For when Elis needs to transact any business with one of the cities, she always approaches me first among her citizens, and chooses me to represent her, since she regards me as the ablest judge and interpreter of the pronouncements of each city. So I have often represented her in other cities, but most often, and on the most numerous and important matters, in Lacedaemon. So much for your question why I do not come often to these parts.[109]

Prodicus, finally, who came from Ceos, is said to have gone on numerous embassies as a representative of his native city.[110]

From this list we can conclude that some of the sophists were highly regarded in their own as well as other *poleis* for their legal and diplomatic expertise. It seems safe to assume that they owed much of their authority precisely to their ability to perform successful mediations in inter-*poleis* disputes. Read together with their promotion of concord, the sophists exhibit analogies in practices with Solon and Lycurgus. Like them, their reputation for wisdom paved the way for their involvement in legal and diplomatic activities aimed at curbing civil strife and promoting concord. But are those analogies merely coincidental, or are they revealing of qualities typically associated with early Greek *sophoi* in their roles as publicly sanctioned mediators and legal experts? To attempt to address that question, we shall briefly review the legal involvement and expertise of the Presocratics.

Diogenes Laertius gives us three accounts regarding this topic. He first reports that Pythagoras left his native Samos to go to Croton, at that time the leading colony in southern Italy. There he is said to have given the Italians a constitution (νόμους θεὶς τοῖς Ἰταλιώταις).[111] Second, Parmenides is said to have served his citizens as a legislator (λέγεται δὲ καὶ νόμους θεῖναι τοῖς πολίταις).[112] Finally, Heraclitus was deemed worthy of granting legislation by his citizens, but showed contempt for the laws on the grounds that the city was already dominated by a bad constitution (ἀξιούμενος δὲ καὶ νόμους θεῖναι πρὸς αὐτῶν ὑπερεῖδε διὰ τὸ ἤδη κεκρατῆσθαι τῇ πονηρᾷ πολιτείᾳ τὴν πόλιν).[113]

There thus existed a tradition in antiquity that at least some of the Presocratics were involved in drawing up laws for their *poleis*. We have already

---

[109] *Hippias Major* 281a = DK 86A6.

[110] Philostratus *Lives of the Sophists* 1.12 = DK 84A1a; *Hippias Major* 282c = DK 84A3.

[111] Diogenes Laertius 8.3, not in DK.

[112] Diogenes Laertius 9.23 = DK 28A1; see also Strabo 6.1.1 and Plutarch *Against Coletes* 1126a = DK 28A12.

[113] Diogenes Laertius 9.2 = DK 22A1.

seen that some of them were involved in acts of political mediation, as promoters of concord. This pattern shows affinities with the traditions about the two lawgivers Lycurgus and Solon, but also with the activities of the sophists. Taken together, these traditions shed new light on the sophists. Instead of being seen as the first promoters of concord they are now located in a traditional discourse that dates back at least to the early lawgivers. It is by drawing on this continuity in practices, one may assume, that the sophists could claim authority and present themselves as ideal conveyors of concord.

But let us return to the early lawgivers and investigate what we know about their activities. Dissatisfied with the direction in scholarship that distinguishes between historical traditions of the early lawgivers and purely legendary ones,[114] Andrew Szegedy-Maszak has adopted an approach that outlines a typology of the lawgivers as portrayed in our sources, thus taking seriously the cultural attitudes and representations surrounding these figures.[115] The material presents us with a coherent picture of a movement from *anomia* (lawlessness) to *eunomia* (good order). In the sources, the intervention of the lawgiver is a process consisting of three stages. The first phase is characterized by a crisis, often identified with *stasis* and civil war. In the next phase, the lawgiver appears and manages to settle the conflict through his authority and wisdom. The success of the intervention is predicated on the lawgiver's expertise, determined in no small degree by his education, which is described as being acquired in two, often connected ways: "extensive travel and study with one of the great philosophers."[116] Finally, when the new laws are implemented, the lawgiver typically removes himself from the *polis* so as not to interfere with the supremacy of the laws.

Two things are of special interest to us in this typology. First, the interventions of the lawgivers are often introduced in reference to a social crisis, and the word στάσις is used to portray this crisis.[117] This is familiar territory for us from our survey of the material on ὁμόνοια. There is a close affinity between ὁμόνοια and στάσις, and the qualifications of the proponent of concord seem only to be fully appreciated when discussed against the backdrop of civil strife. This framing highlights the relevance of the intervention and simultaneously brings into focus the lawgiver's unique capacity to turn the present turmoil into unanimity. We appear to be dealing with a *topos*, where measures to promote the well-being of a community (a new law code, legislative reform, call to concord, etc.) were carefully framed within the context of social strife. If this is right, the frequent appeals to στάσις in our material on the sophists take on a different light. We no longer have to assume that they always respond

---

[114] This criticism applies especially to the work of Adcock 1927.
[115] Szegedy-Maszak 1978.
[116] Szegedy-Maszak 1978:202.
[117] See Gagarin 1986:58–60.

to historical realities.[118] Instead, the appeals to στάσις can be understood as a reference to a traditional discourse and a sign of the proponent's indebtedness to this tradition. In other words, we should take seriously the representational value of στάσις—how it is frequently used as foil to introduce and make relevant the succeeding discourse on concord—without necessarily inferring from this that it directly responds to, or is motivated by, an actual civil war.

The second feature of relevance is the description of the education of the lawgivers: travel and instruction from a *sophos*. This again resonates with what we have seen in connection with the sophists. One of their most recognizable features is their itinerant status, and we will discuss this at greater length in the next chapter. For now, however, it is sufficient to highlight the connection between lawgivers and philosophers, especially the fact that instruction from philosophers was a valued commodity to bring into the arena of legislative reforms. Szegedy-Maszak mentions Thales and Pythagoras as two philosophers who were especially suited to instruct lawgivers, since "both were known to have performed as practicing statesmen."[119] But these are not the only philosophers involved in legislative activities, as our survey has brought to light. This is where I think the typology of Szegedy-Maszak is too schematic: it downplays the overlaps that existed between philosophers and lawgivers and so overlooks various instances when philosophers are engaged in legal activities. It strives for a precise taxonomy of *sophoi* but is not sufficiently sensitive to the resistance of the material to such divisions. In fact, it makes little sense to draw up too distinct borders between the various groups of *sophoi*. It is perhaps more productive to focus on the underlying authority that lends legitimacy to their practices, and to that extent Szegedy-Maszak's analysis is valuable, since it invites us to pursue such an investigation.

We have thus seen how legal expertise, acts of mediation, and the reversal of the political fortunes of the community from *anomia* to *eunomia* constitute key facets of the ideological motivations for the practitioners of wisdom, and we have also outlined how this theme goes all the way back to the Presocratics and the early lawgivers, including such figures as Solon and Thales. Another significant connection in this context is that both Solon and Thales were thought of as members of the Seven Sages. Next we shall turn our attention to this group of *sophoi* in search for further clues—in addition to the material we have already explored on Solon and Thales—of the relationship between the Seven Sages and the theme of mediation and concord explored thus far.[120]

---

[118] Romilly (1972:200) expresses well this point of view. Regarding the discourse on concord she writes: "Et il s'explique par la nécessité où l'on se trouvait de defendre la cité contre une désagrégation alors imminente."

[119] Szegedy-Maszak 1978:203.

[120] For the Seven Sages, see Snell 1971, Fehling 1985, Martin 1993, and Busine 2002.

When discussing the Seven Sages, Diogenes Laertius refers to the opinion of Dicaearchus:

ὁ δὲ Δικαίαρχος οὔτε σοφοὺς οὔτε φιλοσόφους φησὶν αὐτοὺς γεγονέναι, συνετοὺς δε τινας καὶ νομοθετικούς.

Dicaearchus says that they were neither sages nor philosophers, but that they were intelligent legislators.[121]

He continues by saying that some say that they met both at the Pan-Ionian festival and at Corinth and Delphi (ἐν Πανιωνίῳ καὶ ἐν Κορίνθῳ καὶ εν Δελφοῖς συνελθεῖν αὐτούς). According to Aristotle, Pittacus, one of the Seven Sages,[122] was appointed an arbitrator (αἰσυμνήτης) for ten years, and he was involved in overthrowing Melanchrus, the tyrant of Lesbos.[123] Diogenes Laertius emphasizes his legal expertise and refers to his laws (νόμους δὲ ἔθηκε),[124] as do Aristotle (νόμων δημιουργός) and Diodorus (νομοθέτης τε γὰρ ἀγαθός).[125] As has been widely recognized, his legislation was less sweeping than the constitutional reforms of Lycurgus and Solon,[126] but it was substantial enough to earn him a reputation for wisdom and a place among the early lawgivers.[127] But Diodorus adds an interesting piece of information. In the same sentences where he relates Pittacus' fame as legislator he writes that he removed from his fatherland three of the greatest afflictions: tyranny, civil strife, and war (τὴν πατρίδα τριῶν τῶν μεγίστων συμφορῶν ἀπέλυσε, τυραννίδος, στάσεως, πολέμου). Diodorus here stresses the connection between Pittacus' ability as a lawgiver and his capacity to free the state from war and tyranny. In the next paragraph (9.12) he tells how, after Pittacus conquered Phrynon in single combat and procured victory for Mytilene over Athens, the Mityleneans wanted to give Pittacus half of the land they had gained through his victory.[128] But he declined the offer. Diodorus continues:

---

[121] Diogenes Laertius 1.40.

[122] *Protagoras* 343a–b.

[123] *Politics* 1285a30. Whatever the precise meaning of the term αἰσυμνήτης is, it is clear that Mytilene was deeply immersed in civic turmoil and that Pittacus' appointment as αἰσυμνήτης was intended to restore civic accord and mediate between the warring factions. But see Romer's (1982:40) hesitation about the "nature of Pittacus' actual 'mediation.'" For the meaning of αἰσυμνήτης and for a discussion of Mytilene's political situation, see Page 1955:149–161 and 239–240; Andrewes 1974:96–99; Romer 1982; and Gagarin 1986:59–60.

[124] Diogenes Laertius 1.76.

[125] *Politics* 1274b18. Diodorus Siculus 9.11.1.

[126] See, for example, Andrewes 1974:98.

[127] See Bowra 1961:136; Andrewes 1974:97–98; Gagarin 1986:59; and Hölkeskamp 1992.

[128] For a discussion of the different and conflicting versions of this story, see Page 1955:152–161; cf. Andrewes 1974:92–99. For the ancient sources on the Sigean War, see Herodotus 5.95; Strabo 13.1.38; Diodorus Siculus 9.12; Diogenes Laertius 1.74.

συνέταξε δὲ ἑκάστῳ κληρῶσαι τὸ ἴσον, ἐπιφθεγξάμενος ὡς τὸ ἴσον ἐστὶ τοῦ πλείονος πλεῖον. μετρῶν γὰρ ἐπιεικείᾳ τὸ πλεῖον οὐ κέρδει σοφῶς ἐγίνωσκεν· τῇ μὲν γὰρ ἰσότητι δόξαν καὶ ἀσφάλειαν ἀκολουθήσειν, τῇ δὲ πλεονεξίᾳ βλασφημίαν καὶ φόβον, δι᾽ ὧν ταχέως ἂν αὐτοῦ τὴν δωρεὰν ἀφείλαντο.

He ordered that an equal share be assigned to each by lot, having pronounced that the equal share is more than the greater. For by measuring the greater in terms of fairness and not profit he made a wise decision, thinking that fame and certainty would follow upon equality, but that fear and slander would follow upon greed, through which they would quickly have taken away his gift.

This passage resonates well with the material discussed above: Pittacus, through his wisdom—he was one of the Seven—keeps *stasis* in check.[129] By not giving in to greed (πλεονεξία), which generates *stasis,* but by upholding equality (τὸ ἴσον, ἰσότης), he procures a well-governed and prosperous state for the Mytileneans. Compare this to Archytas' view, quoted above. He argues that his particular branch of *sophia* (λογισμός) is ideally suited to restore a society torn by civil conflicts to a state of unity and accord. It is significant that in outlining the positive effects of his interventions he appears to make little distinction between τὸ ἴσον/ἰσότας and ὁμόνοια. This semantic coupling—especially when understood against the thematic backdrop of greed and civil strife—strengthens the connection between the accounts of Pittacus and Lycurgus, where τὸ ἴσον and ἰσότης are employed as the ideal state in the former, and ὁμόνοια in the latter.[130] In other words, τὸ ἴσον/ἰσότης and ὁμόνοια fulfill similar functions as the intellectual antidote to greed and civil strife.

Bias, also one of the Seven Sages,[131] was known for his success in arguing legal cases,[132] and he was sent on a diplomatic mission (πρεσβεύσας) to solve a

---

[129] Pittacus is frequently mentioned as one of the early practitioners of wisdom. See, for example, Simonides 542 *PMG;* Herodotus 1.27; Plato *Republic* 335e and *Hippias Major* 281c; Aristotle *Politics* 1274b and 1285a–b; Diodorus Siculus 9.11–12, 26–28; Strabo 13.2.3; Plutarch *Dinner of the Seven Wise Men;* Dionysius of Halicarnassus *Antiquitates Romanae* 2.26; Diogenes Laertius 1.74–81.

[130] This connection with the earlier material, especially the lawgivers, becomes even stronger when considering a story from Aristoxenos' *Life of Archytas* that relates the encounter between Archytas and Polyarchus. In this meeting Polyarchus argues that the extinction of πλεονεξία is the goal of lawgiving and justice. Aristoxenus' *Life* is preserved in Athenaeus 12.545a = DK 47A9. See Huffman 2005:307–337.

[131] In the story of the tripod as told by Diogenes Laertius 1.28, the Seven Sages are invoked as arbitrators between Milesian fishermen and Ionian youths over the rightful possession of the tripod. For a discussion of the tripod narrative, see Gernet 1981:78–81; and Humphreys 1983a:249–250; and Martin 1993:120.

[132] Diogenes Laertius 1.84.

dispute over borders between Priene and Samos.[133] Lysimachus mentions this mission in a letter to the Samians, where he writes that Bias was sent by the people of Priene to Samos as an ambassador with full powers (αὐτοκράτωρ) to negotiate peace between them (περὶ διαλύσεων).[134] Periander is said to have arbitrated between Pittacus' Mytilene and Athens after the Sigean War,[135] and Aristotle mentions that he was engaged as a witness in a dispute between Tenedos and Sigeion.[136]

In our sources on *sophia*, the Seven Sages constitute the beginning of the Greek wisdom tradition—the functional predecessors to the Presocratics and later *sophoi*. It is significant that many of the practices associated with later *sophoi*—such as legislative involvement, political mediation, and gravitation to the Panhellenic festivals—figure already in our sources on the Sages. If we are right in emphasizing the theme of the wise man as an ideal purveyor of concord and the corollary cancellation of *stasis*, it seems possible to establish a genealogy of intellectual practices—at least with respect to concord—that commences with the Seven Sages and includes the sophists. This genealogy, in turn, unites different groups of *sophoi* that are typically thought of as qualitatively different or even mutually incompatible, such as poets, the Seven Sages, lawgivers, Presocratics, and sophists.

These practices seem to have taken place on a Panhellenic stage and gone well beyond individual *poleis*. The insistence that the sophistic movement was triggered by needs internal to Athens, as some scholars have argued, does not take into account the precedence and Panhellenic scope that the discourse on concord displays. If we pay attention to this genealogy of practices, it seems reasonable to suggest that, while there are significant differences among the different *sophoi* surveyed—geographical, temporal, and intellectual—there are nevertheless compelling thematic continuities that help account for the cultural authority that later *sophoi* could claim for themselves. It is against the backdrop of these intellectual continuities that I suggest we understand the sophists.

*

Stasis and civic turmoil become the rhetorical triggers, as it were, for *sophoi* in their appeals to a civic context for the significance and application of their *sophia*. They exert their *sophia* by directly inserting themselves into the political sphere of the *polis*. This civic involvement contradicts Plato's assertion in the

---

[133] Plutarch *Quaestiones Graecae* 20; cf. Humphreys 1983a:250 and Martin 1993:110.

[134] Quoted from Snell 1971:26.

[135] Bias: Plutarch *Quaestiones Graecae* 20, Diogenes Laertius 1.87, *Letter of Lysimachus to Samos* (RC 7 = Snell 1971:24–26); Periander: Herodotus 5.95, Aristotle *Rhetoric* 1375b, Diogenes Laertius 1.74. For early sages as judges, see Humphreys 1983a:249–251.

[136] *Rhetoric* 1375b.

Hippias Major (281c) that philosophers of old—"Pittacus, and Bias, and Milesian Thales and his followers, and also the later ones up to Anaxagoras"—refrained from participating in politics.[137] Indeed, Plato's efforts to characterize philosophers as distanced from politics and dedicated to the contemplative life—ὁ βίος θεωρητικός—appear questionable when viewed against the concord/equality tradition, where the lines are not so clearly drawn between philosophy and politics, and where practitioners of wisdom find the civic sphere a perfectly fertile avenue for their *sophia.*[138]

This chapter, then, is an attempt to bring out the permeability in the categories of *sophoi.* As a corollary, we need to look for alternate explanations for the impetus of the sophistic movement. It will no longer be sufficient to approach the sophists as qualitatively different from the Presocratics, and to assume that these divisions will be reflected one way or another in their thinking. If we no longer can trace the origin of the sophistic movement exclusively to Athens but to intellectual developments throughout Greece, and if we can attest significant areas of continuity among *sophoi,* then it seems reasonable that we take these findings into consideration when trying to account for their intellectual practices.

I hope to have shown in this chapter that there existed precedents for the sophists to draw on in the concord discourse. We shall continue this exploration of continuity in the next chapters. At this point, however, we need to consider the particularity of the sophists' use of ὁμόνοια. More specifically, why did they choose to adopt this word instead of earlier expressions, such as τὸ ἴσον, ἡσυχία, εὐνομία, ὁμοφρονέω, and what was the cultural significance of this choice?

I have argued at length that the claims of Kramer and Romilly—that the sophists were the first to use the word ὁμόνοια and that it directly related to the political turmoil at the end of the fifth century BCE—do not adequately address the tradition of similar activities on the part of the sophists' predecessors. The invocation of concord was almost always legitimized by the threat of *stasis,* civil strife. This is not to say that the threat of *stasis* was not present or real at each occasion when the appeals to concord were made, only that this was a *topos* that the *sophoi* could (and often did) tap into in order to validate their own interventions.

The field of wisdom was agonistic, as we shall consider more fully in chapter six. *Sophoi* participated in competitive behavior to outperform each other and to achieve preeminent positions for themselves. In this agonistic climate, fierce competition induced individual practitioners to push for distinctions among

---

[137] See my discussion in chapter one, 27–31.

[138] For a discussion of the concepts of the contemplative and political life in Presocratic philosophy, see Zeppi 1972.

themselves, and the coinage of new words was one aspect of such behavior. This, I argue, is what precipitated the adoption of the word ὁμόνοια. While the traditional typology of the avoidance of *stasis* and implementation of concord was still maintained—as well as the traditional ways to achieve this, such as warfare against the barbarians, redistribution of wealth, and new legislation—the terminology to describe this typology changed.

Given that our material is so meager, however, it is very difficult to evaluate the precise cultural significance in this shift in diction. But the choice to avoid older words and to coin new ones presumably signifies more than mere verbal distinctions. It entailed agonistic stabs at earlier proponents and attempts at unabashed self-promotion. In some cases, however, such as Archytas, the old and the new diction are used hand in hand, almost interchangeably.

As far as the early uses of concord are concerned—particularly with respect to Heraclitus and the Delphic Oracle—Romilly's conclusion that ὁμόνοια was a term that was projected back onto earlier times anachronistically seems sound. What is significant with these occurrences, however, is that they reinforce the idea of a thematic link between concord and wisdom, a link so strong that it later led Plutarch to use the word ὁμόνοια to describe the activities of Heraclitus. Ὁμόνοια had thus become synonymous with the long history of intellectual practices performed by *sophoi*, a tradition in which Heraclitus was seen as a natural participant.

4

Itinerant *Sophoi*

ONE OF THE MOST DISTINCTIVE FEATURES of the sophists is their itinerant status, and it will be the focus of this chapter.[1] We shall start by reviewing the evidence of the sophists' travel to understand better its scope and character. We shall then explore the theme of travel in our sources on other practitioners of wisdom, prior to or contemporary with the sophists, to see to what degree they shared this traveling disposition. Next we shall attempt to outline the institutional framework within which these travels took place. The underlying assumption is that travel was difficult in the ancient world, and that there needs to have existed rudimentary institutions that provided an infrastructure that made travel both feasible and safe. I will suggest that the association between travel and wisdom was strong from the archaic period and onward, and that many *sophoi* traveled extensively precisely in their capacity as practitioners of wisdom. If anything, the sophists' itinerant disposition is a sign of how integrated their practices were into Greek intellectual life. This investigation into the significance of travel will yield at best a sketchy picture, given the patchy and unreliable nature of our evidence. But we shall try to develop it in greater depth in the next chapter when we consider the Panhellenic sanctuaries as destinations for philosophical travel.

Sophistic Travel

Plato is probably the best source to convey just how essential travel was for the sophists. In the *Apology*, Socrates says about Gorgias, Prodicus, and Hippias that:

> Every one of them can go into each of the cities (εἰς ἑκάστην τῶν πόλεων) and persuade the young men, who can associate with

---

[1] Remarkably little has been written about travel, especially as it pertains to the travels of *sophoi*. The standard introduction in English to travel in antiquity is Casson 1994. See Dougherty 2001 for an exploration of the metaphorical use of travel, especially in relation to (poetic) wisdom, in the *Odyssey*. See also Hartog 2001 and, for an anthropological and cross-cultural account of travel, Helms 1988.

whomever of their citizens they please at no cost, to leave their company and affiliate with them instead, paying a fee and thanking them besides (χρήματα διδόντας καὶ χάριν προσειδέναι).[2]

Most of the sophists came from cities other than Athens,[3] and they are repeatedly reported to have belonged to rich and influential families with heavy political responsibilities in their city-states of origin. Protagoras, for example, came from Abdera, and Philostratus well illustrates his family's prominent position:

The sophist Protagoras of Abdera was, at home, a student of Democritus and also consorted with the Persian Magi (ὡμίλησε δὲ καὶ τοῖς ἐκ Περσῶν μάγοις) at the time of Xerxes' expedition against Greece. For his father was Maeandrius, one of the richest men in Thrace (πλούτῳ κατεσκευασμένος παρὰ πολλοὺς τῶν ἐν τῇ Θρᾴκῃ). He entertained Xerxes in his house (δεξάμενος δὲ καὶ τὸν Ξέρξην οἰκίᾳ) and secured from him by means of gifts the privilege for his son to consort with the Magi (δώροις τὴν ξυνουσίαν τῶν μάγων τῷ παιδὶ παρ' αὐτοῦ εὕρετο).[4]

We also know that Protagoras was commissioned to write the laws for the Athenian colony at Thurii, and we hear about his travel to and stay in Sicily.[5] In the *Protagoras* Plato has him comment on his traveling status:

A foreigner (ξένον γὰρ ἄνδρα) who goes to great cities and there persuades the best of the young men (τῶν νέων τοὺς βελτίστους) to give up the association of others, relatives or strangers, old or young, and consort with himself to become better through his intercourse (ὡς βελτίους ἐσομένους διὰ τὴν ἑαυτοῦ συνουσίαν)—he who does that has to be careful.[6]

In the same dialogue the young man who desires to be Protagoras' disciple, Hippocrates, stresses to Socrates the importance of being introduced to him right away:

---

[2]   *Apology* 19e–20a.

[3]   Only two of those who are traditionally included among the sophists, Antiphon and Critias, came from Athens. The list of sophists is fluid, however, and Critias is often left out. See, for example, Kerferd 1981:52.

[4]   Philostratus *Lives of the Sophists* 1.10 = DK 80A2.

[5]   Heraclides Ponticus apud Diogenes Laertius 9.50 = DK 80A1; Hesychius *Onomatologus* in scholia on Plato's *Republic* 600c = DK 80A3; *Hippias Major* 282d–e = DK 80A9.

[6]   *Protagoras* 316c–d.

For I am young and I have never seen or heard Protagoras. I was still a child when he visited Athens last time.[7]

From this it is clear that a number of years must have elapsed between Protagoras' visits to Athens, and that he was active in other Greek communities during his absence. It was presumably the fame he had won elsewhere that motivated the Athenians to solicit his services for Thurii.

In the case of Gorgias of Leontini, Philostratus provides us with a vivid account of his public appearances throughout Greece:

Conspicuous also at the festivals of the Greeks he delivered his *Pythian Speech* from the altar in the temple of the Pythian god, on which a golden statue of him was also erected. His *Olympic Speech* had a most serious content. For seeing that Greece was distracted by factions he became a counselor of concord to them, turning them against the barbarians and convincing them to make as prizes of their weapons not each others' cities, but the land of the barbarians. The *Funeral Oration*, which he delivered at Athens, was spoken over those who had fallen in the wars, whom the Athenians buried at public expense with eulogies, and it is written with exceeding skill.[8]

It is also reported that he was sent as an ambassador by his own city to Athens in 427 BCE to ask for their assistance, since the people of Leontini were involved in a war with the Syracusans.[9] This was supposedly his first trip to Athens, and he is said to have been already sixty years old.[10] He gave a public performance in the theater of the Athenians apart from the funeral oration mentioned above, and there is also a story about him performing together with Hippias in purple clothes.[11] He taught in Argos, where he was so hated that his students had to pay fines, and he was active as a teacher in Boeotia and in Thessaly.[12] Isocrates, finally, mentions that he failed to inhabit any one city steadily.[13]

---

[7] *Protagoras* 310e.

[8] Philostratus *Lives of the Sophists* 1.9 = DK 82A1. See the discussion of this passage in chapter three, 61–78.

[9] Diodorus Siculus 12.53 = DK 82A4.

[10] Guthrie 1971:270.

[11] Philostratus *Lives of the Sophists* 1.1 = DK 82A1a; Aelian *Varia Historia* 12.32 = DK 82A9. This story is further discussed in chapter five, 118.

[12] Argos: DK vol. 2, p425:26 = Olympiodorus on Plato's *Gorgias* 46:11; Thessaly: *Meno* 70a–71b, Isocrates *Antidosis* 155 = DK 82A18; Argos and Boeotia: Untersteiner 1954:93 with notes, and Schmid-Stählin 1940:59n10, cf. Guthrie 1971:270n2.

[13] Isocrates *Antidosis* 156 = DK 82A18.

Prodicus came from Ceos and went on numerous embassies as a representative of his city.[14] Plato mentions him in the passage from the *Apology* quoted above (19e) as one who could go into each of the cities and persuade young men to consort with him. Philostratus says that Xenophon, when a prisoner in Boeotia, was released on bail to go to hear lectures delivered by Prodicus.[15] Plato tells us that he managed to combine his public duties with his activities as a teacher.[16]

Hippias of Elis traveled widely throughout Greece on diplomatic missions, and he earned a reputation for his service, as witness the account given by Philostratus:

> Although he went on the most embassies (πρεσβεύσας) on behalf of Elis, nowhere did he destroy his reputation when speaking in public and discoursing, but he amassed great wealth and was enrolled in the tribes of cities both great and small.[17]

Philostratus also mentions Hippias' travels to Sparta, to a small city in Sicily called Inycus, and to Olympia. In the *Hippias Major*, Socrates greets Hippias by saying, "Hippias, the handsome and wise, how long it has been since you put in to us in Athens." In response to which Hippias answers:

> I have not had time, Socrates. For when Elis needs to transact any business with one of the cities, she always approaches me first among her citizens, and chooses me to represent her, since she regards me as the ablest judge and interpreter of the pronouncements of each city. So I have often represented her in other cities, but most often, and on the most numerous and important matters, in Lacedaemon. So much for your question why I do not come often to these parts.[18]

In the *Hippias Minor*, Hippias says that:

> When the time of the celebration of the Olympic Games comes around I always go to Olympia to the festival of the Greeks from my home in Elis. I offer myself to speak at the temple on whatever topic anyone may want to hear of those I have prepared for display (ἐπίδειξιν), and to answer any question anyone may want to ask.[19]

---

[14] Suda = DK 84A1; *Hippias Major* 282c = DK 84A3.
[15] Philostratus *Lives of the Sophists* 1.12 = DK 84A1a.
[16] *Hippias Major* 282c = DK 84A3
[17] Philostratus *Lives of the Sophists* 1.11 = DK 86A2. See also discussion in chapter three, 84–90.
[18] *Hippias Major* 281a = DK 86A6.
[19] *Hippias Minor* 363c = DK 86A8.

Plato mentions that Hippias visited Olympia wearing clothes all of which he had made for himself: ring, skin-scraper, oil-flask, sandals, cloak, tunic, and girdle, and that, besides this, he had with him poems, epics, tragedies, dithyrambs, and many prose writings.[20] He is also said to have published a *List of Olympic Victors*.[21] When asked by Socrates what he was teaching in Sparta, he answers that they very much enjoy hearing:

> about the families of heroes and men and the founding of cities (περὶ τῶν γενῶν ... τῶν τε ἡρώων καὶ τῶν ἀνθρώπων, καὶ τῶν κατοικίσεων), how the cities were first established. In short, they take delight in listening to the whole study of ancient legends and history (καὶ συλλήβδην πάσης τῆς ἀρχαιολογίας ἥδιστα ἀκροῶνται). So because of them I have been forced to learn and memorize all such things.[22]

Finally, Xenophon mentions a discussion between Socrates and Hippias, who he says had arrived in Athens after a long absence.[23]

Hippias, then, traveled widely in Greece. The information we have from Plato and Xenophon implies that he only made sporadic visits to Athens. We are also informed about what kind of activities he was engaged in at Sparta and at the Olympic Games.

From this survey it is clear that for many of the sophists Athens was not their permanent residence, nor did they spend most of their time there. Further, their activities do not seem to be exclusively targeted towards Athens (or any other democratic city, for that matter). Hippias had developed a particular repertoire for Sparta, and it seems reasonable to assume that other sophists had a similar curricular variety. But if the sophists spent much of their time in other cities than Athens, how are we to account for their ability to travel from city to city and be hospitably received? There existed a great, though intermittent, hostility between many of the city-states, and it cannot have been easy or straightforward to walk into any city in the manner described in our sources. To give just one example of the precariousness of traveling to, not to mention crossing over, the territory of neighboring states, Thucydides mentions the situation of Brasidas and his Spartan troops in 424 when marching through Thessaly to Thrace in support of Perdiccas. He explains why the Spartans took precautions to secure escort for their journey:

> For it was normally not easy to cross through Thessaly without escort, and especially so when carrying arms; and it was suspicious to all

---

[20] *Hippias Major* 368b–d = DK 86A12. See discussion in chapter 5, 113–115.
[21] Plutarch *Numa* 1 = DK 86B3.
[22] *Hippias Major* 285d–e = DK 86A11.
[23] *Memorabilia* 4.4.5 = DK 86A14.

Greeks alike to cross through the territory of one's neighbor without permission (καὶ τοῖς πᾶσί γε ὁμοίως Ἕλλησιν ὕποπτον καθειστήκει τὴν τῶν πέλας μὴ πείσαντας διιέναι).[24]

In order to appreciate better how the sophists could travel the Greek world and why they were held in such high regard as teachers, we shall survey our primary material for historical predecessors. We shall be on the lookout for itinerant *sophoi* who exhibited similar educational expertise as the sophists.

Presocratic Travel

Many of the Presocratic philosophers conducted travels far and wide, but few paid visits to Athens. We can document their itineraries in some detail.

Thales is reported to have visited and even spent a long time in Egypt in the pursuit of wisdom.[25] Plutarch mentions that he traveled to Periander in Corinth to be part of a meeting of the Seven Sages.[26]

Anaximander is mentioned in two sources as having connections with Sparta: Diogenes Laertius attributes to him the discovery of the *gnomon* and reports that he set one up on the sundials in Sparta to mark solstices and equinoxes.[27] Cicero mentions that he warned the Spartans about an earthquake and thus saved many lives.[28] Finally, we are told by Aelian that he led a Milesian colonizing expedition to Apollonia on the Black Sea.[29]

Xenophanes describes himself as having "tossed [his] cares up and down the land of Greece" for sixty-seven years,[30] and we know that he left his native city of Colophon at the coming of the Medes and spent the remainder of his life traveling in Southern Italy and Sicily. He is also reported to have written epics on the foundation of Colophon and Elea.[31]

Pythagoras left Samos and the rule of the tyrant Polycrates and went to the leading Achaean colony in Southern Italy, Croton. We hear about many travels. Diogenes Laertius tells us that:

> When young and eager for learning he traveled from his country and was initiated into all Greek and foreign mysteries. He was in Egypt

---

24 Thucydides 4.78.2. Cf. Herman 1987:119.
25 DK 11A11.
26 Plutarch *Dinner of the Seven Wise Men* 2d–e.
27 Diogenes Laertius 2.1 = DK 12A1.
28 Cicero *De Divinatione* 1.50.112 = DK 12A5a.
29 Aelian *Varia Historia* 3.17 = DK 12A3.
30 DK 21B8.
31 Diogenes Laertius 9.20 = DK 21A1. For a general discussion of archaic foundation (κτίσις) poetry and argument against its autonomy as a literary genre, see Dougherty 1994.

when Polycrates recommended him to Amasis [the pharaoh] by way of letter ... and he spent time among the Chaldaeans and Magi.[32]

Diogenes also tells us in the same place that he went to Crete before going back to Samos only to leave again for Croton. Isocrates (*Busiris* 28), too, attests to Pythagoras' pursuit of wisdom through his travels. He writes that Pythagoras went to Egypt and became a disciple of the Egyptians (μαθητής). Herodotus (2.81) also links Pythagoras with Egyptian religious practices and seems to have him in mind in a similar reference in 2.123.[33]

Plato writes in *Parmenides* (127a-c) that Zeno and Parmenides once came to Athens for the Great Panathenaea and that they stayed in Pythodorus' house.

Empedocles originated from the Sicilian city of Acragas and is reported to have visited Thurii, the Athenian colony, shortly after its foundation in 444/443, and the Peloponnesus and Olympia, where he hired a rhapsode to recite his poems. There is also a story in Diogenes Laertius according to which Empedocles went to attend a festival in Messene.[34]

Anaxagoras came from Clazomenae near Smyrna in Ionia, but he left this place for Athens, where he is said to have spent 30 years. There is a story told by Diogenes Laertius that he visited Olympia. In old age he was allegedly expelled from Athens and went to Lampsacus.[35]

Democritus (like Protagoras) was a native of Abdera and traveled far and wide in the known world. In fragment 299, he says that:

> I wandered over the most land of the men of my day, inquiring into the greatest things and I saw the most airs and lands and I listened to the most erudite men, and no one ever exceeded me in composition of treatises with proofs, not even those Egyptians called Arpedonaptae.[36]

Democritus mentions a visit to Athens in fragment 116 and talks about living abroad in fragment 246. Diogenes Laertius narrates that his father entertained king Xerxes, and that he in return left Magi and Chaldaeans behind to instruct

---

[32] Diogenes Laertius 8.2–3.

[33] Peter Kingsley (1994) argues that the reports of Pythagoras' travels should be taken seriously, especially since the sources (Herodotus 2.81 and Isocrates *Busiris* 28) date back to the fifth and fourth centuries BCE. Kingsley sees already in Heraclitus (DK 22B129) an implicit reference to Pythagorean travel. See also Guthrie (1962:163n2) who argues that Isocrates did not invent Pythagoras' travel to Egypt but that it went back at least to Herodotus 2.123. For Isocrates' *Busiris*, see Livingstone 2001.

[34] Diogenes Laertius 8.52, 63, 66–67, 71, and 73 = DK 31A1; Athenaeus 14.620d = DK 31A12.

[35] Diogenes Laertius 2.6–15 = DK 59A1.

[36] DK 68B299.

the young Democritus.[37] We also hear that he went to Egypt and was instructed by priests, that he visited the Chaldaeans in Persia, and that he made it to the Red Sea. Some also add that he went to India as well as to Ethiopia.[38]

When looking at the travels reported in these sources, one can draw a distinction between *sophoi* who seem to have traveled more extensively and whose fame partially rested on their travels, such as Thales, Xenophanes, Pythagoras, and Democritus, and those who are said to have made a few but significant travels, such as Anaximander, Anaxagoras, and Empedocles. Despite the different degrees of intensity of their travels, I still think that we can legitimately compare them in so far as they all had similar expertise and undertook their travels as practitioners of this expertise. We will explore the Panhellenic centers as destinations for such travels in the next chapter, but for now we can draw some preliminary conclusions from the material we have reviewed.

There existed a long-standing tradition of contacts between the cities in the Greek-speaking world, and these contacts extended as far as Egypt and Persia. Given these established channels, it seems reasonable to assume that the sophists did not have to create new networks when traveling, but employed already existing ones. But these insights only take us so far. We have only pushed the question of authority from the sophists to an earlier generation of *sophoi*. To pursue this question further, we shall consult Herodotus' account of the encounter between Solon and Croesus in Book 1.29–30. There Herodotus gives an extensive description of how Solon came to Sardis and Croesus:

> When all these nations had been added to the Lydian empire, and Sardis was at the height of her wealth and prosperity, all the Greek wise men (σοφισταί) of that epoch, one after another, paid visits to the capital. Much the most distinguished of them was Solon the Athenian, the man who at the request of his country had made a code of laws for Athens. He was on his travels at the time, intending to be away for ten years, in order to avoid the necessity of repealing any of the laws he had made. That, at any rate, was the real reason of his absence, though he gave it out that what he wanted was just to see the world. The Athenians could not alter any of Solon's laws without him, because they had solemnly sworn to give them a ten years' trial. For this reason, then—and also no doubt for the pleasure of foreign travel—Solon left home and, after a visit to the court of Amasis in Egypt, went to Sardis to see Croesus. Croesus received him as a guest-friend (ἐξεινίζετο) in the palace, and

---

[37] Note that this story is also associated with Protagoras (Diogenes Laertius 9.34 = DK 68A1), quoted earlier on 94. See discussion below, 109n78.

[38] Diogenes Laertius 9.35 = DK 68A1; Strabo 15.703 = DK 68A12; Cicero *De Finibus Bonorum et Malorum* 9.19.50 = DK 68A13; Aelian *Varia Historia* 4.20 = DK 68A16.

three or four days after his arrival instructed some servants to take him to a tour of the royal treasuries and point out the richness and magnificence of everything. When Solon had made as thorough an inspection as opportunity allowed, Croesus said: "Well, my Athenian guest-friend (Ξεῖνε Ἀθηναῖε), I have heard a great deal about your wisdom, and how widely you have traveled in the pursuit of knowledge. I cannot resist my desire to ask you a question: who is the happiest man you have ever seen?"

Trans. Selincourt, modified[39]

This encounter has been questioned on chronological grounds.[40] What interests me, however, is less the historicity of the meeting than Herodotus' conceptualization of the encounter. Solon travels from Athens to Sardis and is received by Croesus because of his reputation for wisdom—he is one of the Seven Sages—to validate Croesus' claims to happiness (εὐδαιμονία). Croesus' reception of Solon invokes the framework of guest-friendship (ξενία): it is as his guest-friend that Croesus receives and entertains Solon at his court in Sardis and it is in this capacity that he asks him to assess his fortunes. In the Herodotean narrative, then, Solon's travel to and reception by Croesus are predicated on and mediated through the cultural networks provided by ξενία. Is the prominence of ξενία limited to this encounter in Herodotus, or can we find this association between ξενία and σοφία even in the material on the Presocratics and sophists? We shall attempt to address these questions next.

Ξενία and Σοφία

As Gabriel Herman has well documented in *Ritualised Friendship and the Greek City*, there existed in ancient Greece a developed network of interactions among what we might call an international elite (ξενία). Herman defines ξενία "as a bond of solidarity manifesting itself in an exchange of goods and services between individuals originating from separate social units."[41] Within this network, the elite of Greece established relations that often were of crucial importance to their ability to maintain their positions both abroad and within their own *poleis*.[42] One of the fundamental principles for the workings of *xenia* was the institution of gift-exchange and reciprocity—a closed market of exchanges within which

---

[39] Diodorus Siculus (9.26.1) also mentions a meeting between Solon and Croesus, but there Solon is part of a larger delegation of the Seven Sages.

[40] For the problem of chronology that this encounter poses, see How and Wells 1912, 1:66–67; and Asheri, Lloyd, and Corcella 2007:99, with bibliography.

[41] Herman 1987:10.

[42] "Ritual friendship appears as an overwhelmingly upper-class institution ... People of humbler standing are significantly rare," Herman 1987:34.

transactions of material and symbolic capital took place.[43] One of the commodities circulating in such a system, I would argue, was wisdom.[44]

Xenia flourished in the Homeric world but came under intense scrutiny after the emergence of the city-states, when it was seen as a threat to their autonomy.[45] Despite being questioned, however, *xenia* was still a strong operating force in Greek social life long after the rise of the city-states.[46] In the classical period there existed a tension between an older, mainly elite, code of behavior promoted by *xenia* and a more modern one (often explicitly democratic) in line with the demands of the *polis*.[47] But the *polis* could never entirely stamp out the *xenia* framework: "Both inside the city and even more outside it, older social groupings and archaic ideals maintained themselves alongside the new ones with remarkable tenacity."[48] On a more practical level, *xenia* was not only a network that tied together members of separate communities. It also facilitated visits between these members, and the channels between guest-friends allowed them to extend their influence and power base well beyond their own communities. Since guest-friends were always from separate social units, the ability to sustain these relationships was predicated on the ability of guest-friends to travel to their hosts and receive their guest-friends in turn.[49]

---

[43] For the concept of symbolic capital, see the general discussion of how Bourdieu figures in my work, in the introduction, above, 17–19. Symbolic capital implies an expansion of the notion of economic capital. Resources available to agents in a field are not exclusively material but take the form of other rewards, such as recognition, honor, consecration, and prestige. Just like economic capital, symbolic capital is highly sought after and can be accumulated to assure profit (though not always economic) for its holders. For a concise statement of the significance of symbolic capital in Bourdieu's sociology, see Bourdieu 1991:14–16. For an application of the concept of symbolic capital to Greek philosophy, see Nightingale 2000:157; see also Nightingale 1995 and 2004.

[44] It seems to me that Marcel Mauss in his classic study *The Gift* outlines a pattern of exchange in "economic and legal systems that have preceded our own" that fits well with the Greek institution of *xenia*. He writes: "what they exchange is not solely property and wealth, movable and immovable goods, and things economically useful. In particular, such exchanges are acts of politeness: banquets, rituals, military services, women, children, dances, festivals, and fairs, in which economic transaction is only one element, and in which the passing on of wealth is only one feature of a much more general and enduring contract," 5.

[45] For manifestations of such threats, see examples in Herman 1987:1–5.

[46] "Overtly or covertly, guest-friendship continued to act as a powerful bond between citizens of different cities and between citizens and members of various apolitical bodies. And by this persistence in the age of the cities, it became involved in actively shaping the value system of the *polis* and in formulating some of its most basic concepts and patterns of action," Herman 1987:7.

[47] It is important to note here that *elite* in this context does not have as its opposite *democratic*; rather, it is the opposite of forms of government that place the communal interests of the *polis* above the prosperity of individual members of the elite, which, of course, includes an oligarchy like Sparta. For an example of this, see Herman 1987:1.

[48] Herman 1987:6.

[49] The relationships developed within the *xenia* framework were in no way limited to the Greek world: "*xenia* relationships could exist between members of different Greek cities; between

Xenia was successively appropriated by the *polis* for purposes of inter-*polis* diplomacy, so that the personal relationships engaged in by two aristocrats from separate social units were later modified by the *polis*. The larger community appropriated the position of one member and collectively engaged in an agreement with an individual outsider.[50] Herman discusses the propensity of such relationships of proxeny to be built upon already existing ties of *xenia*, and this observation further emphasizes the development of the former from the latter.[51]

Within the *xenia* network, the elite traveled to, entertained, and sustained one another with remarkable efficiency—so much so that one can legitimately talk about an exchange system of goods and services circulating among guest-friends.[52] Herman classifies these exchanges under the headings of material goods and non-material services, and he divides the latter group into three subcategories: "ritual services, private services and services carried out within the context of political institutions."[53] As an example of the non-material services, he refers to Herodotus (3.125), where the affiliates of Polycrates, the tyrant of Samos, are described. We hear of a number of people connected to the tyrant. Of most interest for our purposes are Democedes of Crotona, the best physician of his day, and an unspecified number of soothsayers. To explain the relationship between Polycrates and his associates, Herman suggests a model of social organization that contained elite coalitions headed by a leader who was in turn surrounded by a variety of local supporters as well as guest-friends in other communities.[54] Loosely attached to these leaders and their entourage were a number of specialists, such as physicians, soothsayers, artists, and poets. Among these affiliates, I suggest, we should also include wise men, *sophoi*, who served in a variety of roles, such as political and legal advisors as well as educators.[55] They would be invited by the local leader, travel, and be entertained within the framework of *xenia*. It would also be within this context that they could interact with other practitioners of wisdom and participate in more or less structured exchanges of wisdom.

---

members of Greek cities and members of Greek *ethne* (for example, Macedonians, Epirotes); between Greeks and non-Greeks (for example, Persians, Lydians, Egyptians, Phoenicians, Romans); and finally, between different non-Greeks," Herman 1987:12.

[50] "The concepts, outlook and symbols of guest-friendship were transferred from the personal level to the level of the whole community and, invested with new meanings, they provided the city with a framework for interacting with foreign individuals and communities," Herman 1987:8.

[51] Herman 1987:139.

[52] For a full discussion of the nature and content of such an exchange system, see Herman 1987:73–106.

[53] Herman 1987:81.

[54] Herman 1987:150.

[55] Very often these roles would of course overlap: Solon, for example, was a wise man, a lawgiver and legislative expert, and a poet.

Xenia, then, was an ancient institution that operated primarily, if not exclusively, on what we may call an international level. It was conducive to the establishment of connections between various social units, and it facilitated safe travel among the members of these units. As Herman maintains:

> Ritualised friendship thus became a formula for bringing together a wide variety of people of different social origin, and provided links in elaborate chains of horizontal and vertical integration.[56]

I suggest that early *sophoi* conducted much of their travel within the network of *xenia*, and that the sophists were simply continuing a longstanding practice that had considerable historical resonance.[57]

Scholars have long commented on the propensity of wise men for travel, but not much work has been done to explain how such travel was socially feasible beyond an assessment of a general desire on the part of philosophers to tour and explore the world.[58] Humphreys has addressed the question of Greek intellectuals and observed that poets, as part of that group, "may travel from one part of the Greek world to another and find a welcome everywhere because of their skills." When describing the poet's social role, she writes that he is "a hanger-on of the noble *oikos*."[59] This observation, although vague as to the precise nature of the relationship between poets and nobles and the practicalities of travel, emphasizes the role of the noble *oikoi* as destinations for poetic travel and as parts in an international network that tied together geographically disparate patrons. Humphreys also stresses how crucial travel was to the emerging field of "Greek intellectuals" in the fifth century:

> In the fifth century, philosophers, like other intellectuals, traveled from city to city, expounding their views in the houses of leading citizens or in the public gymnasium. They were the traveling *gurus* of ancient Greece, each with his own theory to expound and his own reputation to build. The type of the philosopher was not yet fixed, the audience's expectations were plastic; the only necessity was, as Louis Gernet has said, that the philosophers should not look like everybody else—and, one might add, should not think like anybody else.[60]

---

[56] Herman 1987:84.
[57] The cultural affiliation between *xenia* and travel will become more apparent in chapter five, when we explore the relevance of *xenia* for the travels to and activities at the Panhellenic centers.
[58] Montiglio 2000:88 is a typical representative of this view: "[T]he first philosophers who took to wandering did so under no other compulsion than their intellectual curiosity." See also Montiglio 2005.
[59] Humphreys 1978:213–214.
[60] Humphreys 1978:225.

Rosalind Thomas has also considered the role of traveling *sophoi*. She outlines the intellectual milieu in which Herodotus participated and against which she believes his work should be understood; and she paints a picture of extensive intellectual travel in the fifth century:

> This suggests that the period was one in which intellectuals, and not only the sophists gathering their crop of pupils, visited many cities in the Greek world—of which Athens was only the most powerful. Other cities benefited—or suffered—from the visits of philosophers ... Herodotus was presumably another of such travelling intellectuals.[61]

It seems safe to conclude that travel was extremely important for practitioners of wisdom in the fifth century. But what do we know about the situation in the archaic period? Montiglio has conducted a broader exploration of the link between travel and philosophy, and she emphasizes the importance of travel for wise men from Odysseus onward. Montiglio highlights what an undesirable and anomalous activity travel was in the Greek world: it is often connected with suffering, supplication, and exile in epic and tragedy, and when associated with trade it is often represented as a great evil.[62] Within such cultural attitudes, Montiglio distinguishes between two types of travel, one positive and one negative. The positive one is linked with knowledge, embraced by the example of Odysseus, who "learns from his toilsome wanderings."[63] Later Solon came to personify this link between travel and learning, so much so that he "inaugurates a tradition which eventually spreads so widely that Diogenes Laertius regards the philosopher who loathes travelling as an exception." This "love of knowledge" that Solon's travels represent, in the words of Montiglio, "is the motive that drove several other Presocratics to travel extensively." She continues:

> Although these sages were also called upon to share their wisdom, as Solon's example alone shows, they primarily went about to learn for themselves rather than to teach others. Their wanderings are a 'Bildungsreise.'[64]

The other form of travel is motivated by the need to work and earn money, and here we find the sophists.[65] This type of travel is modeled on the merchant, where need or greed motivates travel, and, in the case of the sophists, teaching

---

[61] Thomas 2000:12.
[62] Montiglio 2000, esp. 87–88 and 93; and 2005, esp. 24–41.
[63] Montiglio 2000:88; and 2005:91–117.
[64] Montiglio 2000:88.
[65] "But unlike Solon or Democritus, the Sophists did not travel in order to acquire knowledge. Hardly any 'theory,' any abstract curiosity or ethnographic interest motivated their travels. Rather, the Sophists travelled to sell their skill," Montiglio 2000:92; and 2005:105–117.

and money-making—not desire to see the world and learn, as with the Presocratics—are given as the determining factors for them going from city to city. But in establishing these models and in seeking to reconstruct the cultural attitudes associated with them, Montiglio relies heavily on the judgment of Plato. She thus concludes—just as Plato did—that the sophists had no philosophical ambitions, that they only traveled to make money, and that they were generally despised in the Greek world.[66]

Despite her heavy Platonic bias in assessing the sophists, there are two important points in Montiglio's argument that I would like to build on. First, she establishes the ancient connection between travel and wisdom, dating back at least to the archaic period—though I would be reluctant to support her distinction between the two contrasting models of travel. Second, she stresses the negative connotations that existed in relation to travel, and how anyone undertaking travel exposed himself to potential danger. These observations underscore the importance of understanding the social mechanism that made travel possible.

Another, and entirely different, approach to travel comes from the field of archeology. Colin Renfrew and John Cherry outline in *Peer Polity Interaction* a theory of understanding the development of complex societies. This they do in an attempt to avoid the constraints entailed by the two predominant models in archaeology that emphasize either "diffusion of cultures" or "autonomy and local innovation." Instead of this "either-or thinking" they believe that the key to understanding the developments of certain societies lies elsewhere, namely in the communications, processes, and interactions that take place between neighboring, autonomous communities. Though these communities are independent and self-regulating they share "structural homologies" with their neighboring communities, that is:

> similar political institutions, a common system of weights and measures, the same system of writing (if any), essentially the same structure of religious beliefs (albeit with local variations, such as a special patron deity), the same spoken language, and indeed generally what the archaeologist would call the same "culture", in whatever sense he might choose to use that term.[67]

---

[66] "The wanderings of the Sophist within the wandering realm of opinion highlight his unphilosophical nature and match his ability to assume any shape, like a wizard. Wandering is a manifestation of the Sophist's fleeting mutability, which in turn gives rise to a multiplication of definitions. In sum, the Sophist's wanderings connote verbal deceits, greed, and an evasive, slippery nature," Montiglio 2000:93.

[67] Renfrew and Cherry 1986:2.

The origin of these structural homologies can be found neither by looking exclusively at outside influences nor at endogenous developments, but by analyzing "the interaction between the polities—the peer polity interactions." The corollary of this statement is that no single place can be pinpointed as the origin of a particular cultural form. Rather, "the different communities developed simultaneously and their structural homologies developed with them."

The relational mode of thinking introduced in this approach is particularly well-suited to our material. It stresses the analysis of the relationships among the various autonomous polities and how these interactions come to shape the development of the polities and their belief systems.[68] What is more, the relations between the social units are not to be confined to transactions of material commodities, but emphasis should rather be placed on "the flow of information of various kinds between the polities."[69]

But what were the types of interaction that took place in the Greek context and what sorts of communication can we identify? In the words of Renfrew and Cherry:

> If we are studying peer polity interaction, it is thus of particular importance to consider the circumstances in which individual members of different polities are likely to have met, circumstances where competition and emulation could operate, and where symbolic utterances or displays could have their effect. Obviously this could happen on neutral ground, and one may suggest that the whole phenomenon of pan-polity gatherings is one of special interest. The pan-Hellenic games and festivals at centres such as Olympia, Isthmia, Nemea, Delphi and Delos are an excellent example, and no doubt many other early state societies had some kind of framework where members of different polities came into contact.[70]

On the regional level, the Panhellenic sites played an important part in furthering contacts between polities, and we will explore this in the next chapter. But the most pervasive and multidimensional network to promote communication and interaction is the *xenia* network outlined above.[71] Through this network, we see precisely the preoccupation with competition, emulation, and exchanges that pertain to a cultural framework shared by a larger group of autonomous *poleis*.

---

[68] "The significant unit is thus seen, in this perspective, to be the larger community beyond the polity level, comprised of loosely related, yet politically independent, interacting groups," Renfrew and Cherry 1986:7.

[69] Renfrew and Cherry 1986:8.

[70] Renfrew and Cherry 1986:16.

[71] This is not to deny the operation of *xenia* in the visits to the Panhellenic centers, only to emphasize its more pervasive influence as a social institution.

But who where the dominant players participating in these exchanges? When addressing this issue, Renfrew and Cherry downplay the importance of traders, saying instead that the "travels of the decision-makers may have been more important, some undertaken, no doubt, in the course of arranging marriage alliances, or simply in gift-exchange."[72] The locus of interest is thus on interactions between the decision-makers in the various social units. But this raises the question of how, where, and under what circumstances they met. It becomes especially important if we are to attribute to this type of interaction the shaping and influencing of the social structures of the participating communities. Renfrew and Cherry do not explore these aspects of their theory. Instead they point out that this kind of research is in need of further pursuit, the lack of which they deplore:

> In any case, the question of travel, in non-hierarchical as well as hierarchical societies, is an important one which seems to have been considered relatively little. Yet when we are talking about the way symbolic structures in one polity had an influence upon those of another, the existence of interaction and its mechanism is of crucial importance.[73]

Let us pause for a moment to recapitulate the main points of the argument thus far. We have assessed the importance of travel for the sophists and linked it to the general theme of travel by other *sophoi*. Rather than assuming the Platonic bias and distinguishing between the Presocratics who traveled for knowledge and the sophists who traveled for pay, it seems reasonable to assume that the same motivations that induced early *sophoi* to travel were still at play in the time of the sophists. We have further suggested that it was within the framework of *xenia* that much of the philosophical travel occurred. By drawing on the peer polity interaction model, we have called attention to the importance of the inter-*polis* interaction engaged in by decision-makers and the flow of information resulting from their interactions. Here *xenia* becomes crucial in understanding how interactions between the elites in the various communities took place. In the remainder of this chapter, I will try to map out how all of this played out in the time of the sophists. We shall explore what role the *xenia* system had in their travels, and we will also try to push the question of historical predecessors in the direction of the Seven Sages.

Ξενία in the Time of the Sophists

We find many of the *sophoi* engaged in *xenia*-relationships or see their travels described in words that conjure up these elite connections. Isocrates, for

---

[72] Renfrew and Cherry 1986:158.
[73] Renfrew and Cherry 1986:158.

108

example, offers a clear articulation of the connection between his *sophia* and *xenia*. As Too has demonstrated, he repeatedly characterizes his relationship with students "as an extension of a friendship (*philia*) or a guest-host relationship (*xenia*)."[74] In *Epistle* 6, he reassures his addressees (Thebe and Tisiphonus) of his support as a result of his *xenia*-relationship with their deceased father (Jason, the tyrant of Pherae), and he goes on to pledge that his present advice is motivated by his *xenia*-relationship toward them.[75] In *Epistle* 7, he offers advice to Timotheus, whose father, Clearchus, had been one of his students. He begins the letter by invoking his intimate relationship with Clearchus, and concludes by instructing Timotheus to dispatch a letter to him renewing their former friendship and *xenia*-relationship (τὴν φιλίαν καὶ ξενίαν τὴν πρότερον ὑπάρχουσαν).[76] He furthermore conjures up the framework of *xenia* in his repeated categorizations of his own advice as a gift (δῶρον/δωρεά) that he presents to his students.[77] In these instances, then, Isocrates chooses to situate his pedagogical role as an expert counselor in the context of *xenia*; it is the basis for his relationship with his advisees and the sole motivation for his counsel.

The link between ξενία and σοφία is also strong in connection with Protagoras. According to Philostratus, the father of Protagoras established ties to Xerxes as a guest-friend and acquired by means of gifts the opportunity for Protagoras to learn from the Magi.[78] Herodotus (8.120) corroborates the connection between Xerxes and Abdera:

> It is plain that Xerxes came to Abdera on his return back and made a pact of friendship with them (ξεινίην τέ σφι συνθέμενος) and gave them as gifts (δωρησάμενος) a golden sword and gold-sprinkled tiara.

In this passage, we find the same language as in Herodotus' narrative on Croesus and Solon, that is, the language of *xenia* and gift-exchange. It places Protagoras in a similar relationship to Xerxes as Solon to Croesus. Note Philostratus' emphasis on the wealth of Protagoras' father (πλούτῳ κατεσκευασμένος), a prerequisite

---

[74] "In several works he insists that by offering counsel to certain individuals he is continuing the friendship which he had with their fathers (cf. *Epistle* 5.1; *Epistle* 6.1). He specifically asks the addressees of *Epistle* 6 to consider the epistle as *xenia*, as a token of guest-friendship (4)," Too 1995:110.

[75] Isocrates *Epistle* 6.1 and 6.4.

[76] *Epistle* 7.13.

[77] *To Nicocles* 2 and *To Demonicus* 2. Cf. Too 1995:110–111.

[78] See passage quoted earlier on 94 (Philostratus *Lives of the Sophists* 1.10. = DK 80A2). Note that Diogenes Laertius attributes this story to Democritus (9.34), and he also emphasizes how important the relationship of *xenia* was between Democritus' father and Xerxes to bring about the interaction with the Magi. The fact that this account of the affiliation with the Magi is attributed both to Protagoras and Democritus does not in any way, I think, decrease its value as evidence for the importance of *xenia* for the sophists. If anything, it supports the claim that the sharp division between the Presocratics and the sophists is a false one.

for acts of *xenia*. In the *Protagoras* (316c7) we hear that the sophist's audience are the best young men (οἱ βέλτιστοι τῶν νέων), and here βέλτιστοι is a class marker to indicate the young men's social standing as aristocrats.[79]

In general when we hear of a sophist's visit to Athens, he is staying in the household of an aristocrat—an arrangement difficult to understand outside the framework of *xenia*. In Plato's *Protagoras*, for example, we are told that the sophists are staying in the house of Callias, a known Athenian aristocrat. The audience at Callias' house is, in the words of Martin Ostwald:

> a 'Who's Who' of the upper class: Pericles' sons Paralus and Xanthippus, Alcibiades, Critias, Charmides, Phaedrus, Eryximachus, Pausanias, Agathon, Adeimantus son of Cepis, and his namesake, son of Leucolophides.[80]

Plutarch (*Pericles* 36.2–3) also gives evidence for Pericles' association with sophists in general and Protagoras in particular. In Plato's *Gorgias* (447b), Callicles houses the great sophist, and although Callicles' historicity is disputed, it is safe to say that he is meant to belong to the upper stratum in Athenian life.[81]

As we have already observed, we hear of a strong involvement in diplomatic activities on the part of many of the sophists,[82] and this sphere of activities also had strong ties to *xenia*. According to Herman, *xenia* was successively appropriated by the *poleis* for purposes of inter-*polis* diplomacy,[83] and ambassadors were regularly chosen based on their personal hereditary ties of *xenia*.[84] Although we know very little about the specifics surrounding the ambassadorial undertakings of the sophists, it seems likely that their appointments in some measure depended on their ability to draw on private relationships of *xenia*. The evidence of diplomatic expertise, then, is another indication of the sophists' participation and membership in the elite *xenia* network.

---

[79] Cf. Adkins 1973:10, who notes that "βέλτιστοι certainly has socio-political overtones."

[80] Ostwald 1992:343.

[81] See Dodds 1959:12–15, esp. 13n2.

[82] Gorgias: Diodorus Siculus 12.53 = DK 82A4; Prodicus: Philostratus *Lives of the Sophists* 1.12 = DK 84A1a, *Hippias Major* 282c = DK 84A3; Hippias: Philostratus *Lives of the Sophists* 1.11 = DK 86A2.

[83] "The concepts, outlook and symbols of guest-friendship were transferred from the personal level to the level of the whole community and, invested with new meanings, they provided the city with a framework for interacting with foreign individuals and communities," Herman 1987:8.

[84] Herman 1987:139: "time and again, [Greek states] included in their embassies people who already stood in some warm and enduring relationship with the persons to be approached." Cf. Humphreys' discussion of the process of selecting ambassadors in fifth-century Athens. She highlights some important qualifications: wealth, sympathetic disposition to the party involved, and "ties of hereditary proxeny or other personal links with the state to which the embassy was dispatched," Humphreys 1977–1978:100.

The Presocratics, too, seem to belong to this exclusive circle, at least if we take seriously the frequent attestations of their families' prominent stature. For example, Thales is said to have been from a distinguished family (γένος λάμπρον, Diogenes Laertius 1.22), and Anaxagoras is reported to have been "eminent for wealth and noble birth" (οὗτος εὐγενείᾳ καὶ πλούτῳ διαφέρων ἦν, Diogenes Laertius 2.6). Heraclitus was of royal descent but gave up his claim to kingship in favor of his brother (ἐκχωρῆσαι γὰρ τἀδελφῷ τῆς βασιλείας, Diogenes Laertius 9.6). Empedocles, likewise, is said to be of an illustrious family (λαμπρᾶς ἦν οἰκίας, Diogenes Laertius 8.51) and to have once rejected an offer of kingship (τὴν βασιλείαν αὐτῷ διδομένην παρῃτήσατο, Diogenes Laertius 8.63), and we also possess evidence that Parmenides was of noble birth and wealth (γένους τε ὑπάρχων λαμπροῦ καὶ πλούτου, Diogenes Laertius 9.21). When he visited Athens with Zeno, they stayed at the house of Pythodorus, a known Athenian aristocrat (Plato *Parmenides* 127c).

Ξενία and the Seven Sages

But this thematic link between *sophia* and *xenia* does not begin with nor is exclusively restricted to the sources on the sophists. We have seen how Solon was greeted and received as a guest-friend by Croesus in Herodotus. Indeed, he was invited by the Lydian king in his capacity as a practitioner of wisdom, and Croesus comments on his reputation for wisdom and travel (πλάνη). We have also heard of Thales' reputed travel to Egypt, where he allegedly learned geometry,[85] and of his participation in the banquet of the Seven Sages at Corinth. Another member in the stories surrounding the Seven Sages was Anacharsis, and we have interesting attestations of his travels.[86] Herodotus (4.76) relates how he traveled extensively and made displays of his wisdom during his travels (Ἀνάχαρσις, ἐπείτε γῆν πολλὴν θεωρήσας καὶ ἀποδεξάμενος κατ᾽ αὐτὴν σοφίην πολλήν). Diogenes Laertius also attests to his many travels in 1.103 (πολλὰ πλανηθείς). Jan Fredrik Kindstrand has collected the sources for his travels in the Greek world and beyond, and he is said to have visited Sparta, Delphi, Myson in Chen, Periander, and Croesus.[87] Diogenes Laertius writes that he also went to Athens to visit Solon to become, if possible, his guest-friend (βούλοιτο αὐτὸν θεάσασθαι, ξένος τε, εἰ οἷόν τε, γενέσθαι).[88] Solon's initial response was to dismiss him but, struck by his readiness of wit (καταπλαγεὶς τὴν ἑτοιμότητα), he changed his mind and befriended him. Here again we see the thematic link between travel,

---

[85] Diogenes Laertius 1.24.
[86] For a general discussion of the Seven Sages, see Snell 1971; Martin 1993; and Busine 2002. See also discussion in chapter five. For Anacharsis, see Kindstrand 1981.
[87] Kindstrand 1981:8.
[88] Diogenes Laertius 1.101.

wisdom, and *xenia*. We have already explored this link with respect to the sophists and Presocratics, and now I would like to push the analysis even further back to the Seven Sages.

We have scant ancient sources on the Seven Sages, and the material is often problematic. But there still seem to be important themes that fit well with what we have outlined above. Thales, Solon, and Anacharsis all figured in accounts that designate them as members of the *collegium* of the Seven Sages.[89] They were famous for their wisdom and travels. Further, *xenia* seems to have constituted an important institutional framework for their travels: Solon was hospitably received by Croesus, and Anacharsis established a guest-friend relationship to Solon.[90] Diodorus Siculus (9.2) develops this thematic link in a passage where he writes that Croesus used to summon the wisest Greeks and, after spending time with them and benefiting from their wisdom, would send them away with many gifts (Κροῖσος ὁ Λυδῶν βασιλεὺς ... μετεπέμπετο τῶν Ἑλλήνων τοὺς σοφωτάτους, καὶ συνδιατρίβων αὐτοῖς μετὰ πολλῶν δώρων ἐξέπεμψε καὶ αὐτὸς πρὸς ἀρετὴν ὠφελεῖτο πολλά). Later in the same book (9.26), Diodorus repeats the same passage but goes on to name the wise men invited: Solon, Anacharsis, Bias, and Pittacus. Apart from the names of the sages, what these passages add to Herodotus' account is the mention of gifts. Herodotus invokes the language of gift-exchange only to problematize the commodification of wisdom suggested by Croesus. In the Herodotean version, Croesus sends Solon away giftless, deeming him unworthy of any compensation. Diodorus, on the other hand, describes an unproblematic exchange that leads to lavish compensation. Together, these two passages paint a picture of traveling sages hospitably received and generously rewarded for their services. Already in our sources on the Seven Sages, then, we see a quasi-institutionalized role of a wise man, *sophos*. He is a highly sought-after traveling practitioner of wisdom who journeys the Greek world and beyond through connections established through *xenia*. We also encounter these practitioners at banquets and symposia for the Seven Sages, and at the Panhellenic centers, with an emphasis on Delphi. This is a connection that we shall explore further in the next chapter.

---

[89] Anacharsis was first included in this group by Ephorus (ca. 350 BCE) according to Diogenes Laertius 1.41, but Kindstrand 1981:38, argues that he was "closely associated with it at an early date." For a fuller discussion and relevant bibliography, see Kindstrand 1981:33–50.

[90] In this context, we might mention what Plutarch has to say about Solon (*Solon* 26.3; cf. Herodotus 5.113). He came to Cyprus and was well received by one of the kings, Philocyprus. Solon took such a liking to the king that he advised him to move his city to a more favorable place on a nearby plain, and he stayed to manage the founding of the new city (ἐπεμελήθη τοῦ συνοικισμοῦ). In return, Philocyprus thanked Solon by giving the new city, formerly known as Aipeia, the name of Soli. This is the foundation Solon refers to in fragment 19 (West).

5

Sages at the Games

IN ONE OF THE STRANGER ACCOUNTS of sophists at work, we hear how Hippias of Elis made a conspicuous appearance at Olympia. In the words of Plato (*Hippias Minor* 368b-e):

πάντως δὲ πλείστας τέχνας πάντων σοφώτατος εἶ ἀνθρώπων, ὡς ἐγώ ποτέ σου ἤκουον μεγαλαυχουμένου, πολλὴν σοφίαν καὶ ζηλωτὴν σαυτοῦ διεξιόντος ἐν ἀγορᾷ ἐπὶ ταῖς τραπέζαις. ἔφησθα δὲ ἀφικέσθαι ποτὲ εἰς Ὀλυμπίαν ἃ εἶχες περὶ τὸ σῶμα ἅπαντα σαυτοῦ ἔργα ἔχων· πρῶτον μὲν δακτύλιον—ἐντεῦθεν γὰρ ἤρχου—ὃν εἶχες σαυτοῦ ἔχειν ἔργον, ὡς ἐπιστάμενος δακτυλίους γλύφειν, καὶ ἄλλην σφραγῖδα σὸν ἔργον, καὶ στλεγγίδα καὶ λήκυθον, ἃ αὐτὸς ἠργάσω· ἔπειτα ὑποδήματα ἃ εἶχες ἔφησθα αὐτὸς σκυτοτομῆσαι, καὶ τὸ ἱμάτιον ὑφῆναι καὶ τὸν χιτωνίσκον· καὶ ὅ γε πᾶσιν ἔδοξεν ἀτοπώτατον καὶ σοφίας πλείστης ἐπίδειγμα, ἐπειδὴ τὴν ζώνην ἔφησθα τοῦ χιτωνίσκου, ἣν εἶχες, εἶναι μὲν οἵαι αἱ Περσικαὶ τῶν πολυτελῶν, ταύτην δὲ αὐτὸς πλέξαι· πρὸς δὲ τούτοις ποιήματα ἔχων ἐλθεῖν, καὶ ἔπη καὶ τραγῳδίας καὶ διθυράμβους, καὶ καταλογάδην πολλοὺς λόγους καὶ παντοδαποὺς συγκειμένους· καὶ περὶ τῶν τεχνῶν δὴ ὧν ἄρτι ἐγὼ ἔλεγον ἐπιστήμων ἀφικέσθαι διαφερόντως τῶν ἄλλων, καὶ περὶ ῥυθμῶν καὶ ἁρμονιῶν καὶ γραμμάτων ὀρθότητος, καὶ ἄλλα ἔτι πρὸς τούτοις πάνυ πολλά, ὡς ἐγὼ δοκῶ μνημονεύειν· καίτοι τό γε μνημονικὸν ἐπελαθόμην σου, ὡς ἔοικε, τέχνημα, ἐν ᾧ σὺ οἴει λαμπρότατος εἶναι· οἶμαι δὲ καὶ ἄλλα πάμπολλα ἐπιλελῆσθαι.

You most certainly are the wisest of all men in the greatest number of skills, as I once heard you boast about yourself, when you were recounting your great and enviable wisdom at the bankers' tables in the marketplace. You said that once, when you went to Olympia, everything you had on your person was your own work; first the ring—for you began with that—which you had was your own work, showing that

you knew how to engrave rings, and another seal was your work, and
a strigil and an oil-flask were your works; then you said that you yourself had made the sandals you had on, and had woven your cloak and
tunic; and, what seemed to every one most unusual and display of the
most wisdom, was when you said that the girdle you wore about your
tunic was like the Persian girdles of the costliest kind, and that you
had made it yourself. And in addition you said that you brought with
you poems, epics and tragedies and dithyrambs, and many writings
of all sorts composed in prose; and that you were there excelling all
others in knowledge of the arts of which I was speaking [viz. arithmetic, geometry, and astronomy] just now, and in rhythms, harmonies,
and in the correctness of letters, and many other things besides, as I
seem to remember; and yet I forgot your art of memory, as it seems, in
which you think you are most brilliant; and I fancy I have forgotten a
great many other things.

Trans. Gallop, modified[1]

This passage highlights the surprising juxtaposition of Hippias' self-made attire
and the cross-generic compilation of literature that he brought with him—
all described and subsumed under the somewhat flexible rubric of the Greek
word for wisdom, *sophia*, perhaps better translated as 'expertise.'[2] As if that
were not enough, we also hear of his proficiency in a number of other specialized disciplines, such as geometry, astronomy, rhythms, correctness of letters,
and mnemonics. All of this—his attire, literature, and "scientific" expertise—
was prepared for competitive display and consumption. Indeed, we hear that
Hippias outshone all his rivals. Hippias was thus not alone in making an appearance at Olympia, but we are to understand that other people also attended,
if not similarly equipped, at least outfitted with a view to making a similarly
impressive appearance. Our source gives an equal importance to physical and
intellectual self-presentation, and it seems as if conspicuous garments were
as vital for one's competitive standing and success as the proper intellectual
disposition. Given that Hippias outperformed the competition, we could reason-
ably assume that there was a congregation of like-minded *sophoi* at Olympia,
one of the most important Panhellenic centers. Why there? More specifically,
except for its geographical proximity to Elis (Hippias' *polis* of origin), were there
other significant factors that made it an ideal arena for the types of displays of
wisdom—in the full sense of the word—attributed to Hippias in our passage? Do
we hear of similar meetings at other Panhellenic sites, or is it simply a Platonic

---

[1]   As mentioned in chapter two (40n5), the authenticity of the *Hippias Minor* seems well established.
[2]   For a discussion of the semantic range of σοφία, see the introduction, 15–17.

fictional device to discredit Hippias as a flashy and intellectually insubstantial sophist? Finally, are these types of performances exclusively sophistic, that is, limited to the historical figures we traditionally associate with the label sophist, or do they have a broader application to other types of practitioners of wisdom as well?

This passage perfectly illustrates the strangeness of the material on the sophists, and it also draws attention to how little we know about the performance context of their activities. It thus invites us to explore this context further, but it also raises questions about the larger issue of dissemination of wisdom in the ancient Greek world, and the function of the Panhellenic centers in this process. Specifically, I shall try to shed light on the context for intellectual displays at the Panhellenic sanctuaries by documenting the evidence we have for the presence of *sophoi* at these places.[3] Special emphasis will be placed on the repeated claim of the *sophoi*'s self-presentation and charismatic attraction of the audience. The examination is not limited to the sophists, but will also cover material on other practitioners of wisdom. Initial stress will be placed on Delphi in order to outline in greater detail what role that center played as a facilitator in the circulation of *sophia*, and I will suggest that this functional model of Delphi is valid, at least partially, for the workings of other Panhellenic centers, especially Olympia. Next, we shall look at the unique status of Apollo at Delphi in authenticating claims to wisdom, and at the ways in which *sophoi* sought to appropriate for themselves that authority.

Let us start by reviewing the evidence for the presence of *sophoi* at the Panhellenic sanctuaries.

Sophoi at the Panhellenic Centers

We have many testimonials of visits by *sophoi* to the festivals. Some of the most famous visits are those of Empedocles and Anaxagoras. According to Diogenes Laertius, Empedocles had the rhapsode Cleomenes recite his work at Olympia (8.63), and Diogenes adds that Empedocles' presence at the games was such that he outshone all others (8.66). Diogenes also relates that Empedocles' death

---

3 Little work has been done on this topic. Most recently, Tarrant 2003 addresses the presence of the sophists at the games, but his interest is focused on how the sophists would go on to appropriate and "shift the pre-existing competitive ethic away from physical towards verbal competition" (355). In his view Socrates and Plato later continued this process of "redirecting the competitive spirit" (357) by diminishing the importance on competition and winning, a process triggered in response "to the need of democracy to develop a co-operative excellence" (360). Some important discussions can be found in Guthrie 1971:42–43; Lloyd 1987:90–91, esp. n146, and 2005:71–72; and Nightingale 2000 (esp. 168) and 2001, where she argues that Greek "theoretical" philosophy as a cultural practice developed out of the civic institution of *theoria*, and that the "panhellenic space" of sanctuaries played an important part in this process. This exploration is continued and expanded in Nightingale 2004.

occurred after an accident which befell him on his way to a festival (πανήγυρις) in Messene (8.73). He further makes it clear that Empedocles' family had a long-standing tradition of involvement with the Olympic Games: his grandfather kept racehorses (ἱπποτροφηκώς) and was a victor in the seventy-first Olympiad (8.51).[4] Anaxagoras is also alleged to have made an equally impressive appearance at Olympia by dressing himself in a coat in anticipation of the rain, which indeed came (Diogenes Laertius 2.10). We also hear of visits to Olympia by Plato and Diogenes the Cynic, both of whom caught everybody's attention by their celebrity (Diogenes Laertius 3.25 and 6.43).

In the case of Diogenes the Cynic (i.e. in early to mid fourth century BCE), we have an elaborate description of his presence at the Isthmian Games by Dio Chrysostom (8.6–7):

> ἐπεὶ δὲ ἧκεν ὁ τῶν Ἰσθμίων χρόνος καὶ πάντες ἦσαν ἐν Ἰσθμῷ, κατέβη καὶ αὐτός. εἰώθει γὰρ ἐπισκοπεῖν ἐν ταῖς πανηγύρεσι τὰς σπουδὰς τῶν ἀνθρώπων καὶ τὰς ἐπιθυμίας καὶ ὧν ἕνεκα ἀποδημοῦσι καὶ ἐπὶ τίσι μέγα φρονοῦσι. παρέσχε δὲ καὶ αὐτὸν τῷ βουλομένῳ ἐντυγχάνειν.

> So, when the time for the Isthmian games arrived, and everybody was at the Isthmus, he went down also. For it was his custom at the great festivals to make a study of the pursuits and ambitions of men, of their reasons for being abroad, and of the things on which they prided themselves. He gave his time also to any who wished to converse with him.

> Trans. Cohoon, slightly modified

Diogenes made it a habit to frequent the festivals (πανηγύρεις) and took this opportunity to meet with others and offer his wisdom. What sorts of conversation would he engage in, and what advice would he offer his interlocutors? Dio Chrysostom writes that he promised to cure his followers from foolishness, wickedness, and intemperance (ἄγνοια, πονηρία, ἀκολασία 8.8). A little later in his narrative (8.9), Dio Chrysostom depicts other attractions at the Isthmian Games:

> καὶ δὴ καὶ τότε ἦν περὶ τὸν νεὼν τοῦ Ποσειδῶνος ἀκούειν πολλῶν μὲν σοφιστῶν κακοδαιμόνων βοώντων καὶ λοιδορουμένων ἀλλήλοις, καὶ τῶν λεγομένων μαθητῶν ἄλλου ἄλλῳ μαχομένων, πολλῶν δὲ συγγραφέων ἀναγιγνωσκόντων ἀναίσθητα συγγράμματα, πολλῶν δὲ ποιητῶν ποιήματα ᾀδόντων, καὶ τούτους ἐπαινούντων ἑτέρων, πολλῶν

---

[4]   On the authority of Satyrus, Diogenes further reports that Empedocles and his son Exaenetus were both victorious in the same Olympiad, Empedocles in the horse race, and Exaenetus in wrestling (8.53). Whatever the historical veracity of this account may be, it nevertheless serves to highlight and reinforce the strong affiliation of Empedocles' family with Olympia.

δὲ θαυματοποιῶν θαύματα ἐπιδεικνύντων, πολλῶν δὲ τερατοσκόπων τέρατα κρινόντων, μυρίων δὲ ῥητόρων δίκας στρεφόντων, οὐκ ὀλίγων δὲ καπήλων διακαπηλευόντων ὅτι τύχοιεν ἕκαστος.

That was also the time to hear crowds of wretched sophists around the Temple of Poseidon as they shouted and heaped abuse on each other, and their so-called students as they fought with one another, and many historians reading out their dumb writings, and many poets reciting poetry to the applause of others, and many magicians showing their tricks, many fortune-tellers telling fortunes, countless orators perverting justice, and not a few peddlers peddling whatever came to hand.

Trans. Miller

This passage, which purports to describe the situation at the Isthmian Games in mid-fourth century BCE,[5] offers good testimony to the variety of *sophoi* present at the games: sophists, historians, poets, magicians, etc. The context for their activities is described as highly competitive (βοώντων καὶ λοιδορουμένων ἀλλήλοις; μαχομένων). Of particular interest is that Dio Chrysostom gives us a description of the state of affairs at a big festival other than Delphi and Olympia, and that the picture is so consistent with the evidence we have from those places. Just as in the passage from the *Hippias Minor* discussed earlier, we hear of "scientific" and "literary" competitive performances, in which emphasis is placed on the individual *sophos'* ability to outdo the competition and to attract disciples. And the context for these performances is described in both instances as a formalized competition similar to the athletic contests.[6]

A similar picture emerges from the material on the individual sophists and their visits to the games. Both Gorgias and Hippias visited Olympia, and our sources, mainly Plato, give us a multifaceted description of the sorts of activities in which they took part. Hippias, for example, while at Olympia, offered to speak

---

[5]   Miller 1979:51 dates the episode to 359 BCE.

[6]   For discussions of competition in wisdom, see Lloyd 1979 (esp. 92–98) and 1987:50–108; Richardson 1981; Griffith 1990; and Graziosi 2001. Cf. the picture that emerges from the *Contest of Homer and Hesiod*. Here, we hear of a highly formalized competition in wisdom, alongside other more traditional athletic competitions, where what counts is one's ability to answer any possible question. The winner is crowned (322) and rewarded with a prize in the same manner as the athletes: the words ἀγωνίζομαι, ἀγών, νικάω, and νίκη (315 and 322) are used to describe the competition between Hesiod and Homer. The statues of Gorgias at Olympia and Delphi offer another good example of the analogy between athletic and intellectual competition. A base of a statue dated to the early fourth century BCE was excavated at Olympia in 1876, which contained an epigram in honor of Gorgias. The inscription eulogizes Gorgias for "training the soul for the contests of virtue" (ἀσκῆσαι ψυχὴν ἀρετῆς ἐς ἀγῶνας). See Morgan 1994 for discussion and bibliography.

on any topic he had prepared and to take questions afterwards (*Hippias Minor* 363c-d),[7] and he refers to his activities at Olympia as competitive (Ὀλυμπίασιν ἀγωνίζεσθαι; ibid. 364a). Philostratus (*Lives of the Sophists* 1.11) adds that "he used to charm Greece at Olympia with his ornate and well-devised speeches":

> ἔθελγε τὴν Ἑλλάδα ἐν Ὀλυμπίᾳ λόγοις ποικίλοις καὶ πεφροντισμένοις εὖ.

Here we are reintroduced to the theme of quasi-formalized contests in wisdom and flamboyant displays with an eye to attracting listeners and students. This emphasis on self-presentation is a recurring motif in our sources on *sophoi*. Aelian (*Varia Historia* 12.32) writes that Pythagoras wore white clothing, a golden garland (στέφανον χρυσοῦν), and Persian or Scythian trousers (ἀναξυρίδας);[8] and in the same paragraph he also comments that Hippias and Gorgias appeared in purple robes (πορφυραῖς ἐσθῆσι).[9] We find a similar emphasis on attire in Diogenes Laertius' description of Empedocles' public demeanor (8.73):

> διὸ δὴ πορφύραν τε ἀναλαβεῖν αὐτὸν καὶ στρόφιον ἐπιθέσθαι χρυσοῦν, ὡς Φαβωρῖνος ἐν Ἀπομνημονεύμασιν· ἔτι τ' ἐμβάδας χαλκᾶς καὶ στέμμα Δελφικόν. κόμη τε ἦν αὐτῷ βαθεῖα καὶ παῖδες ἀκόλουθοι· καὶ αὐτὸς ἀεὶ σκυθρωπὸς ἐφ' ἑνὸς σχήματος ἦν. τοιοῦτος δὴ προήει.

> No doubt it was the same means that enabled him to don a purple robe and over it a golden girdle, as Favorinus relates in his *Memorabilia*, and again slippers of bronze and a Delphic laurel-wreath. He had thick hair, and a train of boy attendants. He himself was always grave, and kept his gravity of demeanor unshaken. In such sort would he appear in public.

> Trans. Hicks

These passages all call attention to the physical appearance of the different *sophoi* in public. There are striking similarities between the outfits of Hippias

---

[7] Similar practices were shared by Ion in Plato's *Ion*, who claimed to be able to explain and elaborate on any point in Homer before an audience.

[8] For the ethnic connotations of ἀναξυρίδας, see Burkert 1972:165n250 and 112n16. See also Miller 1991, who argues from the iconographic portrayal in Attic vase-painting of symposiasts and komasts wearing the *kidaris*, an Oriental hat, that it is representative of "the deliberate adoption of a select range of Oriental objects by wealthy Athenians as an effective statement of elitism," 71. From such a perspective, it is tempting to understand the embracing of Oriental wear as an elite marker intended for a "domestic" audience, not as an indicator of personal exposure to the Orient (intellectual or otherwise).

[9] For the purple robe, see Morrison 1949:58n21. For Athenian male dress norms in the fifth century BCE, see Geddes 1987.

and Empedocles: the purple robe, girdle, and sandals.[10] Hippias wore a Persian girdle, and the trousers of Pythagoras are likely to have been of Persian origin and design. The mention of a group of attendant boys is also striking—highlighting the effectiveness of the outfit in captivating the audience and pupils. This question of followers is addressed in fragment 112 (DK 31B112), where Empedocles describes his reception in the various cities he enters:

ἐγὼ δ᾽ ὑμῖν θεὸς ἄμβροτος, οὐκέτι θνητός
πωλεῦμαι μετὰ πᾶσι τετιμένος, ὥσπερ ἔοικα,
ταινίαις τε περίστεπτος στέφεσίν τε θαλείοις.
τοῖσιν † ἄμ᾽ † ἂν ἴκωμαι ἐς ἄστεα τηλεθάοντα,
ἀνδράσιν ἠδὲ γυναιξί, σεβίζομαι· οἱ δ᾽ ἄμ᾽ ἕπονται
μυρίοι ἐξερέοντες, ὅπη πρὸς κέρδος ἀταρπός,
οἱ μὲν μαντοσυνέων κεχρημένοι, οἱ δ᾽ ἐπὶ νούσων
παντοίων ἐπύθοντο κλυεῖν εὐηκέα βάξιν,
δηρὸν δὴ χαλεπῇσι πεπαρμένοι <ἀμφ᾽ ὀδύνῃσιν>.

But I go up and down among you an immortal god,
No longer mortal, held in honor among all, as it seems,
Crowned with both fillets and blooming garlands.
Men and women worship me, when I enter their flourishing towns;
And they follow me in countless numbers, asking where the path to
    profit lies.
Some want divinations; others, pierced for a long time by harsh
    pains,
Asked to hear a healing utterance against all kinds of diseases.

Trans. McKirahan, modified[11]

According to his own account, Empedocles is met by thousands of people in every city he enters.[12] His appearance displays a magnetism that exerts a pull on his surroundings, and he has a great throng of people accompanying him during his stay in the city. In the Platonic dialogue *Protagoras* (315a–b), Plato says that Protagoras had a similar effect on his audience:

---

[10] Kingsley 1995 interprets the sandals of bronze as a "magical 'symbol'" that represents Empedocles' "ability to descend to the underworld at will," 289.

[11] Kingsley 1995:220 argues that we should take seriously Empedocles' statement of immortality, and he questions modern attempts at dismissing it as ironic: "In fact it is quite clear that any attempt at denying the fragment its literal, obvious meaning is wrong." Cf. Long 1966:259n1.

[12] It is intriguing that he apparently traveled from city to city; this is another feature that is normally attributed to the sophists.

τούτων δὲ οἳ ὄπισθεν ἠκολούθουν ἐπακούοντες τῶν λεγομένων, τὸ μὲν πολὺ ξένοι ἐφαίνοντο, οὓς ἄγει ἐξ ἑκάστων τῶν πόλεων ὁ Πρωταγόρας, δι' ὧν διεξέρχεται, κηλῶν τῇ φωνῇ ὥσπερ Ὀρφεύς, οἱ δὲ κατὰ τὴν φωνὴν ἕπονται κεκηλημένοι.

Behind them many followed listening to the things said—they seemed for the most part to be strangers—whom Protagoras brings with him from each of the cities he passes through, charming them with his voice like Orpheus. And they, being charmed, follow in pursuit of his voice.[13]

Recall that this type of Orphic attraction on his followers is also attributed to Hippias by Philostratus in the passage quoted earlier (*Lives of the Sophists* 1.11), in which Philostratus uses the verb θέλγω ("charm," "spell-bind") to describe Hippias' power over his audience. This attraction is envisioned in the passage from the *Protagoras* through the use of the verb κηλέω ("charm," "enchant," "spell-bind"). Thrasymachus also uses the same verb to describe the efficacy of his own oratory on an audience, as Plato quotes him in the *Phaedrus* (267c–d):

ὀργίσαι τε αὖ πολλοὺς ἅμα δεινὸς ἀνὴρ γέγονεν καὶ πάλιν ὠργισμένοις ἐπᾴδων κηλεῖν, ὡς ἔφη.

The man was skilled at stirring up many and, once stirred up, at enchanting them again through his charms, as he said.

All these mentions of charms and spells might seem to take us off track from the theme of *sophoi* and Panhellenic centers. But we shall return to this topic in the next section to see how appropriate it is to the context of displays of wisdom at Delphi and the other Panhellenic sanctuaries.

In addition to the examples we have reviewed thus far, there is much more textual evidence for the presence of *sophoi* at the games. Gorgias, for example, is said to have appeared at the festivals of Greece. Our source, Philostratus (*Lives of the Sophists* 1.9), singles out Delphi, Olympia, and Athens—without making any qualitative distinctions among the centers, thereby implying that there would be no substantial difference in terms of the performance context at the different sites. Philostratus is careful to note that Gorgias adapted his wording depending on where he performed, but he stresses that his overall messages remained the same. The Platonic dialogue *Meno* opens with Socrates saying

---

[13] For poetic inspiration and voice, see Schadewaldt 1944; Sperduti 1950; Dodds 1951:80–82; Tigerstedt 1970; Murray 1981; Walsh 1984; Ritook 1989; Ford 1992:31–89. On Orpheus, see Linforth 1941; Guthrie 1952; West 1983; Graf 1987; and Segal 1989. On magic and rhetoric, see Romilly 1975 and Gellrich 1993.

that Gorgias brought wisdom to Thessaly and, in describing his habits when in Thessaly, Socrates tells us that Gorgias offered himself to any Greek who wanted to question him on any subject (70a–c):

παρέχων αὐτὸν ἐρωτᾶν τῶν Ἑλλήνων τῷ βουλομένῳ ὅ τι ἄν τις βούληται.

This procedure of making oneself available for questioning echoes Dio Chrysostom's description of Diogenes the Cynic's behavior at the Isthmian Games (8.7)—παρέσχε δὲ καὶ αὐτὸν τῷ βουλομένῳ ἐντυγχάνειν.[14]

It thus seems reasonable to suppose that the context for formal displays and dissemination of wisdom would look similar at many of the Panhellenic festivals.[15] But attendance of *sophoi* at the games does not begin with Hippias and Gorgias, or even with Empedocles and Anaxagoras. We can trace the precedent for such later activities by the Presocratics and sophists back at least to the Seven Sages.[16] We have numerous sources discussing how they frequented the Panhellenic festivals. Diogenes Laertius (1.40), for example, firmly locates them within a Panhellenic framework:

φασὶ δέ τινες καὶ ἐν Πανιωνίῳ καὶ ἐν Κορίνθῳ καὶ ἐν Δελφοῖς συνελθεῖν αὐτούς.

Some people say that they met at the Panionian festival, at Corinth, and at Delphi.

Plutarch (*Solon* 4) provides a similar assessment:

γενέσθαι δὲ μετ' ἀλλήλων ἔν τε Δελφοῖς ὁμοῦ λέγονται καὶ πάλιν ἐν Κορίνθῳ, Περιάνδρου σύλλογόν τινα κοινὸν αὐτῶν καὶ συμπόσιον κατασκευάσαντος.

---

[14] In the *Apology*, Socrates, too, describes his practice of making himself available to rich and poor alike for questioning: ὁμοίως καὶ πλουσίῳ καὶ πένητι παρέχω ἐμαυτὸν ἐρωτᾶν (33b).

[15] Richardson (1992:225) gives a good description of the range of activities that took place at Olympia: "It had already come to be used as a place for debate between cities when a dispute arose, for arbitration, and for the publication of treaties. It became also a place where orators, philosophers and literary men could display their talents, by speeches or recitation of their works. It was said that Herodotus read parts of his history here, in the *opisthodomos* of the temple of Zeus (Lucian *Herodotus* 1). Gorgias appealed for unity against Persia here in 408, and Lysias and Isocrates composed speeches for delivery at Olympia in the early fourth century." As the examples from the *Protagoras* and the *Meno* demonstrate, the context for the intellectual displays of sophists should not be thought of as being exclusively that of the Panhellenic sanctuaries; but they constituted a significant and major venue for these displays, as I hope that the documentation of *sophoi* at the games has shown.

[16] On the Seven Sages, see Martin 1993.

They are said to have met together at Delphi and again in Corinth, where Periander prepared some common assembly for them and a symposium.

In the *Protagoras* (343a–b), we hear that they met at Delphi and that, as a first-fruit offering of their wisdom to Apollo, they inscribed their sayings there.[17] The Seven Sages, through their offering, defer their wisdom to the legitimizing power that Apollo's temple at Delphi could confer on it; and by inscribing their aphorisms in the temple, they simultaneously award the sanctuary the role of a repository for their *sophia*.

But there is yet another area in which the Seven Sages can be said to have sought to obtain the authority from Delphi for their activities and to have deferred to the oracle as the guarantor and authenticator of *sophia*, namely, in the narratives about the tripod.[18] According to one version of this story (Diogenes Laertius 1.28), some Milesian fishermen, not knowing that a tripod had been caught in their nets, sold their catch to Ionian youths. When they later learned about the tripod, they started a dispute over its ownership with the Ionians, and they finally referred the question to the Delphic oracle, and the god answered:

τρίποδος πέρι Φοῖβον ἐρωτᾷς;
τίς σοφίῃ πάντων πρῶτος, τούτου τρίποδ' αὐδῶ.

Are you asking Phoebus regarding the tripod?
Who is the wisest of all men, I proclaim the tripod to be his.

Diogenes continues:

διδοῦσιν οὖν Θαλῇ· ὁ δὲ ἄλλῳ καὶ ἄλλος ἄλλῳ ἕως Σόλωνος. ὁ δὲ ἔφη σοφίᾳ πρῶτον εἶναι τὸν θεὸν καὶ ἀπέστειλεν εἰς Δελφούς.

And so they gave it to Thales; and he gave it to another who, in turn, gave it to another, until it came into the possession of Solon. But he said that the god was wisest and sent it off to Delphi.[19]

---

[17] For a full discussion of the aphorisms of the Seven Sages, see Schutz 1866 and Oikonomides 1980 and 1987.

[18] For a discussion of the tripod narrative, see Gernet 1981:78–81; Humphreys 1983a:249–250; and Martin 1993:120. For an etiological explanation of the myth traced back to Sumerian texts, see Reiner 1961. Martin 1993:122 also discusses the tripod story within a comparative framework.

[19] Diogenes gives us many more variants of the story. Some accounts describe the origin of the tripod: It was a bridal gift presented at Pelops' wedding by Hephaestus. It was later passed on to Menelaus and then carried off by Paris along with Helen. She later threw it into the ocean, saying that it would be a cause of strife. In another account Periander sent the tripod on a ship to Thrasybulus. The ship was wrecked and the tripod was later found by fishermen. In yet other versions, it was not a tripod, but a bowl or golden goblet. One version relates how a certain

Louis Gernet has called attention to the competitive aspects of the transmission of the tripod among the sages, and how athletic contests at the games constitute the immediate context for its circulation. Thus, in the words of Gernet, "The tripod or the vase is regarded as a prize awarded on the basis of a competition of wisdom, indeed, a contest of happiness."[20] Here the emphasis on Delphi as the meeting place of the sages seems particularly appropriate to express this emulation of athletic competition that figures in the tripod narrative. Plutarch's account (*Solon* 4) adds to this description:

> ἔτι δὲ μᾶλλον εἰς ἀξίωμα καὶ δόξαν αὐτοὺς κατέστησεν ἡ τοῦ τρίποδος
> περίοδος καὶ διὰ πάντων ἀνακύκλησις καὶ ἀνθύπειξις μετ' εὐμενείας
> φιλοτίμου γενομένη.

But the circulation of the tripod brought them still more fame and reputation, its circulation among all of them, and their mutual yielding of it with competitive yet generous grace.[21]

We find a number of other accounts in which the affiliation of the Seven Sages with Delphi is stressed, but they are also frequently mentioned in relation to other festivals; for example, Chilon appears at Olympia,[22] and Thales supposedly died while watching an athletic contest in his old age.[23]

To sum up: up to this point we have seen how the Panhellenic centers were the meeting places for *sophoi*, and that there is evidence for a continuity of practices going back to the Seven Sages. This was where *sophoi* attracted listeners and students, where they read their works, and where they, in turn, could familiarize themselves with the work of others.[24] Such activities would occur at a number of Panhellenic festivals, not just at Delphi. The descriptions of the presence of *sophoi* at the games place a surprising emphasis on their mass appeal and

---

Bathycles from Arcadia left a bowl (φιάλη) at his death to be given to the one who had been most useful with his wisdom (δοῦναι τῶν σοφῶν ὀνήϊστῳ). A second version tells that Croesus, king of Lydia, gave a golden goblet (ποτήριον χρυσοῦν) to a friend to be bestowed upon the wisest of the Greeks. Plutarch, following the first version of Diogenes Laertius, makes the fishermen come from Cos and the buyers of the catch from Miletus. He adds that Helen threw the tripod into the ocean on her way back from Troy in accordance with an old prophecy. See Wiersma 1934 for the different versions.

20 Gernet 1981:79.
21 This is of course not to imply that this is the only way to interpret the tripod story. Indeed, there are other versions where the tripod does not circulate among the Seven Sages or has no affiliation with Apollo at Delphi. For more on the tripod and the Seven Sages, see Wiersma 1934, Snell 1971, Gernet 1981, Fehling 1985, Martin 1993, and Busine 2002.
22 Hermippus in Diogenes Laertius 1.72.
23 Diogenes Laertius 1.39.
24 Delphi was also the occasion for musical/poetical recitations, which undoubtedly many *sophoi* would attend and make an object of interpretation and criticism. For more on the musical performances at Delphi, see Richardson 1992.

ability to attract listeners. Next, we shall return to the theme of philosophical magnetism, that is, to the attraction that *sophoi* are repeatedly described as wielding over their listeners.

Philosophical Magnetism

Empedocles, Protagoras, Hippias, and Thrasymachus all figure in contexts where they are said to have enchanted or made their audience possessed. I will try to show how this Orphic power of attraction is intrinsically linked to their connection with Delphi, and consequently, to its divine protector as the ultimate authority and guarantor of their *sophia*. The route we are going to use to explore this theme goes through some fragmentary lines of Pindar's Eighth Paean. By comparing the descriptions of the power of attraction of the *sophoi* to Pindar's poem, we shall see how uniquely appropriate the usages of the verbs κηλέω and θέλγω are in the context of displays of wisdom at Panhellenic festivals.

Pausanias gives us the mythological background to Paean 8 which elaborates on the succession of the four temples at Delphi.[25] The first temple, he writes (10.5.9–12), was made out of laurel wood. After its demise, a second temple was built by bees out of beeswax and feathers. Apollo sent it to the Hyperboreans, and so the third temple was constructed by Athena and Hephaestus, this time out of bronze, presumably to make it a more durable sanctuary. This was in turn hidden by the gods in a chasm in the earth. Finally, Trophonius and Agamedes built the fourth temple out of stone. Particularly relevant for us are the third temple and its main attraction, the Charmers (Κηληδόνες). These were female creatures—possibly with some affiliation to the winged Sphinx[26]—who sat on the temple gable and, as their name suggests (derived from the same root as the verb κηλέω), entranced visitors with their voices. This destructive behavior angered the gods who destroyed the temple and hid it under the earth.

Pindar (105–116, Rutherford) describes the Charmers and the detrimental results of listening to their songs in Paean 8:

> χάλκεοι μὲν τοῖχοι χάλκ[εαί
>   θ' ὑπὸ κίονες ἔστασαν,
> χρύσεαι δ' ἐξ ὑπὲρ αἰετοῦ
>   ἄειδον Κηληδόνες.
> ἀλλά μιν Κρόνου παῖ[δες
>   κεραυνῷ χθόν' ἀνοιξάμ[ε]νο[ι
> ἔκρυψαν τὸ [π]άντων ἔργων ἱερώτ[ατον

---

[25] For textual edition and commentary of Pindar's paeans, and discussion of the Delphic temples, see Rutherford 2001:210–232.

[26] Rutherford 2001:219. See Dickie 1997, who suggests a common ancient source.

γλυκείας ὀπὸς ἀγασ[θ]έντες
ὅτι ξένοι ἔφ[θ]<ι>νον
ἄτερθεν τεκέων
ἀλόχων τε μελ[ί]φρονι
αὐδ[ᾷ θυ]μὸν ἀνακρίμναντες.

Bronze were the walls, bronze pillars stood beneath, and six golden Charmers sang above the gable. But the sons of Cronus opened the ground with a thunderbolt and hid it, the most sacred of all works ...

... astonished at the sweet voice, that foreigners wasted away apart from children and wives, hanging up their spirit as a dedication to the sweet voice.

Trans. Rutherford

There are some remarkable features in Pindar's poem that can help further our understanding of Delphi as a site of particular interest to *sophoi*, on the one hand, and of the intriguing and charismatic bond between these *sophoi* and their audience, on the other. As Ian Rutherford has shown, Pindar presents us with a mythological account of the interconnectedness of prophetic song and Delphi that predates the establishment of the Delphic oracle.[27] The song of the Κηληδόνες has been likened to that of the Sirens in the *Odyssey*,[28] whose utterances Rutherford calls "a narration of universal knowledge."[29] There are several overlaps between Paean 8 and the material on *sophoi* reviewed earlier. First, there is a strong emphasis on the element of voice in our accounts. In Pindar, it is repeated twice (ὀπός and αὐδᾷ) in lines 112 and 116. The audience is astonished at the sweet voice of the Κηληδόνες, and they dedicate their

---

[27] Rutherford 2001:220. For other instances of the connection between prophetic song and Delphi, see, e.g. Pindar fr. 150 (μαντεύεο, Μοῖσα, προφατεύσω δ' ἐγώ, "Deliver your prophesy, Muse, and I will interpret."). Dodds 1951:82 comments that the "words he uses are the technical terms of Delphi; implicit in them is the old analogy between poetry and divination." See also Paean 6.6 (ἀοίδιμον Πιερίδων προφάταν) and Bacchylides 9.3 (θεῖος προφάτας). Murray 1981:97, and Rutherford 2001:307 discuss these passages. For a more general discussion on poetry and prophecy, see Chadwick 1952, and Kugel 1990.

[28] Pausanias (10.5.12) and Philostratus (*Vita Apollonii* 6.11) both make this connection. It also occurs at *Vita Sophoclea* 64.

[29] Rutherford 2001:220, referring to the *Odyssey* 12.189–191:

ἴδμεν γάρ τοι πάνθ', ὅσ' ἐνὶ Τροίῃ εὐρείῃ
Ἀργεῖοι Τρῶές τε θεῶν ἰότητι μόγησαν,
ἴδμεν δ' ὅσσα γένηται ἐπὶ χθονὶ πουλυβοτείρῃ.

For we know all the toils that the Argives and the Trojans suffered
At spacious Troy by the will of the gods,
And we know all that happens on the all-nourishing earth.

spirit to it.[30] In the Platonic dialogue *Protagoras*, people are enchanted with Protagoras as he enters their city and follow him in pursuit of his voice (κατὰ τὴν φωνὴν ἕπονται κεκηλημένοι). Although φωνή is not used for "voice" in the lines quoted from Pindar, it occurs a little later in the poem, in line 120. Scholars have debated what it refers to, given the fragmentary state of the text, but Rutherford, following Charles Segal, argues that the use may figure in lines that "constitute a flash-back and refer to the construction of the Κηληδόνες and the third temple."[31] It is thus very likely that it is yet another reference to the Κηληδόνες, and as such it suggestively mirrors the Platonic use in the *Protagoras*. And this connection between the temple at Delphi and φωνή is further elaborated in a fragment of Heraclitus, preserved by Plutarch (DK 22B92):

Σίβυλλα δὲ μαινομένῳ στόματι καθ' Ἡράκλειτον ἀγέλαστα καὶ ἀκαλλώπιστα καὶ ἀμύριστα φθεγγομένη χιλίων ἐτῶν ἐξικνεῖται τῇ φωνῇ διὰ τὸν θεόν.[32]

The Sibyl with frenzied mouth, according to Heraclitus, uttering words that are without laughter, without adornment, and without incense reaches over a thousand years with her voice through the god.[33]

The voice of the Κηληδόνες and the voice of *sophoi* thus produce similar reactions in their listeners, that is, a feeling of entrancement and enchantment; and the etymological affinity between Κηληδόνες and κηλέω further illuminates this connection on the verbal level. This is surely similar to the effect that is envisioned also in the passages about Thrasymachus and Hippias, although in the Hippias passage λόγος is substituted for φωνή.

The participle ἀνακρίμναντες in line 116 of Paean 8, used to describe the dedication of the spirit that the listeners make to the Κηληδόνες, is derived from the verb that in Attic Greek is ἀνακρεμάννυμι. It means either "to hang up on a thing" or "to make dependent." Rutherford translates is as "hang up in

---

[30] Compare this to Hesiod's Muses (*Theogony* 26–34), who breathed a divine voice into the poet (ἐνέπνευσαν δέ μοι αὐδὴν θέσπιν) and thus enabled him to celebrate in song things to come and things that had been (ἵνα κλείοιμι τά τ' ἐσσόμενα πρό τ' ἐόντα). For bibliography, see footnote 13 above.

[31] Rutherford 2001:222 and n38.

[32] This quotation comes from Plutarch, and there is a vivid scholarly debate about how much of the quotation is authentic and how much derives from Plutarch himself. See Kahn 1979:124–125 and Guthrie 1962:414n1.

[33] It is perhaps significant that Plutarch, when introducing this quotation, refers to it as a counter-example to the charm of Sappho's poetry, which spell-binds and enchants the listeners (κηλοῦντα καὶ καταθέλγοντα τοὺς ἀκρωμένους), *De Pythiae Oraculis* 6. Thus it seems that Plutarch has displaced the motif of charming and spell-binding from Delphi to Sappho's poetry.

dedication to," and when discussing this passage in his commentary (220), he expands on his translation by saying that *xenoi* are "hanging up their souls as an offering to the voice, in a metaphor that suggests both a religious dedication and psychological dependency." He thus brings out the twofold meaning of the verb and emphasizes the reciprocal relationship implied in the act of dedication as a result of dependency. In Plato's *Ion*,[34] Socrates postulates that it is divine power (θεία δύναμις), not art (τέχνη), that makes it possible for Ion to speak well on Homer, and he goes on to liken the power to the force found in magnetic stones (533d–e):

> καὶ γὰρ αὕτη ἡ λίθος οὐ μόνον αὐτοὺς τοὺς δακτυλίους ἄγει τοὺς
> σιδηροῦς, ἀλλὰ καὶ δύναμιν ἐντίθησι τοῖς δακτυλίοις, ὥστ' αὖ δύνασθαι
> ταὐτὸν τοῦτο ποιεῖν ὅπερ ἡ λίθος, ἄλλους ἄγειν δακτυλίους, ὥστ' ἐνίοτε
> ὁρμαθὸς μακρὸς πάνυ σιδηρίων καὶ δακτυλίων ἐξ ἀλλήλων ἤρτηται·
> πᾶσι δὲ τούτοις ἐξ ἐκείνης τῆς λίθου ἡ δύναμις ἀνήρτηται. οὕτω δὲ καὶ
> ἡ Μοῦσα ἐνθέους μὲν ποιεῖ αὐτή, διὰ δὲ τῶν ἐνθέων τούτων ἄλλων
> ἐνθουσιαζόντων ὁρμαθὸς ἐξαρτᾶται.

> For this stone not only moves the iron rings themselves, but it also instills a power into the rings so that they in turn can do the same thing as the stone, to move other rings, so that sometimes a long chain entirely of bits of iron and rings hang upon each other. And all of them are dependent upon that stone for their power. In the same way the Muse makes men possessed herself, and through these possessed people, a chain is being hung from other persons who are being possessed.

In this passage, Plato uses the verb ἀρτάω and the compounds ἀναρτάω and ἐξαρτάω to designate how the pieces of iron and men are attached to one another. These verbs have basically the same semantic range as ἀνακρεμάννυμι: "to hang upon" or "make dependent upon." The original source, the magnetic stone or the Muse, channels its power through chains of dependency to its followers and links them together, one depending upon the other. A little later in the dialogue (535e–536a), Socrates turns to Ion to explain where he sees the rhapsode's role in this series of dependency:

> οἶσθα οὖν ὅτι οὗτός ἐστιν ὁ θεατὴς τῶν δακτυλίων ὁ ἔσχατος, ὧν
> ἐγὼ ἔλεγον ὑπὸ τῆς Ἡρακλειώτιδος λίθου ἀπ' ἀλλήλων τὴν δύναμιν
> λαμβάνειν; ὁ δὲ μέσος σὺ ὁ ῥαψῳδὸς καὶ ὑποκριτής, ὁ δὲ πρῶτος αὐτὸς

---

[34] For text, commentary, and discussion of Plato's attitude towards poetry, see Murray 1996.

ὁ ποιητής· ὁ δὲ θεὸς διὰ πάντων τούτων ἕλκει τὴν ψυχὴν ὅποι ἂν
βούληται τῶν ἀνθρώπων, ἀνακρεμαννὺς ἐξ ἀλλήλων τὴν δύναμιν.

You are aware then that this spectator of yours is the last of the rings,
of which I said that they receive the power from each other through
the Heraclean stone? You, the rhapsode and actor, are the middle ring,
and the poet himself is the first. But the god draws the souls of men
through all these rings wherever he wants, making the power of one
depend on the other.

Ion holds an intermediary position, poised between the poet and his audience.
When addressing the inspiration that emanates from the poets and enraptures
the listeners, Socrates says (536b):

ἐκ δὲ τούτων τῶν πρώτων δακτυλίων, τῶν ποιητῶν, ἄλλοι ἐξ ἄλλου
αὖ ἠρτημένοι εἰσὶ καὶ ἐνθουσιάζουσιν, οἱ μὲν ἐξ Ὀρφέως, οἱ δὲ ἐκ
Μουσαίου· οἱ δὲ πολλοὶ ἐξ Ὁμήρου κατέχονταί τε καὶ ἔχονται.

As to these first rings—the poets—different people are dependent upon
and inspired by different ones; some are dependent upon Orpheus,
others upon Musaeus; but the majority is possessed and held by Homer.

This resonates well with the passage quoted from the *Protagoras* earlier, where
Protagoras is said to have a similar attraction on his followers as Orpheus; he
charms them with his voice and draws them with him from city to city.[35] In
the present passage, Orpheus, Musaeus, and Homer all make their audience
possessed, as do the rhapsodes, in turn, when reciting their poetry in public.
Implicit is also the notion of charm and enchantment (θέλγω, κηλέω) similar to
that discussed above in relation to the attraction of the Κηληδόνες and certain
sophoi on their audience.

Beyond the chain of rings is the god, who draws the souls of men in any
direction he pleases. By instilling divine power (θεία δύναμις) into the voice of
poets and thus inspiring anyone hearing it, he establishes a particular relationship whereby he controls the souls of men (ἕλκει τὴν ψυχὴν τῶν ἀνθρώπων).
This is reminiscent of lines 115–116 of Paean 8, where ξένοι are said to hang up
their souls in dedication to the sweet voice of the Κηληδόνες (μελ[ί]φρονι αὐδ[ᾶ
θυ]μὸν ἀνακρίμναντες). What is more, in the *Ion* passage cited earlier (535e–
536a), the god is described as "making the power of one depend on the other"
(ἀνακρεμαννὺς ἐξ ἀλλήλων τὴν δύναμιν), that is, he channels divine power
through the rings and in so doing connects the various levels to each other. Plato
is here using the same participle as in Pindar. In both passages, the verb carries

---

35 For Orpheus and Orphism, see n13 above.

the meaning of dependency; in Pindar, it denotes the dependency that the ξένοι experience listening to the divinely inspired voice of the Κηληδόνες; in the *Ion*, it pertains to the mutual dependency among the different levels of audience of the divine voice. In both instances, the ultimate source of dependency is the god, and this is clearly illustrated in the description of divine manipulation of mortal souls as a result of exposure to the divine power.

This power of attraction articulated in Pindar and Plato shares similarities with that of the *sophoi* discussed above. First, it contains the element of enchantment of the audience. Further, the magnetism that they all display is closely affiliated with the performance context at the games and festivals in general, and at Delphi in particular.[36] Much emphasis is placed on the outfit of the rhapsode in the *Ion*; how he is dressed up in many-colored clothes and wears golden crowns (κεκοσμημένος ἐσθῆτι ποικίλῃ καὶ χρυσοῖς στεφάνοις; 535d), and Socrates explicitly mentions festivals and sacrifices as the places where the rhapsode inspires his listeners (ἐν θυσίαις καὶ ἑορταῖς; 535d).[37]

The seat of the Κηληδόνες is at Delphi, and the authority of their charismatic song, I suggest, must be understood with reference to their connection with that sanctuary. And this link could also be extended to the charismatic power of *sophoi*;[38] through their affiliation with Delphi and other Panhellenic centers, they tap into the authority these places have to legitimize prophetic speech. The Heraclitean passage quoted earlier (DK 22B92) is a good example of this link. The fragment mentions the timeless truths uttered by the oracle through the mediation of Apollo, and it stresses the idea of Delphi as the center of dissemination from and out of which those utterances emanate; Delphi becomes the seat of the voice. In fragment 93, this connection is further elaborated:

ὁ ἄναξ, οὗ τὸ μαντεῖόν ἐστι τὸ ἐν Δελφοῖς, οὔτε λέγει οὔτε κρύπτει ἀλλὰ σημαίνει.

The lord whose oracle is that at Delphi neither speaks nor hides, but gives signs.

---

[36] In this context, one could also include other key terms such as ἐπῳδαί, γοητεία, and ψυχαγωγία, all of which are used in relation to magicians, poets, and sophists. For a discussion of these terms, see Romilly 1975.

[37] See also 530b and 541c.

[38] By using the term "charismatic power," I draw heavily upon the Weberian term "charisma," which he defines as, "a certain quality of an individual personality by virtue of which he is considered extraordinary and treated as endowed with supernatural, superhuman, or at least specifically exceptional powers or qualities. These are such as are not accessible to the ordinary person, but are regarded as of divine origin or as exemplary, and on the basis of them the individual concerned is treated as a 'leader.' In primitive circumstances this peculiar kind of quality is thought of as resting on magical powers, whether of prophets, persons with reputation for therapeutic or legal wisdom, leaders in the hunt, or heroes in war." Weber 1978:241.

Here Heraclitus juxtaposes his own oracular and enigmatic style to that of the Delphic oracle, thereby paralleling his own voice to Delphi's and invoking it as the ultimate authority for his own *sophia*.[39] It is also significant how well fragment 101 (ἐδιζησάμην ἐμεωυτόν, "I searched myself")[40] resonates with one of the emblems of Delphic wisdom, "Know thyself" (γνῶθι σαυτόν), and Guthrie points out that the verb used by Heraclitus, δίζημαι, also means "to seek the meaning of an oracle."[41] Empedocles, in fragment 112 quoted above, describes how part of his expertise was to deliver oracles (μαντοσύνη and βάξις) to his audience. Socrates likewise had strong ties with Delphi and claimed that his reputation for wisdom, if not the wisdom itself, ultimately derived from Apollo:

τῆς γὰρ ἐμῆς, εἰ δή τίς ἐστιν σοφία καὶ οἵα, μάρτυρα ὑμῖν παρέξομαι τὸν θεὸν τὸν ἐν Δελφοῖς.

I will provide the god at Delphi as witness to my wisdom (such as it is), if indeed I possess any.[42]

In like manner, Diogenes Laertius (8.8), citing Aristoxenus, reports that, "Pythagoras got most of his ethical doctrines from the Delphic priestess Themistoclea." It is not relevant to our investigation whether this is historically true or not; we are more interested in the reputation Delphi had for defining and validating wisdom.

There is plenty of material to support the view that *sophoi*, through tapping into the repository of *sophia* that Delphi constituted and through aligning themselves with its authority, were seen as themselves being a conduit for a similar type of charismatic speech. The verbal and thematic echoes between Paean 8 and the *Protagoras* are examples of this overlap of authority, and Pindar's poem provides us with the context to understand the *sophoi*'s almost uncanny, yet highly conventional abilities to attract listeners and enchant them with their verbal performances.

In the final part, we shall consider the exploration undertaken thus far in light of the findings of last chapter. We shall explore the role of *xenia* as a facilitator in the circulation of *sophia*, and demonstrate how intrinsically linked this network was with the Panhellenic centers.

---

[39] As Kahn 1979:23 notes, it has been thought since antiquity that "the Delphic mode" was "a paradigm for Heraclitus' own riddling style." For the parallelism between Heraclitus' style and that of the Delphic oracle, see Guthrie 1962:414, esp. n2; cf. Nightingale 2000:164.

[40] Heraclitus DK 22B101.

[41] Guthrie 1962:418.

[42] Plato *Apology* 20e. Lloyd 1987 notes that Plato, although often portraying Socrates as interested in oracular knowledge, "frequently undercuts references to Socrates as some kind of μάντις," 86–87n134.

Xenia and the Panhellenic Centers

The aim of this section is to direct attention to the importance of the elite network of *xenia* for establishing formal channels of interaction that enabled *sophoi* to meet. One might object that there seems to be an inconsistency in my argument in the apparent discrepancy between the mass appeal of the *sophoi*, on the one hand, and the emphasis on the importance of the elite network of *xenia*, on the other. But these aspects stand in no way in a contradictory relationship to each other. Participation in the *xenia* network assures the acquisition of symbolic capital that enables (and even authenticates) *sophoi* to present themselves to a larger audience as charismatic figures capable of dazzling intellectual performances. It is thus their exclusive position as practitioners of wisdom that is owed to the elite network of *xenia*. One of the characteristics of this position is the ability to enchant and enthrall a mass audience.

As I argued in the last chapter, there is a strong link in our primary sources between *xenia* and dissemination of wisdom, or, to phrase it differently, the ability of *sophoi* to travel and participate in intellectual exchanges appears to be contingent upon their utilization of the formal channels of interaction already established through the *xenia*-system. In this context, the Panhellenic centers were crucial meeting places for *sophoi* as well as important arenas for intellectual interaction and dissemination. Isocrates (*Panegyricus* 4.43) gives us a good insight into the significance of these festivals in the maintenance and renewal of *xenia* relationships:

τῶν τοίνυν τὰς πανηγύρεις καταστησάντων δικαίως ἐπαινουμένων ὅτι τοιοῦτον ἔθος ἡμῖν παρέδοσαν, ὥστε σπεισαμένους πρὸς ἀλλήλους καὶ τὰς ἔχθρας τὰς ἐνεστηκυίας διαλυσαμένους συνελθεῖν εἰς ταὐτόν, καὶ μετὰ ταῦτ᾽ εὐχὰς καὶ θυσίας κοινὰς ποιησαμένους ἀναμνησθῆναι μὲν τῆς συγγενείας τῆς πρὸς ἀλλήλους ὑπαρχούσης, εὐμενεστέρως δ᾽ εἰς τὸν λοιπὸν χρόνον διατεθῆναι πρὸς ἡμᾶς αὐτούς, καὶ τάς τε παλαιὰς ξενίας ἀνανεώσασθαι καὶ καινὰς ἑτέρας ποιήσασθαι.

Now the founders of our great festivals are justly praised for handing down to us a custom by which, having proclaimed a truce toward each other and resolved our pending quarrels, we come together in one place, where, as we make our prayers and sacrifices in common, we are reminded of the kinship (*syngeneia*) which exists among us and are made to feel more kindly towards each other for the future, reviving old *xeniai* and establishing new ones.

Trans. Herman, modified

To judge from this Isocratean characterization, the Panhellenic centers were of particular importance in the maintenance of *xenia*-relationships. In the last chapter we considered the significance of *xenia* in providing an institutional framework of interaction for *sophoi*, and we have up till now explored the strong presence of *sophoi* at the Panhellenic centers. It is time to bring these observations together in an attempt to explore the Panhellenic sanctuaries as central meeting places for *sophoi*. We shall do this through the insights of Anthony Snodgrass' work on peer polity interaction. When exploring the peer polity interaction approach developed by Colin Renfrew and John Cherry, he addresses the role of meeting places at the supra-polity level. In this context, he talks about the significance of Delphi in the areas of codification of law and colonization, not only to give approval to proposals, but also to provide the impetus for action:

> The function of the Delphic oracle is perhaps seen at its most remarkable in the context of colonisation. Most important Greek colonies boasted a foundation legend which began with a consultation of the oracle ... Delphi was evidently acting as the main central clearinghouse for information of a geographical and political kind which was of potential value to many different cities and their governments.[43]

Snodgrass proposes a systemic and institutional analysis of Delphi as a central hub on a supra-polity level in a broader circulation pattern of knowledge among the Greek *poleis*. He concludes that Delphi gathered, authenticated, and distributed various kinds of information. Although he makes no mention of the sophists or any other practitioner of wisdom, I nonetheless suggest that we extend his findings and draw an analogy to the model outlined here of the Panhellenic centers as focal points in the interaction of *sophoi* and circulation of *sophia* in the Greek world.

A powerful illustration of this model was already provided in the tripod narrative involving the Seven Sages, discussed earlier. The connection between *sophoi*, in this case the Seven Sages, and Delphi is already established in this account. In addition to this association, Plutarch's narrative (*Solon* 4) adds emphatic allusions to the terminology of *xenia*. First we have the twofold repetition of circulation (περίοδος and ἀνακύκλησις). The prize passes from hand to hand (as does the narrative on the tripod itself) in successive acts of generous giving, acts that serve to enhance the status of both recipient and giver alike. The gift is declined only to be passed on to the next person in line, until it is finally returned to the god. The words designating how the tripod is passed on, "with competitive yet generous grace" (εὐμένεια φιλότιμος) invoke the kind

---

[43] Snodgrass 1986:53–54.

of relationship established through lavish acts of (competitive) gift-giving, namely, that of guest-friends (ξένοι). This relationship is further emphasized through the history of the object: Diogenes writes that it is of divine origin, made by Hephaestus, given to Pelops, passed on to Menelaus, stolen by Paris, and then miraculously recovered from the ocean. Gernet notes that this history gives the object "an almost civic status, as is often the case with prize objects in Homer."[44] It is thus well suited to serve in these narratives as a precious object of the highest order to be passed generously among guest-friends. In the words of Martin: "The provenance of tripod dedications at Delphi suggests they were prestige items circulating in an aristocratic gift-exchange network. I suggest such a network is represented in the tale of the sages."[45]

Plutarch's tripod narrative expresses the thematic association that existed in antiquity among *sophoi*, Panhellenic centers, and *xenia*. Such an association seems especially relevant, since these centers, Delphi in particular, were closely connected with the authentication and distribution of wisdom. The Panhellenic sanctuaries thus functioned as clearinghouses, analogous to the role of Delphi in the area of colonization and law as outlined by Snodgrass. The proposed institutional function of *xenia* as a facilitator of travel and intellectual interaction also affords the most plausible way of accounting for the strong presence, as documented in our primary sources, of *sophoi* at the Panhellenic centers. In the last chapter, I explored the frequent involvement in and allusions to *xenia*-relationships on the part of *sophoi* in other contexts. It seems probable that this institutional framework is equally significant in the Panhellenic setting.[46]

---

[44] Gernet 1981:80.

[45] Martin 1993:127n42. Morgan 1990 gives support to such a view. When discussing tripods as dedications, she writes, "It is possible, for example, that their social value depended upon their previous role as gifts or prestige items within an elite exchange network," 46. This network could also be said to be at work in the sympotic context of the Seven Sages as portrayed by Plutarch's *Dinner of the Seven Wise Men*. The symposium, of course, would be the site *par excellence* for aristocratic activities and for the same elite ethos that fueled the operation of *xenia*. For a social analysis of the institution of the symposium, see Murray 1990; see also Griffith 2001:56–59.

[46] The scarcity of primary sources presents unique challenges in attempting a full-scale investigation of the subject matter at hand, and I have often settled for a "circumstantial" picture of the institutional framework that facilitated travel and interaction among *sophoi*. See the appendix for a longer discussion of how the fragmentary nature of the sources has affected my argument.

6

Competition in Wisdom

THE AIM OF THIS CHAPTER is to examine in closer detail the elements of competition involved in the ancient Greek wisdom tradition.[1] This aspect of Greek intellectual life is particularly relevant since there is in our material a close affiliation on the part of *sophoi* with the Panhellenic games, the sites of competition *par excellence*.[2] An exploration of this subject will also help us achieve a better understanding of the agonistic elements of the teachings present in our sources on the sophists: Protagoras, for example, wrote two works called *Overthrowing Arguments* (Καταβάλλοντες) and *Contradictory Arguments* (Ἀντιλογικοί);[3] we are told that Hippias was ready to lecture at Olympia on any subject he had prepared for exhibition and afterwards to answer any questions raised by his audience.[4] Gorgias also offered to answer any question asked by his listeners after he was done lecturing.[5] Another example of this agonistic genre is the anonymous work we have preserved under the name *Twofold Arguments* (Δισσοὶ

---

[1] The material considered in this chapter is very selective. I have tried not to cast my net too widely and have thus often—but by no means always—ignored elements of competition manifested in the poetic tradition. Instead, I have sought to outline a set of competitive practices in whose tradition the sophists later operated. For a fuller account that considers the whole poetic tradition and material, see Griffith 1990.

[2] Although there exist numerous studies on every possible aspect of the athletic competitions, not much attention has been paid to the Panhellenic games as places for agonistic public performances and debates on topics ranging from poetry to natural philosophy and human anatomy. Some notable exceptions are Lloyd 1979, esp. 92–98, and 1987:50–108 to whose excellent discussion and references my argument is greatly indebted; Richardson 1981; Griffith 1990; Osborne 1993; and Graziosi 2001. For a discussion of the athletic competitions at the Panhellenic games, see, for example, Gardiner 1910; Kyle 1987; Tzachou-Alexandri 1989; and Golden 1998. The gravitation of practitioners of wisdom towards the Panhellenic centers is further explored in chapter five.

[3] Sextus Empiricus *Adversus Mathematicos* 7.60 = DK 80B1 and Diogenes Laertius 3.37 = DK 80B5. For καταβάλλω as a wrestling metaphor borrowed from athletics, see Gagarin 2001:171–186, esp. n6; and Hawhee 2004:35–39.

[4] *Hippias Minor* 363c-d = DK 86A8.

[5] *Gorgias* 449c = DK 82A20. Similar practices were shared by Ion in Plato's *Ion*, who claimed to be able to explain and elaborate on any point in Homer before an audience.

Λόγοι).[6] Finally, this sort of investigation will help us place the activities of the sophists in a more nuanced cultural context and acquire a better sense of how their works related to traditional genres and discourses.

We shall proceed by reviewing the sources we have for competition in wisdom. Special attention will be given to the recurring contrast between intellectual and athletic achievements and their due rewards. The material on the sophists will then be considered against the backdrop of this discourse. We shall suggest that the competitive elements present in the sophistic material should be understood as traditional and in line with the practices of earlier *sophoi*. In fact, competitiveness and contestation will prove to be some of the most pervasive characteristics of the Greek wisdom tradition.

Hesiod supplies us with early evidence for competition in wisdom. In the *Works and Days* he discusses his (un)familiarity with sailing and concedes that he has only sailed from Aulis to Euboea—a distance of some 65 meters.[7] He continues:

> ἔνθα δ’ ἐγὼν ἐπ’ ἄεθλα δαΐφρονος Ἀμφιδάμαντος
> Χαλκίδα [τ’] εἰσεπέρησα. τὰ δὲ προπεφραδμένα πολλὰ
> ἄεθλ’ ἔθεσαν παῖδες μεγαλήτορες. ἔνθα μέ φημι
> ὕμνῳ νικήσαντα φέρειν τρίποδ’ ὠτώεντα.

There I passed across into Chalchis to the contests for warlike Amphidamas. His great-hearted sons set forth many prizes that had been announced beforehand. There I say that I was victorious in song and won a tripod with ears.[8]

In the Homeric *Hymn to Apollo* (149–150, Allen) we hear of a similar competition:

> οἱ δέ σε πυγμαχίῃ τε καὶ ὀρχηθμῷ καὶ ἀοιδῇ
> μνησάμενοι τέρπουσιν ὅταν στήσωνται ἀγῶνα.

---

[6] DK 90 1–9.

[7] West 1978:20.

[8] *Works and Days* 654–657, West. Hesiod makes another mention of the competition between singers (ἀοιδοί) at the very beginning of the same poem (lines 24–26), where it stands as a model for good strife (cf. Lloyd 1987:58n29):

> ἀγαθὴ δ’ Ἔρις ἥδε βροτοῖσιν.
> καὶ κεραμεὺς κεραμεῖ κοτέει καὶ τέκτονι τέκτων,
> καὶ πτωχὸς πτωχῷ φθονέει καὶ ἀοιδὸς ἀοιδῷ.

> This *eris* ('emulation', 'competition') is good for mortals.
> Potter bears a grudge against potter and craftsman against craftsman,
> And beggar envies beggar and singer singer.

But with boxing and dancing and song they remember and delight you,
whenever they arrange a contest.

Later, the poet asks the maidens who are his audience to remember him in
the future (ἐμεῖο δὲ καὶ μετόπισθε μνήσασθ'), and to say that his songs are the
best in times to come (τοῦ πᾶσαι μετόπισθεν ἀριστεύουσιν ἀοιδαί), whenever a
stranger asks them.[9]

There is also some interesting information in the work that has come down
to us under the name *Contest of Homer and Hesiod*. This piece was composed close
to the time of Hadrian, but it is clear that the author draws upon sources that go
back at least to the *Museum* of Alcidamas in the early fourth century BCE.[10] The
setting for the *Contest of Homer and Hesiod* is the funeral games of Amphidamas,
king of Euboea, and in addition to trials in bodily strength and speed, there is
also a competition in wisdom (σοφία), lines 62–66:

> κατὰ δὲ τὸν αὐτὸν
> χρόνον Γανύκτωρ ἐπιτάφιον τοῦ πατρὸς Ἀμφιδάμαντος
> βασιλέως Εὐβοίας ἐπιτελῶν πάντας τοὺς ἐπισήμους ἄνδρας
> οὐ μόνον ῥώμῃ καὶ τάχει, ἀλλὰ καὶ σοφίᾳ ἐπὶ τὸν ἀγῶνα
> μεγάλαις δωρεαῖς τιμῶν συνεκάλεσεν.

At the same time, Ganuctor was celebrating the funeral games of his
father Amphidamas, king of Euboea, and summoned for a competition
all men who were famous not only for their strength and speed, but
also for wisdom, honoring them with great gifts.

We hear of judges (κριταί, 69) presiding over the contests, as the sages question each other. Whoever gives the best answers is victorious. The capacity to
answer any question is crucial, and this is highlighted in Homer's remark to
Hesiod (160):

> ἄλλο δὲ πᾶν ὅ τι σῷ θυμῷ φίλον ἐστὶν ἐρώτα

Ask anything else that is dear to your heart.

---

[9]   166–173. *Iliad* 2.594–600 also provides evidence for poetic competition in the epic tradition. Here
the Muses in anger remove the ability to sing from Thamyris of Thrace, since he boasted that he
would be victorious (νικησέμεν) against the Muses in song.

[10] For a fuller discussion on the sources for this work, see West 1967, who believes that Alcidamas
invented the narrative on the contest, and Richardson 1981, who argues that Alcidamas' *Museum*
uses an even older account dating back to the sixth century BCE. For the question of how the
Michigan Alcidamas Papyrus relates to the *Museum* and the *Contest of Homer and Hesiod*, see Koniaris
1971 and Renehan 1971.

Hesiod walks away the victor on the grounds that his poetry promotes peace whereas Homer sings of war. His prize is a tripod, which he dedicates to the Muses. In this work, then, we hear of a highly formalized competition in wisdom, alongside other more traditional athletic competitions, where what counts is one's ability to answer any question. Further, the winner is crowned (ἐστεφάνωσεν, 208) and rewarded with a prize in the same manner as the athletes: the words ἀγωνίζομαι and ἀγών (54, 65, 68, 71, and 215), νικάω and νίκη (71, 207, 209, 210, 214, 216, and 255) are used to describe the competition between Hesiod and Homer. These verbs are typically affiliated with athletic prowess.[11] It is worth mentioning that the prize, a tripod, is a familiar element in our sources as a reward for wisdom: Diogenes Laertius tells the story of the tripod and the Seven Sages, where the Delphic oracle declares that the tripod should belong to the wisest man alive.[12] In the *Contest of Homer and Hesiod* we similarly have a wisdom contest with the prize of a tripod and, as we shall see shortly, an important role played by oracular responses.

In the same tradition, Heraclitus expresses his strong disapproval of Homer and Archilochus, and voices his discontent within a framework of competition:

> τόν τε Ὅμηρον ἔφασκεν ἄξιον ἐκ τῶν ἀγώνων
> ἐκβάλλεσθαι καὶ ῥαπίζεσθαι καὶ Ἀρχίλοχον ὁμοίως.

He said that Homer deserved to be thrown out of the games and whipped, and also Archilochus.[13]

In fragment 2, Xenophanes outlines his criticism of athletic competition, and compares the benefits of his own wisdom to those of the athletic competitions:[14]

> ῥώμης γὰρ ἀμείνων
> ἀνδρῶν ἠδ' ἵππων ἡμετέρη σοφίη
> ...
> σμικρὸν δ' ἄν τι πόλει χάρμα γένοιτ' ἐπὶ τῶι,
> εἴ τις ἀεθλεύων νικῶι Πίσαο παρ' ὄχθας·
> οὐ γὰρ πιαίνει ταῦτα μυχοὺς πόλεως.

Our sophia is better than the strength of men and horses.

---

[11] It is also interesting to note that Hesiod wins the competition because his poetry is judged to be more beneficial to society by promoting peace. This is the same criterion that is applied in the *agon* between Aeschylus and Euripides in the *Frogs*. For this theme (rejection of war and praise of peace), see Richardson 1981:2–3.

[12] This theme is discussed at greater length in chapter five, above, 122–123.

[13] Diogenes Laertius 9.1 = DK 22B42.

[14] For a treatment of the tradition critical of athletics, see Bowra 1938; Marcovich1978; Kyle 1987, esp. 124–154; and Larmour 1999:41–55.

...

There would be little benefit to the city from this, if someone should compete and be victorious at the banks of Pisa. For this does not fatten the treasury chambers of the city.[15]

Traditionally, this fragment has been read as Xenophanes' condemnation of athletics. If we put it together with the passage quoted from Heraclitus, however, we can read it as an affirmative declaration of his own wisdom, in which his intelligence is carefully framed to contrast with the benefits of athletic victory. Heraclitus, focusing exclusively on competition in *sophia*, acknowledges that his wisdom participates in an agonistic relationship with earlier and contemporary *sophoi*. Xenophanes, on the other hand, shifts the focus and articulates the benefits of wisdom contrastively by saying what athletics cannot accomplish. Both Heraclitus and Xenophanes, however, promote the pursuit of wisdom as an agonistic activity. Similar sentiments were later expressed in Euripides' *Autolykos*, where the uselessness of athletes is contrasted with the benefit to society of the wise man:

16   τίς γὰρ παλαίσας εὖ, τίς ὠκύπους ἀνὴρ
      ἢ δίσκον ἄρας ἢ γνάθον παίσας καλῶς
      πόλει πατρῴᾳ στέφανον ἤρκεσεν λαβών;

      ...

23   ἄνδρας χρὴ σοφούς τε κἀγαθοὺς
      φύλλοις στέφεσθαι, χὦστις ἡγεῖται πόλει
      κάλλιστα σώφρων καὶ δίκαιος ὢν ἀνήρ,
      ὅστις τε μύθοις ἔργ' ἀπαλλάσσει κακὰ
      μάχας τ' ἀφαιρῶν καὶ στάσεις· τοιαῦτα γὰρ
      πόλει τε πάσῃ πᾶσί θ' Ἕλλησιν καλά.

For what good wrestler, what swift-footed runner or quoits-thrower or excellent boxer has been sufficient to his city with the crown he earned?

...

Wise and noble men should be crowned with leaves, both he who leads the city best, being a prudent and just man, and he who removes evil actions with his words and takes away

---

[15] DK 21B2, 20–22. For a full discussion of this fragment, see Bowra 1938 and Marcovich 1978, esp. 16–26. Similar sentiments were later expressed by Isocrates in *Antidosis* 250: "But what is most astonishing of all is that while they would grant that the mind is superior to the body, nevertheless, in spite of this opinion, they look with greater favour upon training in gymnastics than upon the study of philosophy" (trans. Norlin).

battles and civil strifes. For such things are good both for every city and for all Greeks.[16]

The promised reward when honoring *sophoi* is good order—*eunomia* in Xenophanes, and removal of external and internal conflicts in Euripides—a public good athletes can never produce.[17]

The next set of evidence to consider is what we might refer to as riddle competition.[18] Perhaps the most famous instance of this is preserved in the myth of Oedipus and the Sphinx, but there are other instances. Hesiod, for example, relates the encounter and trial between the two seers (μάντεις) Calchas and Mopsus.[19] This encounter results in the death of Calchas when he is surpassed in prophetic knowledge by Mopsus. Greek literature abounds in references to how it is important for wise men to be able correctly to interpret riddles. This was particularly valued since the riddle was the oracular response *par excellence*: riddles and the enigmatic nature of wisdom and knowledge are recurrent themes in our sources.[20] In the *Contest of Homer and Hesiod*, for example, part of the contest consists of Homer having to finish enigmatic lines of poetry fired at him by Hesiod. Also, in the same work, both sages are said to have died due to their incapacity to correctly interpret riddles, as had been prophesied to them by oracles: Hesiod fails to understand the true meaning of an oracle from Delphi,[21] and Homer falls short of understanding the riddle posed by some young boys.[22]

Lucian's *Herodotus* reveals another outlet for competitive intellectual practices. There Lucian relates how Herodotus recited his work at Olympia.[23] He describes how Herodotus presented himself as an Olympic competitor, not a spectator (οὐ θεατὴν ἀλλ' ἀγωνιστὴν Ὀλυμπίων παρεῖχεν ἑαυτόν) and recited his work before a large audience. The result was that Herodotus became better known than the Olympic victors themselves, and that his name was proclaimed not only by one herald but in every city that had dispatched attendants to the festival. This performance by Herodotus is not only a flashy display of wisdom, but it also

[16] Euripides fr. 282, 23-28 (*Autolykos*) TGF. For a discussion of this fragment, see Marcovich 1978:20; Sutton 1980; and Kyle 1987:128. See also discussion in chapter three, 81.

[17] This theme is discussed at greater length in chapter three, 80–82. For *eunomia*, see Andrewes 1938; Ehrenberg 1946b; Grossmann 1950; Erasmus 1960; Ostwald 1969, esp. 62–85; and Irwin 2005:183–193.

[18] Ohlert 1912; Lloyd 1987:85; Griffith 1990:192 with footnotes 24–27; and Dillery 2005, esp. 176.

[19] Fr. 278, West.

[20] Lloyd 1979:60–61, esp. n6 with bibliography; Lloyd 1987:85–87, esp. n127; Griffith 1990:192; Graziosi 2001:69.

[21] *Contest of Homer and Hesiod* 215–229. Cf. Thucydides 3.96.1.

[22] *Contest of Homer and Hesiod* 323–338. Heraclitus picks up on this failure of Homer to understand what the riddling boys meant in fr. 56 (DK 22B56), where he likens the deception of Homer, the wisest of all Greeks, to the deception of men with respect to their recognition of visible things.

[23] Lucian *Herodotus* 1.

provides an explicit contestation of the worth of athletic accomplishments, especially when contrasted to Herodotus' own practices. After all, Herodotus presents himself as an athletic competitor, wins more fame than the athletes, and has his name proclaimed in every city. All this reinforces the idea of the superiority of his wisdom over the achievements accomplished by the athletes—a theme familiar from the fragments of Xenophanes and Euripides quoted above.[24]

Thucydides offers a perfect illustration of the agonistic aspirations of works such as those of Herodotus in his disclaimer at the beginning of Book 1. There he contrasts these agonistic tendencies in favor of his own goals:

κτῆμά τε ἐς αἰεὶ μᾶλλον ἢ ἀγώνισμα ἐς τὸ παραχρῆμα ἀκούειν ξύγκειται

My work is composed as a possession to last forever rather than as a competitive piece to be heard by an immediate audience.[25]

Thucydides addresses other aspects of this agonistic nature later in his work (3.38.4–7). The context is a deliberation in the assembly over what actions should be taken in the face of the revolt of Mytilene in 427 BCE. Cleon addresses the assembly and criticizes the citizens for allowing the act of political deliberation to turn into an oratorical competition:

> The persons to blame are you who are so foolish as to institute these contests (κακῶς ἀγωνοθετοῦντες); who go to see an oration as you would to see a sight, take your facts on hearsay, judge of the practicability of a project by the wit of its advocates, and trust for the truth as to past events, not to the fact which you saw more than to the clever structures which you heard; the easy victims of newfangled arguments, unwilling to follow received conclusions; slaves to every new paradox, despisers of the commonplace; the first wish of every man being that he could speak himself, the next to rival (ἀνταγωνιζόμενοι) those who can speak by seeming to keep up with their ideas by applauding every hit almost before it is made, and by being as quick in catching an argument as you are slow in foreseeing its consequences; asking, if I may so say, for something different from the conditions under which we live, and yet comprehending inadequately those very conditions; very slaves to the pleasure of the ear, and more like the audience of a rhetorician than the council of a city (ἁπλῶς τε ἀκοῆς ἡδονῇ ἡσσώμενοι καὶ σοφιστῶν θεαταῖς ἐοικότες καθημένοις μᾶλλον ἢ περὶ πόλεως βουλευομένοις).
>
> Trans. Crawley

---

[24] For an exploration of the connection between wisdom and athletics in ancient Greece, see Larmour 1999, esp. 41–55.
[25] 1.22.4.

This passage illustrates how commonplace these competitive performances were, and how, in the eyes of Cleon (and, presumably, Thucydides), they were significant enough to influence negatively the political climate of the time.

But perhaps the most important source for actual competitions in wisdom comes from the medical writers. In the treatise *Nature of Man*, we are told how inadequate are the theories of others who, although they adopt the same opinion (γνώμη τῇ αὐτῇ), nevertheless fail to say the same things (τὰ αὐτά).[26] And the author continues:

> Γνοίη δ' ἄν τις τόδε μάλιστα παραγενόμενος αὐτέοισιν ἀντιλέγουσιν·
> πρὸς γὰρ ἀλλήλους ἀντιλέγοντες οἱ αὐτοὶ ἄνδρες τῶν αὐτέων ἐναντίον
> ἀκροατέων οὐδέποτε τρὶς ἐφεξῆς ὁ αὐτὸς περιγίνεται ἐν τῷ λόγῳ, ἀλλὰ
> ποτὲ μὲν οὗτος ἐπικρατέει, ποτὲ δὲ οὗτος, ποτὲ δὲ ᾧ ἂν τύχῃ μάλιστα ἡ
> γλῶσσα ἐπιρρυεῖσα πρὸς τὸν ὄχλον.

> Someone would best learn this by being present when they debate.
> Although the same people are debating and listening, never does the
> same man win the argument three times in a row, but sometime one is
> victorious, sometime another, and sometime the one who happens to
> have the glibbest tongue before the crowd.[27]

We are left without any doubt that there existed formal debates on a variety of topics that we can loosely collect under the heading of *sophia*, and that these debates bore a close resemblance to other forms of agonistic contests with a developed vocabulary of winning and losing (περιγίνεται, ἐπικρατέει). This is a point stressed by Lloyd:

> This text clearly indicates that even such, as we might suppose,
> specialised or technical topics as the ultimate constituents of man were
> the subject of public debates between contending speakers in front of a
> lay audience in the late fifth or early fourth century BC.[28]

In the *Nature of Man* (1, 23–24) the author goes on to assert that it is the lack of understanding that makes the debaters contradict themselves (αὐτοὶ ἑωυτοὺς καταβάλλειν ... ὑπὸ ἀσυνεσίης). The verbs used to mean "debate" and "contradict" in the passages quoted above (καταβάλλειν and ἀντιλέγειν) correspond to

[26] The date of this treatise is roughly 440–400 BCE. In the words of Jones: "In Chapter I Melissus the Eleatic, who flourished about 440 B.C., is mentioned in such a way as to show that his doctrines were not yet forgotten or out of date, and throughout the first eight chapters the influence of Empedocles is strong. We ought then to postulate for the first section a date not earlier than 440 B.C. and not later than (say) 400 B.C.", Jones 1923, 4:xxvii. See also Lloyd 1979:92–98.

[27] *Nature of Man*, 15–20.

[28] Lloyd 1979:93.

the names of Protagoras' works, the *Overthrowing Arguments* (Καταβάλλοντες) and the *Contradictory Arguments* (Ἀντιλογικοί), and they seem to be appropriately used in the context of competitive debate, where the goal is to overcome one's opponent.[29] Gorgias uses the verb καταβάλλειν in his *Defense on behalf of Palamedes* when he talks about the danger that awaits the judges if they make the wrong decision and condemn him:

ὑμῖν μὲν γὰρ μέγας ὁ κίνδυνος, ἀδίκοις φανεῖσι δόξαν τὴν μὲν καταβαλεῖν, τὴν δὲ κτήσασθαι. τοῖς δὲ ἀγαθοῖς ἀνδράσιν αἱρετώτερος θάνατος δόξης αἰσχρᾶς·

You run the great risk of overthrowing one reputation by seeming unjust, while acquiring another. But for good men death is more desirable then a shameful reputation.[30]

In this passage, καταβάλλειν is employed where reputation is at stake. By winning the argument one's own reputation is enhanced, while that of the opponent is overthrown; and this is clearly the meaning of the passage from the Hippocratic corpus quoted above, where the disputants attack each other in order to be proclaimed victors in the debate. It is also likely that this was the ability that the *Overthrowing Arguments* of Protagoras dealt with, and which he sought to instill in his students. Plutarch preserves the name of one of Thrasymachus' works, Ὑπερβάλλοντες, and though the prefix used here is different, the meaning is likely similar to that of the κατα-prefix.[31]

Lysias, in his *Olympian Speech*, tells how Heracles first founded the Olympic Games, and lists intellectual competition alongside athletic ones:

ἀγῶνα μὲν σωμάτων ἐποίησε, φιλοτιμίαν <δὲ> πλούτου, γνώμης δ' ἐπίδειξιν ἐν τῷ καλλίστῳ τῆς Ἑλλάδος.

He instituted athletic competition, ambitious display of wealth, and an exhibition of intelligence in the most beautiful part of Greece.[32]

Finally, Isocrates mentions the allurements of Athens in the *Panegyricus* and, when enumerating the attractions the city offers, he says that it provides a variety of contests:

ἔτι δ' ἀγῶνας ἰδεῖν μὴ μόνον τάχους καὶ ῥώμης ἀλλὰ καὶ λόγων καὶ γνώμης καὶ τῶν ἄλλων ἔργων ἁπάντων, καὶ τούτων ἆθλα μέγιστα.

---

[29] Pollux 2.120 = DK 87B98 attributes the use of the participle ἀντιλογούμενοι to Antiphon.
[30] DK 82B11a, 35.
[31] DK 85B7.
[32] Lysias *Olympian Speech* 33.2.

[With us, it is possible] further to see competitions, not only in speed and strength, but also in speeches and wisdom and in all other deeds; and [it is possible to see] the greatest prizes for these competitions.[33]

What emerges from the examples above is a pattern of competitive performances of wisdom where such qualities as poetic excellence, riddle-solving capabilities, and specialized expertise were highly valued and rewarded. The competitive venues for these performances employed a language that mirrors the vocabulary we traditionally associate with athletic competition, for example, the use of terms such as "judges," "winners," "crowns," or "prizes." A crucial feature of these performances seems to have consisted in the ability on the part of the sage to answer any questions posed to him. In the surveyed material we witness a clear rivalry between athletic and intellectual accomplishments. The swiftness or strength of athletes is repeatedly juxtaposed to the wisdom of the sages (ταχύτης ποδῶν and ῥώμη vs. σοφίη in Xenophanes; ῥώμη καὶ τάχος vs. σοφία in the *Contest of Homer and Hesiod*; and τάχος καὶ ῥώμη vs. γνώμη καὶ λόγοι in Isocrates). The juxtaposition between athletic and intellectual prowess exhibits a formal characteristic that suggests that this rivalry was a traditional topic.[34] *Sophoi* could be quite jealous of the rewards reaped by athletes. Xenophanes, for example, complains about how athletic victors receive the front seats at the games (καί κε προεδρίην φανερὴν ἐν ἀγῶσιν ἄροιτο) and meals at public expense (καί κεν σῖτ' εἴη δημοσίων κτεάνων ἐκ πόλεως),[35] despite the fact that, in his view at least, his wisdom is more deserving than their accomplishments. This theme is picked up by Socrates who, when asked to suggest an alternative penalty to the death penalty suggested by his accusers, answers:

τί οὖν πρέπει ἀνδρὶ πένητι εὐεργέτῃ δεομένῳ ἄγειν σχολὴν ἐπὶ τῇ ὑμετέρᾳ παρακελεύσει; οὐκ ἔσθ' ὅτι μᾶλλον, ὦ ἄνδρες Ἀθηναῖοι, πρέπει οὕτως ὡς τὸν τοιοῦτον ἄνδρα ἐν πρυτανείῳ σιτεῖσθαι, πολύ γε μᾶλλον ἢ εἴ τις ὑμῶν ἵππῳ ἢ συνωρίδι ἢ ζεύγει νενίκηκεν Ὀλυμπίασιν· ὁ μὲν γὰρ ὑμᾶς ποιεῖ εὐδαίμονας δοκεῖν εἶναι, ἐγὼ δὲ εἶναι.

---

[33] *Panegyricus* 45.

[34] Gorgias, for example, uses this dichotomy in his *Funeral Oration* honoring the Athenians who had died in war. There he praises the Athenians for being able to exercise these two qualities at once (καὶ δισσὰ ἀσκήσαντες μάλιστα ὧν δεῖ, γνώμην <καὶ ῥώμην>), and he later goes on to say that they use their prudence of opinion to check the imprudence of strength (τῶι φρονίμωι τῆς γνώμης παύοντες τὸ ἄφρον <τῆς ῥώμης>), DK 82B6. The problem with this fragment is, of course, that the two uses of ῥώμη are conjectures, but it fits so well with the pattern we have already detected in the quoted sources that I find it a very likely, and thus illustrative, conjecture.

[35] DK 21B2.

What then is befitting for a poor man, who is a benefactor and needs leisure, to exhort you? Nothing is more befitting, men of Athens, than for such a man to be given free meals at the town-hall, much more so than if anyone of you had won a victory at the Olympic Games either with a single horse or with a two-horse chariot or with a four-horse chariot. For he gives you the appearance of happiness, whereas I give real happiness.[36]

Socrates contrasts his own accomplishments and usefulness to the *polis* to the achievements of the athletic victors. By claiming for himself the public recognition normally granted to athletic success he locates himself within the agonistic tradition outlined above. It is interesting to note that Socrates' claim to fame came from the oracle of Apollo at Delphi which, after being asked by Chaerephon whether there was anyone wiser than Socrates, pronounced that there existed no wiser man in the world.[37] Socrates challenges the rewards given to athletes and claims that he is more worthy of them, but he also attributes his reputation for wisdom to the prophetic utterances of Delphi. He thereby acknowledges, at least indirectly, his indebtedness to a long tradition of practitioners of wisdom dating all the way back to the Seven Sages.[38] Furthermore, although he emphasizes the rivalry between athletes and *sophoi*, the question posed to Delphi regarding his wisdom is clearly asked with a view also to the rivalry among *sophoi*—no one is *wiser* (σοφώτερος) than Socrates—and thus stresses the twofold competition seen above: both between athletic and intellectual pursuits and among practitioners of wisdom.

Isocrates also complains that athletic achievements are held in higher regard than intellectual pursuits (*Panegyricus* 1):

Πολλάκις ἐθαύμασα τῶν τὰς πανηγύρεις συναγαγόντων καὶ τοὺς γυμνικοὺς ἀγῶνας καταστησάντων, ὅτι τὰς μὲν τῶν σωμάτων εὐτυχίας οὕτω μεγάλων δωρεῶν ἠξίωσαν, τοῖς δ' ὑπὲρ τῶν κοινῶν ἰδίᾳ πονήσασι καὶ τὰς αὐτῶν ψυχὰς οὕτω παρασκευάσασιν ὥστε καὶ τοὺς ἄλλους ὠφελεῖν δύνασθαι, τούτοις δ' οὐδεμίαν τιμὴν ἀπένειμαν.

I have often wondered over those who convened the Panhellenic festivals and founded the athletic contests, that they deemed success of bodies worthy of so great gifts, whereas to those who privately toiled on behalf of the public and prepared their own minds so as to be able to benefit even others, to them they assigned no honor.

---

36   *Apology* 36d. Cf. Marcovich 1978, esp. 19–20.
37   *Apology* 20e-21a.
38   The connection between Delphi and wisdom is further explored in chapter five.

It is particularly relevant that this complaint is voiced in the context of the games at the Panhellenic sanctuaries. It emphasizes the traditional theme of the opposition between athletic and intellectual pursuits, on the one hand, but it also focuses attention on the games as potential or desired sites for competition in wisdom, on the other.[39] What, then, do the frequent comparative appeals to athletic prowess accomplish? The answer, I suggest, is twofold. It situates intellectual activity within the sphere of public goods—goods that deserve public recognition. But, perhaps more importantly, it construes wisdom as a competitive enterprise—one with winners and losers and with high stakes in the taking for the victor.

*

It is in the light of the competition in wisdom outlined above that I suggest we now review the material on the sophists. Although the main bulk of the evidence concerns only two of the sophists, Gorgias and Hippias, I believe it provides us with a representative view of the intellectual practices of the other sophists. In the case of Gorgias, we have already seen that he made quite a name for himself at the Panhellenic games (ἐμπρέπων δὲ καὶ ταῖς τῶν Ἑλλήνων πανηγύρεσι),[40] where he gave public displays. We also hear of his activities in Athens:

παρελθὼν γὰρ οὗτος ἐς τὸ Ἀθηναίων θέατρον ἐθάρρησεν εἰπεῖν "προβάλλετε" καὶ τὸ κινδύνευμα τοῦτο πρῶτος ἀνεφθέγξατο, ἐνδεικνύμενος δήπου πάντα μὲν εἰδέναι, περὶ παντὸς δ' ἂν εἰπεῖν ἐφιεὶς τῷ καιρῷ.

For he came before the theater of the Athenians and had the confidence to say "propose" and he was the first to call out aloud this bold enterprise, showing presumably that he knew everything, and that, trusting to the right moment, he would talk about everything.[41]

In the *Meno*, he is again said to answer any question any Greek may ask him, not refusing to answer anyone (αὐτὸς παρέχων αὑτὸν ἐρωτᾶν τῶν Ἑλλήνων τῷ βουλομένῳ ὅτι ἄν τις βούληται, καὶ οὐδενὶ ὅτῳ οὐκ ἀποκρινόμενος).[42] Note that any Greek may ask him questions, a fact that stresses the Panhellenic character of the games as well as of the audience for whom he would normally lecture. His promise to answer anyone's questions resonates with what we saw earlier in the *Contest of Homer and Hesiod*, where this ability is also singled out.

---

[39] For a fuller discussion of Isocrates' criticism of athletics, see Kyle 1987, esp. 134–137.
[40] Philostratus *Lives of the Sophists* 1.9.4 = DK 82A1.
[41] Philostratus *Lives of the Sophists* 1.1 = DK 82A1a.
[42] *Meno* 70c.

There is a controversial piece of evidence from Clement of Alexandria.[43] In a discussion on the futility of worldly wisdom, he refers to Gorgias:

καὶ τὸ ἀγώνισμα ἡμῶν κατὰ τὸν Λεοντῖνον Γοργίαν διττῶν [δὲ] ἀρετῶν δεῖται, τόλμης καὶ σοφίας. τόλμης μὲν τὸ κίνδυνον ὑπομεῖναι, σοφίας δὲ τὸ αἴνιγμα γνῶναι. ὁ γάρ τοι λόγος καθάπερ τὸ κήρυγμα τὸ Ὀλυμπίασι καλεῖ μὲν τὸν βουλόμενον, στεφανοῖ δὲ τὸν δυνάμενον.

And our contest needs two virtues, according to Gorgias of Leontini, daring and wisdom; daring, on the one hand, to withstand the danger, and wisdom, on the other, to understand the riddle. For speech, just like the proclamation at Olympia, summons whoever wants [to compete], but crowns only the winner.

Bernays, who saw in this passage the first prose mention of Olympia,[44] was puzzled over the use of αἴνιγμα γνῶναι, and asked if Clement indeed meant to imply that there existed riddling contests at Olympia. He thought not, and suggested instead an emendation of the word that would agree with a line in Homer.[45] Diels also emended αἴνιγμα, but chose a word that meant "to trip up" (πλίγμα), taking the metaphor from the world of wrestling. Ferguson, on the other hand, defended αἴνιγμα and thought that it was "a plain allusion to a famous legendary feat of σοφία," that is, Oedipus' encounter with the Sphinx.[46] Thomas Buchheim likewise sees no reason for emending the text as long as it has not been clearly established what sort of ἀγώνισμα is meant.[47]

Although it is hard to sort out any obvious and undisputed conclusions regarding Clement's quotation of Gorgias, it is still worth the effort to take this passage seriously and compare it to the investigation we have conducted thus far. To begin with, the ability to solve riddles and the designation for such knowledge as σοφία is a well-established pattern that emerges from our sources. Further the positioning of Gorgias' intellectual activities in the context of competitions

---

[43] Clement of Alexandria 1.11.51. I describe it as controversial for several reasons. First, most scholars have wondered why Clement chose to quote Gorgias at this particular point in his work. Second, they have failed to understand the significance of the word αἴνιγμα used in the passage and have thus suggested a variety of emendations (τὰ αἴσιμα "what is fitting" Bernays; πλίγμα "crossing the legs in wrestling, tripping one's opponent" Diels, DK 82B8). Third, no clear consensus has been reached on the quote itself, that is, what should fall within quotation marks and what should not. Finally, it has also been argued that the quote comes from two different places in Gorgias' works. For a full discussion of these problems, see Bernays 1853:432–433; Ferguson 1921:284–287; and Buchheim 1989:192–195.

[44] Bernays 1853:432. The presence of the words τὸ κήρυγμα τὸ Ὀλυμπίασι made Bernays conclude that this passage was indeed taken from the Ὀλυμπικὸς Λόγος.

[45] Bernays 1853:433. The line is from *Iliad* 15.207.

[46] Ferguson 1921:284–287.

[47] Buchheim 1989:192.

(ἀγώνισμα) is also a common theme. Finally, his competitive performance of wisdom at Olympia, one of the most important Panhellenic centers, mirrors a pattern we have detected dating back to the alleged congregation of the Seven Sages at these centers. We may never know the truth about Clement's quotation, but we can perhaps glean from it attitudes regarding wisdom that circulated in antiquity. These attitudes, as far as we can determine, seem to agree to a remarkable degree with other, older, and more reliable sources, such as those voiced in the *Contest of Homer and Hesiod*.

Gorgias also had a golden statue of himself erected at Delphi.[48] This is especially striking in the context of athletic competition and victory celebration. As Leslie Kurke has pointed out, it was the prerogative of the aristocratic victors at the Panhellenic games to erect a statue of themselves to commemorate their success.[49] Thus, one way of understanding the statue of Gorgias is to see it as an act of self-promotion rivaling the dedications made by the athletes. This line of interpretation ties in well with the competition we have already described between athletic and intellectual achievements.

Hippias made innumerable visits to Olympia at the time of the festival and he was ready to speak on any subject he had prepared for display. Plato also mentions that Hippias had visited Olympia wearing clothes all of which he had made for himself: ring, skin-scraper, oil-flask, sandals, cloak, tunic, and girdle, and that, besides this, he had with him poems, epics, tragedies, dithyrambs, and many prose writings. He is also said to have published a *List of Olympic Victors*.[50] Finally, Philostratus says that:

εὐδοκιμῶν δὲ καὶ τὸν ἄλλον χρόνον ἔθελγε τὴν Ἑλλάδα ἐν Ὀλυμπίαι λόγοις ποικίλοις καὶ πεφροντισμένοις εὖ.

Having a good reputation for the whole rest of his time, he enchanted Greece at Olympia with speeches that were both diverse and well devised.[51]

In the case of both Gorgias and Hippias, it seems clear that one of the main arenas for their activities was the Panhellenic games. Moreover, their performances there are clearly competitive and oriented towards winning debates and reputation, and this competitive behavior is often juxtaposed and likened

---

[48] Philostratus *Lives of the Sophists* 1.9.4 = DK 82A1; Pausanias 6.17.7 = 82A7; Pausanias 10.18.7 = DK 82A7; Dio Chrysostom 37.28 = DK 82A7; Cicero *De Oratore* 3.32.129 = DK 82A7; Pliny *Naturalis Historia* 33.83 = DK 82A7; Athenaeus 11.505d–e.

[49] Kurke 1993:141–149 and 1999:315. For a discussion of the significance of Gorgias' statue as a subtext in Plato's *Phaedrus*, see Morgan 1994.

[50] Plutarch *Numa* 1 = DK 86B3.

[51] *Lives of the Sophists* 1.11.7 = DK 86A2.

to athletic competition. Both the performance aspects of their exhibitions, including extravagant clothing and other forms of self-presentation,[52] and their promise to know and answer all questions clearly draw upon traditional features of an earlier wisdom tradition. These elements of thematic continuity have often been ignored in favor of criticism that promotes the uniqueness and innovativeness of the sophists.[53]

[52] *Hippias Minor* 368b = DK 86A12. Compare this to the flamboyant appearance of Empedocles, who, "liked to walk about with a grave expression, wearing a purple robe with a golden girdle, a Delphic wreath, shoes of bronze, and a luxuriant growth of hair, and attended by a train of boys," Guthrie 1965:132. For a fuller discussion on Empedocles, see Kingsley 1995.

[53] Griffith 1990:201n7 has called attention to this feature: "If at times ... I appear to minimize the originality or distinctiveness of the sophists, and of Euripidean 'shock-tactics,' this is only because I think that the continuities have been consistently undervalued by 'progressivist' critics committed to an oversimplified model of a developing Greek 'consciousness' and an accompanying rise and fall (decadence) in literary practice and taste."

APPENDIX
Primary Sources for the Sophists

It would be difficult to regard the story of the tripod as legend, since it seems to have been invented simply as an illustration of a type of wisdom. Still, it remains a legend because of the recognizable persistence of certain traditional ideas or images, and because of the mythological basis it retains (more or less faithfully, depending on the authors). Without such a foundation, the narrative would lose the minimum emotional and poetic interest it has.

Louis Gernet *The Anthropology of Ancient Greece*

IN EXPLORING THE CULTURAL AUTHORITY of the sophists, I have repeatedly used Plato, Xenophon, and Aristotle as important sources. This invites the question of how it is possible to use this hostile tradition to draw a nuanced picture of the sophists—especially if its members are, as I argue in chapter one, engrossed in a battle over legitimacy with rival practitioners of wisdom. In addition, the chronological diversity of the material on the Greek wisdom tradition poses numerous problems. For example, how are we to justify the juxtaposition of *testimonia* from Plato and, say, Diogenes Laertius (probably active in the first half of the third century CE) or Stobaeus (early fifth century CE)?

The problem of the potential unreliability of primary sources is of course not unique to this book, but confronts anyone studying Greek culture and literature. Early Greek philosophy is particularly affected, since most of what has come down to us is derived from later, more or less reliable, summaries. In response to this situation, a whole field of study has emerged in an attempt to establish reliable criteria according to which the authenticity of such primary sources can be assessed. Jaap Mansfeld has been active in both chronicling the emergence of doxography as a modern discipline, while simultaneously making substantial contributions to it; and his scholarship is the obvious starting point for anyone interested in understanding the many problems associated with establishing the authenticity of the primary material on early Greek philosophy.

While those of us interested in the sophists must often rely on the findings of doxographical scholarship, we still face difficulties peculiar to the material on them, especially the extent to which Plato's hostility towards sophists disqualifies him as a reliable source for their intellectual practices. The guiding principle that I have adopted in the foregoing pages is to strive for conceptual consistency, that is, for the recurrence of motifs, themes, and homologies that help bring into focus crucial features. I then attempted to corroborate the validity of these themes by chronicling their prevalence in sources that are chronologically and qualitatively diverse. In the case of the sophists' presence at the Panhellenic games, for example, we have evidence from sources as disparate as Plato's *Hippias Minor*, Dio Chrysostom, and Clement of Alexandria. Regarding their preoccupation with the topic of concord (ὁμόνοια), there exists a similar breadth of *testimonia*, including some surviving fragments from Gorgias, Antiphon, and Thrasymachus.

While such chronological diversity in the sources is helpful, it is certainly not sufficient. When discussing accusations against the sophists of teaching for pay in chapter two, for example, my main line of argument is that many of the later sources are directly derivative of the Platonic tradition and therefore offer little new evidence. In that case I instead seek to contrast the Platonic characterization of the sophists with divergent portrayals found in old comedy and Isocrates—precisely to highlight the lack of conceptual consistency. In other words, I have assumed that there exist conceptual connections among temporally disparate passages except when there is strong evidence to the contrary, for example, in passages from independent traditions. I have thus tried not to rely exclusively on the Platonic tradition, but to corroborate characterizations found there with evidence from other traditions or in later authors with access to diverse sources. The treatment of the primary sources in this book is thus far from precise, but given the dearth of material—especially in respect to the sophists—I have attempted throughout to avoid conclusions based on one-sided characterizations.

Despite the presence of conceptual connections, however, there is no guarantee that they necessarily correspond to a factual reality. Even so, they might still be revealing about historical representations; that is, "the way in which the Greeks themselves thought things happened and pictured to themselves the ideal by which they then judged the real."[1] This is especially relevant in the material on the elusive Seven Sages, where there is a particular problem of the reliability of the sources. It has been argued by Detlev Fehling that Plato invented this group of *sophoi* in the *Protagoras*, and that all earlier occurrences of the names of sages in Greek literature refer to individual sages without any notion that they were part of a *collegium*.[2] In Fehling's view, it would be historically flawed to ascribe any cultural significance to the Seven Sages before the

---

[1] Martin 1993:108.
[2] Fehling 1985.

fourth century BCE, and all subsequent references to them are derived from Plato. This view is contrary to that of Bruno Snell, who reached a different conclusion based upon his reading of papyrus *PSI 1093*. There he found fragmentary lines of hexameter poetry that he ascribed to a work on the banquet of the Seven Sages.[3] Citing this papyrus as well as the *scholia* attributed to the Seven Sages (transmitted by Diogenes Laertius)—which, on the basis of meter and content, he dates to no later than to the fifth century BCE—Snell argued that there existed a traditional genre on the Seven Sages that predated Plato; he further suggested that the *Contest of Homer and Hesiod* is a good example of this genre.[4]

Martin similarly defends the antiquity of the tradition of the Seven Sages. Examining the sources surrounding the sages and comparing similar features and characteristics, he argues that "certain traits, certain recurring themes, in the stories of the sages allow us to extrapolate and to reconstruct a world in which the existence of a group of Seven Sages, long before Plato's era, makes good sense."[5] We also have the commandments of the Seven Sages that both Oikonomides and Schultz trace back to an original inscription that they believe was cut on a stele in Apollo's temple at Delphi sometime in the early sixth century BCE.[6] There is thus evidence to suggest that literary and oral accounts of the Seven Sages existed before Plato, and that these rich traditions were readily available for later generations of *sophoi* to appropriate and model themselves upon.

---

[3] Snell 1966.
[4] Cf. Richardson 1981:1, who argues that the story of the contest goes back to the sixth century BCE.
[5] Martin 1993:113.
[6] See Schultz 1866 and Oikonomides 1980 and 1987. Though Schultz's date of the inscriptions may be a bit too early, it is probably safe to suggest a pre-Platonic date for the stele.

Bibliography

Adcock, F. E. 1927. "Literary Tradition and Early Greek Code-Makers." *Cambridge Historical Journal* 2:95–109.

Adkins, A. W. H. 1973. "'Ἀρετή, τέχνη, Democracy and Sophists: Protagoras 316b–328d." *Journal of Hellenic Studies* 93:3–12.

Anderson, W. D. 1966. *Ethos and Education in Greek Music.* Cambridge, MA.

Andrewes, A. 1938. "Eunomia." *Classical Quarterly* 32:89–102.

———. 1974. *The Greek Tyrants.* London.

Asheri, D., Lloyd, A., and Corcella, A. 2007. *A Commentary on Herodotus I-IV.* Ed. O. Murray and A. Moren. Oxford.

Balot, R. K. 2001a. "Aristotle's Critique of Phaleas: Justice, Equality, and Pleonexia." *Hermes* 129:32–44.

———. 2001b. *Greed and Injustice in Classical Athens.* Princeton.

Barney, R. 2006. "The Sophistic Movement." In *A Companion to Ancient Philosophy,* ed. M. L. Gill and P. Pellegrin, 77–97. Malden, MA.

Baulaudé, J.-F. 2006. "Hippias le passeur." In *La costruzione del discorsofilosofico nell' età dei Presocratici,* ed. M. Sassi, 287–304. Pisa.

Bernays, J. 1853. "Zu Gorgias' Ὀλυμπικὸς λόγος." *Rheinische Museum für Philologie* 8:432–433.

Bett, R. 1989. "The Sophists and Relativism." *Phronesis* 34:139–169.

Blank, D. L. 1985. "Socratics Versus Sophists on Payment for Teaching." *Classical Antiquity* 4:1–49.

Boardman, J. 1980. *The Greeks Overseas: Their Early Colonies and Trade.* London.

Bourdieu, P. 1991. *Language and Symbolic Power.* Trans. G. Raymond and M. Adamson. Cambridge, MA.

———. 2000. *Pascalian Meditations.* Stanford.

Bowra, C. M. 1938. "Xenophanes and the Olympian Games." *American Journal of Philology* 59:257–279.

———. 1961. *Greek Lyric Poetry from Alcman to Simonides.* 2nd ed. Oxford.

Bremmer, J. N. 1996. "The Status and Symbolic Capital of the Seer." In *The Role of Religion in the Early Greek Polis: Proceedings of the Third International Seminar* on *Ancient Greek Cult, Organized by the Swedish Institute of Athens, 16-18 October 1992*, ed. R. Hägg, 97–109. Stockholm.

Buchheim, T. 1989. *Gorgias von Leontinoi: Reden, Fragmente und Testimonien.* Hamburg.

Burkert, W. 1972. *Lore and Science in Ancient Pythagoreanism.* Trans. E. L. Minar, Jr. Cambridge, MA.

———. 1983. "Itinerant Diviners and Magicians: A Neglected Element in Cultural Contacts." In *The Greek Renaissance of the Eighth Century B.C.: Tradition and Innovation; Proceedings of the Second International Symposium at the Swedish Institute in Athens, 1-5 June, 1981*, ed. R. Hägg, 115–119. Stockholm.

———. 1985. *Greek Religion.* Trans. J. Raffan. Cambridge, MA.

———. 1987. *Ancient Mystery Cults.* Cambridge, MA.

———. 1992. *The Orientalizing Revolution: Near Eastern Influence on Greek Culture in the Early Archaic Age.* Trans. W. Burkert and M. E. Pinder. Cambridge, MA.

Busine, A. 2002. *Les Sept Sages de la Grèce antique: Transmission et utilisation d'un patrimoine légendaire d'Hérodote à Plutarque.* Paris.

Campbell, D. A. 1982. *Greek Lyric Poetry: A Selection of Early Greek Lyric, Elegiac, and Iambic Poetry.* New ed. Bristol.

———. 1988. *Greek Lyric.* Vol. 2. Loeb Classical Library. Cambridge, MA.

———. 1991. *Greek Lyric.* Vol. 3. Loeb Classical Library. Cambridge, MA.

Carey, C. 2000. "Old Comedy and the Sophists." In *The Rivals of Aristophanes: Studies in Athenian Old Comedy*, ed. F. D. Harvey and J. Wilkins, 419–436. London.

Casson, L. 1994. *Travel in the Ancient World.* Baltimore.

Chadwick, N. K. 1952. *Poetry and Prophecy.* Cambridge.

Classen, C. J. 1965. "Bemerkungen zu zwei griechischen 'Philosophiehistorikern.'" *Philologus* 109:175–181.

———, ed. 1976. *Sophistik.* Wege der Forschung 187. Darmstadt.

Cole, T. 1991. *The Origins of Rhetoric in Ancient Greece.* Baltimore.

Collins, D. 2004. *Master of the Game: Competition and Performance in Greek Poetry.* Hellenic Studies 7. Washington, DC.

Corey, D. 2002. "The Case against Teaching Virtue for Pay: Socrates and the Sophists." *History of Political Thought* 23:89–210.

Denyer, N., ed. 2001. *Plato. Alcibiades.* Cambridge Greek and Latin Classics. Cambridge.

Dickie, M. W. 1997. "Philostratus and Pindar's Eighth Paean." *Bulletin of the American Society of Papyrologists* 34:11–20.

Diels, H., and Kranz, W, eds. 1996. *Die Fragmente der Vorsokratiker.* 6th ed. 3 vols. Zürich.

Dillery, J. 2005. "Chresmologues and Manteis: Independent Diviners and the Problem of Authority." In *Mantikê: Studies in Ancient Divination*, ed. S. I. Johnston and P. T. Struck, 167–232. Leiden.

Dodds, E. R. 1951. *The Greeks and the Irrational.* Berkeley.

———, ed. 1959. *Plato. Gorgias.* Oxford.

Dougherty, C. 1994. "Archaic Greek Foundation Poetry: Questions of Genre and Occasion." *Journal of Hellenic Studies* 114:34–46.

———. 2001. *The Raft of Odysseus: The Ethnographic Imagination of Homer's Odyssey.* Oxford.

Dover, K. J., ed. 1968. *Aristophanes. Clouds.* Oxford.

Drees, L. 1968. *Olympia: Gods, Artists, and Athletes.* Trans. G. Onn. New York.

Edmunds, L. 2006. "What Was Socrates Called?" *Classical Quarterly* 56:414–425.

Ehrenberg, V. 1946a. *Aspects of the Ancient World.* Oxford.

———. 1946b. "Eunomia." In Ehrenberg 1946a:70–93.

———. 1950. "Origins of Democracy." *Historia* 1:515–48.

Erasmus, H. J. 1960. "Eunomia." *Acta Classica* 3:53–64.

Fairweather, J. A. 1974. "Fiction in the Biographies of Ancient Writers." *Ancient Society* 5:231–275.

Fehling, D. 1985. *Die sieben Weisen und die frühgriechische Chronologie: Eine traditionsgeschichtliche Studie.* Bern.

Ferguson, A. S. 1921. "On a Fragment of Gorgias." *Classical Philology* 16:284–287.

Ferguson, J. 1958. *Moral Values in the Ancient World.* London.

Ferrari, G. R. F. 1992. "Platonic Love." In Kraut 1992:248–276.

Finley, M. I. 1977. *The World of Odysseus.* 2nd ed. London.

Flower, M. 2000. "From Simonides to Isocrates: The Fifth-Century Origins of Fourth-Century Panhellenism." *Classical Antiquity* 19:65–101.

———. 2008. *The Seer in Ancient Greece.* Berkeley.

Forbes, C. A. 1942. *Teacher's Pay in Ancient Greece.* Lincoln.

Ford, A. 1992. *Homer: The Poetry of the Past.* Ithaca.

———. 1993. "Sophistic." *Common Knowledge* 1.5:3–47.

Forrest, W. G. 1957. "Colonisation and the Rise of Delphi." *Historia* 6:160–175.

Fränkel, H. 1975. *Early Greek Poetry and Philosophy.* Trans. M. Hadas and J. Willis. Oxford.

Frede, M. 2004. "Aristotle's Account of the Origins of Philosophy." *Rhizai* 1:9–44.

Freeman, K. 1948. *Ancilla to the Pre-Socratic Philosophers: A Complete Translation of the Fragments in Diels, Fragmente der Vorsokratiker.* Cambridge, MA.

Friedländer, P. 1964. *Platon.* 3rd ed. 2 vols. Berlin.

Gagarin, M. 1986. *Early Greek Law.* Berkeley.

———. 2001. "The Truth of Antiphon's Truth." In *Before Plato: Essays in Ancient Greek Philosophy* VI, ed. A. Preus, 171–186. Albany.

Gardiner, E. N. 1910. *Greek Athletic Sports and Festivals.* London.

Geddes, A. G. 1987. "Rags and Riches: The Costume of Athenian Men in the Fifth Century." *Classical Quarterly* 37:307–331.

Gellrich, M. 1993. "Socratic Magic: Enchantment, Irony, and Persuasion in Plato's Dialogues." *Classical World* 87:275–307.

Gernet, L. 1981. *The Anthropology of Ancient Greece.* Trans. J. Hamilton and B. Nagy. Baltimore.

Golden, M. 1998. *Sport and Society in Ancient Greece.* Cambridge.

Gomperz, H. 1912. *Sophistik und Rhetorik.* Stuttgart.

Graf, F. 1987. "Orpheus: A Poet among Men." In *Interpretations of Greek Mythology,* ed. J. Bremmer, 80–106. London.

———. 1997. *Magic in the Ancient World.* Trans. F. Philip. Cambridge, MA.

Grant, A. 1885. *The Ethics of Aristotle.* 4th ed. 2 vols. London.

Gray, V. 2001. "Herodotus' Literary and Historical Method: Arion's Story (1.23–24)." *American Journal of Philology* 122:11–28.

Graziosi, B. 2001. "Competition in Wisdom." In *Homer, Tragedy, and Beyond: Essays in Honour of P. E. Easterling,* ed. F. Budelmann and P. Michelakis, 57–74. London.

Griffith, M. 1990. "Contest and Contradiction in Early Greek Poetry." In *Cabinet of the Muses: Essays on Classical and Comparative Literature in Honor of Thomas G. Rosenmeyer,* ed. M. Griffith and D. J. Mastronarde, 185–207. Atlanta.

———. 2001. "Public and Private in Early Greek Institutions of Education." In *Education in Greek and Roman Antiquity,* ed. Y. L. Too, 23–84 Leiden.

———. Forthcoming. "Apollo, Teiresias, and the Politics of Tragic Prophecy." In *Apolline Politics and Poetics,* ed. V. Karasmanis, L. Athanassaki, et al., Delphi and Athens.

Grossmann, G. 1950. *Politische Schlagwörter aus der Zeit des Peloponnesischen Krieges.* Zürich.

Grote, G. 1872. *A History of Greece.* 4th ed. Vol. 7. London.

Grube, G. M. A. 1961. *The Drama of Euripides.* New York.

Guthrie, W. K. C. 1952. *Orpheus and Greek Religion: A Study of the Orphic Movement.* 2nd ed. London.

———. 1962. *A History of Greek Philosophy.* Vol. 1, *The Earlier Presocratics and the Pythagoreans.* Cambridge.

———. 1965. *A History of Greek Philosophy.* Vol. 2, *The Presocratic Tradition from Parmenides to Democritus.* Cambridge.

———. 1969. *A History of Greek Philosophy.* Vol. 3, *The Fifth-Century Enlightenment.* Cambridge.

———. 1971. *The Sophists.* Cambridge.

Hall, J. M. 1997. *Ethnic Identity in Greek Antiquity.* Cambridge.

Harrison, E. L. 1964. "Was Gorgias a Sophist?" *Phoenix* 18:183–192.

Hartog, F. 2001. *Memories of Odysseus.* Trans. J. Lloyd. Edinburgh.

Harvey, F. D. 1965. "Two Kinds of Equality." *Classica et Mediaevalia* 26:101–146.

————. 1985. "*Dona Ferentes*: Some Aspects of Bribery in Greek Politics." In *Crux: Essays in Greek History Presented to G. E. M. de Ste Croix on his Seventy-fifth Birthday*, ed. P. A. Cartledge and F. D. Harvey, 76–117. London.

Havelock, E. A. 1957. *The Liberal Temper in Greek Politics.* New Haven.

————. 1963. *Preface to Plato.* Cambridge, MA.

Hawhee, D. 2004. *Bodily Arts: Rhetoric and Athletics in Ancient Greece.* Austin.

Hegel, G. W. F. 1892. *Lectures on the History of Philosophy.* Vol. 1. Trans. E. S. Haldane. London.

Helms, M. W. 1988. *Ulysses' Sail: An Ethnographic Odyssey of Power, Knowledge, and Geographical Distance.* Princeton.

Herman, G. 1987. *Ritualised Friendship and the Greek City.* Cambridge.

Hölkeskamp, K.-J. 1992. "The 'Codification of Law' in Archaic Greece." *Métis* 7: 9–81.

————. 2000. "(In-)Schrift und Monument: Zum Begriffs des Gesetzes im archaischen und klassischen Griechenland." *Zeitschrit für Papyrologie und Epigraphik* 132:73–96.

Hornblower, S. 1991. *A Commentary on Thucydides.* Vol. 1, *Books I–III.* Oxford.

————. 1996. *A Commentary on Thucydides.* Vol. 2, *Books IV–V.24.* Oxford.

How, W. W., and Wells, J. 1912. *A Commentary on Herodotus.* 2 vols. Oxford.

Huffman, C. A. 2005. *Archytas of Tarentum: Pythagorean, Philosopher, and Mathematician King.* Cambridge.

Humphreys, S. C. 1977–1978. "Public and Private Interests in Classical Athens." *The Classical Journal* 73:97–104.

————. 1978. *Anthropology and the Greeks.* London.

————. 1983a. "The Evolution of Legal Process in Ancient Attica." In *Tria corda: Scritti in onore di Arnaldo Momigliano*, ed. E. Gabba, 229–251. Como.

————. 1983b. *The Family, Women, and Death.* London.

Imperio, O. 1998. "La figura dell' intellettuale nella commedia greca." In *Tessere: Frammenti della commedia greca; Studi e commenti*, ed. A. M. Belardinelli, O. Imperio, G. Mastromarco, et al., 43–130. Bari.

Irwin, E. 2005. *Solon and Early Greek Poetry: The Politics of Exhortation.* Cambridge.

Irwin, T., trans. 1985. *Aristotle. Nicomachean Ethics.* Indianapolis.

Jaeger, W. 1965. *Paideia: The Ideals of Greek Culture.* 2nd ed. Vol. 1, *Archaic Greece: The Mind of Athens.* Trans. G. Highet. New York.

Jones, W. H. S. 1923. *Hippocrates.* Vol. 2. Loeb Classical Library. Cambridge, MA.

Kahn, C. H. 1979. *The Art and Thought of Heraclitus: An Edition of the Fragments with Translation and Commentary.* Cambridge.

————. 1985. "The Beautiful and the Genuine." *Oxford Studies in Ancient Philosophy* 3:261–287.

Ker, J. 2000. "Solon's *Theôria* and the End of the City." *Classical Antiquity* 19:304–329.

Kerferd, G. B. 1950. "The First Greek Sophists." *Classical Review* 64:8–10.

———. 1976. "The Image of the Wise Man in Greece in the Period before Plato." In *Images of Man in Ancient and Medieval Thought*, ed. F. Bossier et al., 17–28. Leuven.

———. 1981a. *The Sophistic Movement*. Cambridge.

———, ed. 1981b. *The Sophists and their Legacy: Proceedings of the Fourth International Colloquium of Ancient Philosophy at Bad Homburg 1979*. Hermes Einzelschriften 44. Wiesbaden.

Kindstrand, J. F. 1981. *Anacharsis: The Legend and the Apophthegmata*. Studia Graeca Upsaliensia 16. Uppsala.

Kingsley, P. 1994. "From Pythagoras to the *Turba Philosophorum*: Egypt and Pythagorean Tradition." *Journal of the Warburg and Courauld Institutes* 57:1–13.

———. 1995. *Ancient Philosophy, Mystery, and Magic: Empedocles and Pythagorean Tradition*. Oxford.

Kirk, G. S., Raven, J. E., and Schofield, M. 1983. *The Presocratic Philosophers*. 2nd ed. Cambridge.

Koniaris, G. L. 1971. "Michigan Papyrus 2754 and the *Certamen*." *Harvard Studies in Classical Philology* 75:107–129.

Kramer, H. 1915. *Quid valeat ὁμόνοια in litteris Graecis*. Göttingen.

Kraut, R., ed. 1992a. *The Cambridge Companion to Plato*. Cambridge.

———. 1992b. "Introduction to the Study of Plato." In Kraut 1992:1–50.

Kugel, J. L., ed. 1990. *Poetry and Prophecy: The Beginnings of a Literary Tradition*. Ithaca.

Kurke, L. 1991. *The Traffic in Praise: Pindar and the Poetics of Social Economy*. Ithaca.

———. 1993. "The Economy of Kudos." In *Cultural Poetics in Archaic Greece: Cult, Performance, Politics*, ed. C. Dougherty and L. Kurke, 131–163. Cambridge.

———. 1999. *Coins, Bodies, Games, and Gold: The Politics of Meaning in Archaic Greece*. Princeton.

———. 2006. "Plato, Aesop, and the Beginnings of Mimetic Prose." *Representations* 94:6–52.

Kyle, D. 1987. *Athletics in Ancient Athens*. Leiden.

Laks, A. 2006. *Introduction à la philosophie présocratique*. Paris.

Larmour, D. 1999. *Stage and Stadium: Drama and Athletics in Ancient Greece*. Nikephoros Beihefte 4. Hildesheim.

Linforth, I. M. 1941. *The Arts of Orpheus*. Berkeley.

Livingstone, N. 2001. *A Commentary on Isocrates' Busiris*. Mnemosyne Supplement 223. Leiden.

Lloyd, G. E. R. 1979. *Magic, Reason, and Experience*. Cambridge.

———. 1987. *The Revolutions of Wisdom*. Berkeley.

———. 1990. *Demystifying Mentalities*. Cambridge.

———. 2005. *The Delusions of Invulnerability: Wisdom and Morality in Ancient Greece, China, and Today*. London.

Long, A. A. 1966. "Thinking and Sense-Perception in Empedocles: Mysticism or Materialism?" *Classical Quarterly* 16:256–276.

———. 1984. "Methods of Argument in Gorgias' Palamedes." In Ἡ ἀρχαία σοφιστική: *The Sophistic Movement; Proceedings of the 1st International Symposium on the Sophistic Movement*, 233–241. Athens.

———, ed. 1999. *The Cambridge Companion to Early Greek Philosophy*. Cambridge.

Lynch, J. P. 1972. *Aristotle's School: A Study of a Greek Educational Institution*. Berkeley.

MacDonald, M. 2006. "Encomium of Hegel." *Philosophy and Rhetoric* 39:22–44.

MacDowell, D. M. 1982. *Gorgias. Encomium of Helen*. London.

———. 1983. "Athenian Laws about Bribery." *Revue internationale des droits de l'antiquite* 30:57–78.

Malkin, I. 1989. "Delphoi and the Founding of Social Order in Archaic Greece." *Métis* 4:129–153.

Mafredini, M., and Piccirilli, L., eds. 1980. *Plutarco. Le vite di Licurgo e di Numa*. Milan.

Mansfeld, J. 1990. *Studies in the Historiography of Greek Philosophy*. Assen, The Netherlands.

———. 1999. "Sources." In Long 1999:22–44.

———, and Runia, D. T. 1996. *Aetiana: The Method and Intellectual Context of a Doxographer*. Vol. 1, *The Sources*. Leiden.

Marcovich, M. 1978. "Xenophanes on Drinking Parties and the Olympic Games." *Illinois Classical Studies* 3:1–26.

Martin, J. 1976. "Zur Entstehung der Sophistik." *Saeculum* 27:143–164.

Martin, R. P. 1993. "The Seven Sages as Performers of Wisdom." In *Cultural Poetics in Archaic Greece: Cult, Performance, Politics*, ed. C. Dougherty and L. Kurke, 108–128. Cambridge.

Mauss, M. 1967. *The Gift: Forms and Functions of Exchange in Archaic Societies*. Trans. I. Cunnison. New York.

McCoy, M. 2008. *Plato on the Rhetoric of Philosophers and Sophists*. Cambridge.

Meiggs, R., and Lewis, D., eds. 1969. *A Selection of Greek Historical Inscriptions to the End of the Fifth Century B.C.* Oxford.

Mikalson, J. D. 1991. *Honor Thy Gods: Popular Religion in Greek Tragedy*. Chapel Hill.

Miller, M. 1991. "Foreigners at the Greek Symposium?" In *Dining in a Classical Context*, ed. W. J. Slater, 59–81. Ann Arbor.

Miller, S. G. 1979. *Arete: Ancient Writers, Papyri, and Inscriptions on the History and Ideals of Greek Athletics and Games*. Chicago.

Montiglio, S. 2000. "Wandering Philosophers in Classical Greece." *Journal of Hellenic Studies* 120:86–105.

———. 2005. *Wandering in Ancient Greek Culture*. Chicago.

Moreau, J. 1979. "Qu'est-ce qu'un sophiste?" *Les etudes philosophiques* 1979:325–335.

Morgan, C. 1990. *Athletes and Oracles: The Transformation of Olympia and Delphi in the Eighth Century B.C.* Cambridge.

Morgan, K. A. 1994. "Socrates and Gorgias at Delphi and Olympia: *Phaedrus* 235d6–236b4." *Classical Quarterly* 44:375–386.

Morrison J. S. 1949. "An Introductory Chapter in the History of Greek Education." *Durham University Journal* 41:55–63.

———. 1953. "Xenophon, Memorabilia 1:16: The Encounters of Socrates and Antiphon." *Classical Review* 67:36.

———. 1958. "The Origins of Plato's Philosopher-Statesman." *Classical Quarterly* 8:198–218.

Moulakis, A. 1973. *Homonoia: Eintracht und die Entwicklung eines politischen Bewusstseins.* Munich.

Mueller, I. 1992. "Mathematic Method, Philosophical Truth." In Kraut 1992:170–199.

Müller, R. 1986. "Sophistique et démocratie." In *Positions de la sophistique*, ed. B. Cassin, 179-193. Paris.

Murray, O., ed. 1990. *Sympotica: A Symposium on the Symposion.* Oxford.

———. 1993. *Early Greece.* 2nd ed. London.

Murray, P. 1981. "Poetic Inspiration in Early Greece." *Journal of Hellenic Studies* 101:87–100.

———. 1996. *Plato on Poetry.* Cambridge.

Nehamas, A. 1990. "Eristic, Antilogic, Sophistic, Dialectic: Plato's Demarcation of Philosophy from Sophistry." *History of Philosophy Quarterly* 7:3–16.

Nestle, W. 1942. *Vom Mythos zum Logos.* Stuttgart.

Nightingale, A. 1995. *Genres in Dialogue: Plato and the Construct of Philosophy.* Cambridge.

———. 1999. "Plato's Lawcode in Context: Rule by Written Law in Athens and Magnesia." *Classical Quarterly*, n.s., 49:100–122.

———. 2000. "Sages, Sophists, and Philosophers: Greek Wisdom Literature." In *Literature in the Greek and Roman Worlds: A New Perspective*, ed. O. Taplin, 156–191. Oxford.

———. 2001. "On Wandering and Wondering: *Theôria* in Greek Philosophy and Culture." *Arion* 9:23–58.

———. 2004. *Spectacles of Truth in Classical Greek Philosophy: Theoria in Its Cultural Context.* Cambridge.

Ober, J. 1989. *Mass and Elite in Democratic Athens: Rhetoric, Ideology, and the Power of the People.* Princeton.

———. 1998. *Political Dissent in Democratic Athens: Intellectual Critics of Popular Rule.* Princeton.

———. 2004. "I, Socrates ... The Performative Audacity of Isocrates' *Antidosis.*" In *Isocrates and Civic Education*, ed T. Poulakos and D. J. Depew, 21–43. Austin.

Ohlert, K. 1912. *Rätsel und Rätselspiele der alten Griechen.* 2nd ed. Berlin.

Oikonomides, A. 1980. "The Lost Delphic Inscription with the Commandments of the Seven and P. Univ. Athen. 2782." *Zeitschrit für Papyrologie und Epigraphik* 37:179–183.

———. 1987. "Records of the 'Commandments of the Seven Wise Men' in the Third Century B.C." *Classical Bulletin* 63:67–76.

Osborne, R. 1993. "Competitive Festivals and the *Polis.*" In *Tragedy, Comedy and the Polis: Papers from the Greek Drama Conference, Nottingham, 18–20 July 1990*, ed. A. H. Sommerstein et al., 21–38. Bari.

Ostwald, M. 1969. *Nomos and the Beginnings of the Athenian Democracy.* Oxford.

———. 1986. *From Popular Sovereignty to the Sovereignty of Law: Law, Society, and Politics in Fifth-century Athens.* Berkeley.

———. 1990. "*Nomos* and *Phusis* in Antiphon's Περὶ Ἀληθείας." In *Cabinet of the Muses: Essays on Classical and Comparative Literature in Honor of Thomas G. Rosenmeyer*, eds. M. Griffith and D. J. Mastronarde, 293–306. Atlanta.

———. 1992. "Athens as a Cultural Centre." In *The Cambridge Ancient History.* 2nd ed., 5:306–369. London and Cambridge.

Owen, G. E. L. 1986. "Philosophical Invective." In *Logic, Science, and Dialectic: Collected Papers in Greek Philosophy*, ed. M. Nussbaum, 347–364. Ithaca.

Page, D. L. 1955. *Sappho and Alcaeus: An Introduction to the Study of Ancient Lesbian Poetry.* Oxford.

Patzer, A. 1986. *Der Sophist Hippias als Philosophiehistoriker.* Freiburg.

———. 1994. "Sokrates in den Fragmenten der attischen Komödie." In *Orchestra: Drama, Mythos, Bühne*, ed. A. Bierl, P. V. Möllendorff et al., 50–81. Stuttgart.

Pendrick, G. 1998. "Plato and ῥητορική." *Rheinische Museum für Philologie* 141:10–23.

———. 2002. *Antiphon the Sophist: The Fragments.* Cambridge.

Penner, T. 1987. *The Ascent from Nominalism: Some Existence Arguments in Plato's Middle Dialogues.* Dordrecht.

Perlman, P. 2005. "Imagining Crete." In *The Imaginary Polis*, ed. M. H. Hansen, 7:282–334. Copenhagen.

Perlman, S. 1958. "A Note on the Political Implications of *Proxenia* in the Fourth Century BC." *Classical Quarterly* 8:185–191.

———. 1976. "On Bribing Athenian Ambassadors." *Greek Roman and Byzantine Studies* 17:223–233.

Platnauer, M., ed. 1964. *Peace.* Oxford.

Popper, K. R. 1962. *The Open Society and Its Enemies.* 4th ed., rev. 2 vols. London.

Reiner, E. 1961. "The Etiological Myth of the 'Seven Sages.'" *Orientalia* 30:1–11.

Renehan, R. 1971. "The Michigan Alcidamas-Papyrus: A Problem in Methodology." *Harvard Studies in Classical Philology* 75:85–105.

Renfrew, C., and Cherry, J. F., eds. 1986. *Peer Polity Interaction and Socio-Political Change.* Cambridge.

Richardson, N. J. 1975. "Homeric Professors in the Age of the Sophists." *Proceedings of the Cambridge Philological Society*, n.s., 21:65–81.

———. 1981. "The Contest of Homer and Hesiod and Alcidamas' Mouseion." *Classical Quarterly* 31:1–10.

———. 1992. "Panhellenic Cults and Panhellenic Poets." In *The Cambridge Ancient History.* 2nd ed., 5:223–244. London and Cambridge.

Ritook, Z. 1989. "The Views of Early Greek Epic on Poetry and Art." *Mnemosyne* 42:331–348.

Robinson, E. 2007. "The Sophists and Democracy Beyond Athens." *Rhetorica* 35:109–22.

Robinson, T. M. 2000. "The Defining Features of Mind-Body Dualism in the Writings of Plato." In *Psyche and Soma: Physicians and Metaphysicians on the Mind-body Problem from Antiquity to Enlightenment*, ed. J. P. Wright and P. Potter, 37–55. Oxford.

Roller, R. 1931. *Untersuchungen zum Anonymous Iamblichi.* Tübingen.

Romer, F. E. 1982. "The Aisymneteia: A Problem in Aristotle's Historic Method." *American Journal of Philology* 103:25–46.

Romilly, J. de. 1972. "Vocabulaire et propagande ou les premiers emplois du mot ὁμόνοια." In *Mélanges de linguistique et de philologie grecques offerts à Pierre Chantraine*, 199–209. Paris.

———. 1975. *Magic and Rhetoric in Ancient Greece.* Cambridge, MA.

———. 1992. *The Great Sophists in Periclean Athens.* Oxford.

Rosenmeyer, T. G. 1955. "Gorgias, Aeschylus, and 'Apate.'" *American Journal of Philology* 76:225–260.

Ross, W. D. 1953. *Aristotle's Metaphysics: A Revised Text with Introduction and Commentary.* 2 vols. Oxford.

Roth, P. 1984. "Teiresias as *Mantis* and Intellectual in Euripides' *Bacchae.*" *Transactions and Proceedings of the American Philological Association* 114:59–69.

Runciman, W. G. 1982. "Origins of State: The Case of Archaic Greece." *Comparative Studies in Society and History* 24:351–377.

Rutherford, I. 2001. *Pindar's Paeans: A Reading of the Fragments with a Survey of the Genre.* Oxford.

Schadewaldt, W. 1944. *Von Homers Welt und Werk.* Leipzig.

Schiappa, E. 1990. "Did Plato Coin Rhêtorikê?" *American Journal of Philology* 111:460–473.

———. 1991. *Protagoras and Logos: A Study in Greek Philosophy and Rhetoric.* Columbia.

————. 1995. "Isocrates' *Philosophia* and Contemporary Pragmatism." In *Rhetoric, Sophistry, Pragmatism*, ed. S. Mailloux, 33–60. Cambridge.

Schmid, W., and Stählin, O. 1940. *Geschichte der griechischen Literatur.* Munich.

Schofield, M. 1991. *The Stoic Idea of the City.* Cambridge.

Schultz F. 1866. "Die Sprüche der delphischen Säule." *Philologus* 24:193–226.

Seaford, R. 2004. *Money and the Early Greek Mind: Homer, Philosophy, Tragedy.* Cambridge.

Segal, C. 1962. "Gorgias and the Psychology of the *Logos*." *Harvard Studies in Classical Philology* 66:99–155.

————. 1989. *Orpheus: The Myth of the Poet.* Baltimore.

Sidgwick, H. 1872. "The Sophists." *Journal of Philology* 4:288–307.

Smith, N. D. 1989. "Diviners and Divination in Aristophanic Comedy." *Classical Antiquity* 8:140–158.

Snell, B. 1944. "Die Nachrichten über die Lehren des Thales und die Anfänge der griechischen Philosophie- und Literaturgeschichte." *Philologus* 96:170–82.

————. 1953. *The Discovery of the Mind.* Trans. T. G. Rosenmeyer. Cambridge, MA.

————. 1966. "Zur Geschichte vom Gastmahl der Sieben Weisen." In *Gesammelte Schriften*, 115–118. Göttingen.

————. 1971. *Leben und Meinungen der sieben Weisen.* 4th ed. Munich.

Snodgrass, A. 1986. "Interaction by Design: The Greek City State." In *Peer Polity Interaction and Socio-political Change*, ed. C. Renfrew and J. F. Cherry, 47–58. Cambridge.

Sperduti, A. 1950. "The Divine Nature of Poetry in Antiquity." *Transactions and Proceedings of the American Philological Association* 81:209–240.

Sprague, R. K. 1972. *The Older Sophists.* Columbia.

————. 1973. "Sophists and Philosophers: Problems of Classification." *American Journal of Philology* 94:350–364.

Storey, I. C. 2003. *Eupolis: Poet of Old Comedy.* Oxford.

Sutton, D. F. 1980. *The Greek Satyr Play.* Meisenheim am Glan.

Szegedy-Maszak, A. 1978. "Legends of the Greek Lawgivers." *Greek Roman and Byzantine Studies* 19:199–209.

Tarrant, H. 2003. "Athletics, Competition and the Intellectual." In *Sport and Festival in the Ancient Greek World*, ed. D. Phillips and D. Pritchard, 351–363. Swansea.

Taylor, C. 2001a. "Bribery in Athenian Politics Part I: Accusations, Allegations, and Slander." *Greece and Rome* 48:54–66.

————. 2001b. "Bribery in Athenian Politics Part II: Ancient Reaction and Perceptions." *Greece and Rome* 48:154–172.

Taylor, C. C. W. 2006. "Socrates the Sophist." In *Remembering Socrates*, ed. L. Judson and V. Karasmanis, 157–168. Oxford.

Tell, H. P. 2007. "Sages at the Games: Intellectual Displays and Dissemination of Wisdom in Ancient Greece." *Classical Antiquity* 26:249–275.

———. 2009. "Wisdom for Sale? The Sophists and Money." *Classical Philology* 104:13–33.

Thériault, G. 1996. "L'apparition du culte d'Homonoia." *Les Études Classiques* 64:127–150.

Thomas, R. 2000. *Herodotus in Context: Ethnography, Science, and the Art of Persuasion.* Cambridge.

Tigerstedt, E. N. 1965–1978. *The Legend of Sparta in Classical Antiquity.* 3 vols. Stockholm.

———. 1970. "Furor Poeticus: Poetic Inspiration in Greek Literature before Democritus and Plato." *Journal of the History of Ideas* 31:163–178.

Too, Y. L. 1995. *The Rhetoric of Identity in Isocrates: Text, Power, Pedagogy.* Cambridge.

Tzachou-Alexandri, O., ed. 1989. *Mind and Body: Athletic Contest in Ancient Greece.* Athens.

Untersteiner, M. 1954. *The Sophists.* Trans. K. Freeman. Oxford.

Vernant, J-P. 1982. *The Origins of Greek Thought.* Ithaca.

Vlastos, G. 1947. "Equality and Justice in Early Greek Cosmologies." *Classical Philology* 42:156–178.

———. 1953. "Isonomia." *American Journal of Philology* 74:337–366.

———. 1975. "Plato's Testimony concerning Zeno of Elea." *Journal of Hellenic Studies* 95:136–162.

———. 1981. *Platonic Studies.* Princeton.

Wacquant, L. 1998. "Pierre Bourdieu." In *Key Sociological Thinkers*, ed. R. Stones, 215–229. New York.

Waisglass, A. A. I. 1956. "Demonax, ΒΑΣΙΛΕΥΣ ΜΑΝΤΙΝΕΩΝ." *American Journal of Philology* 77:16–76.

Wallace, R. W. 1998. "The Sophists in Athens." In *Democracy, Empire, and the Arts in Fifth-century Athens*, ed. D. Boedeker and K. A. Raaflaub, 203–222. Cambridge, MA.

———. 2007. "Plato's Sophists, Intellectual History after 450, and Sokrates." In *The Cambridge Companion to the Age of Pericles*, ed. L. J. Samons II, 215–237. Cambridge.

Walsh, G. B. 1984. *The Varieties of Enchantment: Early Greek Views of the Nature and Function of Poetry.* Chapel Hill.

Wardy, R. 1996. *The Birth of Rhetoric: Gorgias, Plato, and their Successors.* London.

Weber, M. 1978. *Economy and Society.* Ed. G. Roth and G. Wittich. 2 vols. Berkeley.

Welskopf, E. C. 1974. "Sophisten." In *Hellenische Poleis: Krise, Wandlung, Wirkung*, ed. E. C. Welskopf, 4:1927–1984. Berlin.

West, M. L. 1967. "The Contest of Homer and Hesiod." *Classical Quarterly*, n.s., 17:433–450.

————, ed. 1978. *Hesiod. Works and Days.* Oxford.

————. 1983. *The Orphic Poems.* Oxford.

————, ed. 1989–1992. *Iambi et Elegi Graeci.* 2nd ed. 2 vols. Oxford.

————. 1993. "Simonides Redivivus." *Zeitschrit für Papyrologie und Epigraphik* 8:1–14.

Whitehorne, J. 2002. "Aristophanes' Representation of Intellectuals." *Hermes* 130:28–35.

Whitmarsh, T. 2005. *The Second Sophistic.* Greece & Rome: New Surveys in the Classics 35. Oxford.

Wiersma, W. 1934. "The Seven Sages and the Prize of Wisdom." *Mnemosyne* 3:150–154.

Willetts, R. F. 1982. "Cretan Laws and Society." In *The Cambridge Ancient History,* vol. 3, part 3, *The Expansion of the Greek World, Eighth to Sixth Centuries B.C.,* ed. J. Boardman and N. G. L. Hammond, 234–248. 2nd. ed. London.

Woodruff, P. 1982. *Hippias Major.* Indianapolis.

————. 1999. "Rhetoric and Relativism: Protagoras and Gorgias." In Long 1999:290–310.

Worman, N. 2008. *Abusive Mouths in Classical Athens.* Cambridge.

Wright, J. P., and Potter, P., eds. 2000. *Psyche and Soma: Physicians and Metaphysicians on the Mind-body Problem from Antiquity to Enlightenment.* Oxford.

Wright, M. R. 1981. *Empedocles. The Extant Fragments.* New Haven.

Young, D. C. 1984. *The Olympic Myth of Greek Amateur Athletics.* Chicago.

Zeppi, S. 1972. "Bios theoreticos e bios politicos come ideali di vita nella filosofia preplatonica." *Logos* 219–248.

Index Locorum

Subject Index